D1562654

Agents of Empire

AGENTS OF EMPIRE

*Spanish Ambassadors
in Sixteenth-Century Italy*

MICHAEL J. LEVIN

CORNELL UNIVERSITY PRESS
ITHACA AND LONDON

First published 2005 by Cornell University Press

Printed in the United States of America

Library of Congress Cataloging-in-Publication Data

Levin, Michael Jacob.
    Agents of empire : Spanish ambassadors in sixteenth-century Italy / Michael J. Levin.
        p. cm.
    Includes bibliographical references and index.
    ISBN-13: 978-0-8014-4352-7 (cloth : alk. paper)
    ISBN-10: 0-8014-4352-0 (cloth : alk. paper)
    1. Spain—Foreign relations—Italy—Venice.   2. Venice (Italy)—Foreign relations—Spain.   3. Spain—Foreign relations—Italy—Papal States.   4. Papal States—Foreign relations—Spain.   5. Ambassadors—Italy—Venice—History—16th century.   6. Ambassadors—Italy—Papal States—History—16th century.
7. Spain—Foreign relations—1516–1700.   I. Title.
    DP86.I8L48 2005
    327.46045'09'031—dc22   2005016051

Cornell University Press strives to use environmentally responsible suppliers and materials to the fullest extent possible in the publishing of its books. Such materials include vegetable-based, low-VOC inks and acid-free papers that are recycled, totally chlorine-free, or partly composed of nonwood fibers. For further information, visit our website at www.cornellpress.cornell.edu.

Cloth printing   10 9 8 7 6 5 4 3 2 1

Contents

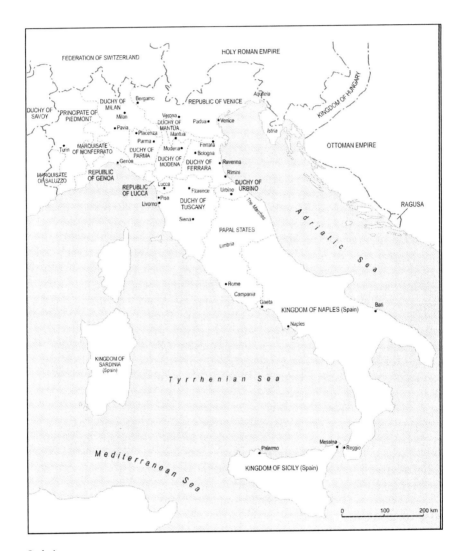

FEDERATION OF SWITZERLAND

HOLY ROMAN EMPIRE

KINGDOM OF HUNGARY

DUCHY OF SAVOY

PRINCIPE OF PIEDMONT

DUCHY OF MILAN

Bergamo

Aquileia

REPUBLIC OF VENICE

Verona

Milan

Pavia

DUCHY OF MANTUA

Padua

Venice

Istria

OTTOMAN EMPIRE

Parma

Placenza

Mantua

MARQUISATE OF MONFERRATO

Turin

DUCHY OF PARMA

Modena

Ferrara

Genoa

DUCHY OF MODENA

Bologna

DUCHY OF FERRARA

Ravenna

MARQUISATE OF SALUZZO

REPUBLIC OF GENOA

Rimini

Lucca

DUCHY OF URBINO

REPUBLIC OF LUCCA

Florence

Urbino

RAGUSA

Livorno

Pisa

DUCHY OF TUSCANY

The Marches

A d r i a t i c   S e a

Siena

PAPAL STATES

Umbria

Rome

Campania

KINGDOM OF NAPLES (Spain)

Gaeta

Bari

Naples

KINGDOM OF SARDINIA (Spain)

T y r r h e n i a n   S e a

M e d i t e r r a n e a n   S e a

Messina

Palermo

Reggio

KINGDOM OF SICILY (Spain)

0   100   200 km

Italy in 1559.

Preface

T his book originated from my interest in the political and cultural relationship between Spain and Italy in the late Renaissance. In order to explore contemporary perspectives on these issues, I decided to focus on Spanish resident ambassadors in Rome and Venice, the two most powerful Italian states. As the official representatives of the Spanish Habsburgs, the ambassadors were the point men in the Crown's campaign to establish hegemony in Italy. Through examination of the correspondence between the ambassadors and their monarchs, I was able to analyze individual opinions and actions, as well as gain insights on larger issues, like the nature of Spanish imperialism and the development of national identity. Diplomatic correspondence is often dry or routine, but the writers' personalities still manage to shine through, and that is where history comes alive.

The ambassadors were sometimes flamboyant, usually arrogant, and always dedicated to their cause. To my surprise, they also seemed anxious. Most historians describe Italy in this period as a region dominated by Spain, so much so that Italy experienced a "pax hispanica" until the late seventeenth century. So why were the Spanish ambassadors so uneasy? I found it difficult to accept that Spanish hegemony in Italy was as absolute as we believed, if the Spanish officials in Italy at the time could be so uncertain. It was their business to dominate the Italians, but they clearly did not believe they had completely succeeded. In this study, I analyze how the ambassadors tried to control Venice and the Papacy, and why they never quite did. In the end, I suggest, the Spaniards' own imperial power and arrogance became a liability. The greater their strength and hubris, the more the Italians feared and resented them. Spanish imperialism, like most such ventures, thus produced ambiguous results.

The long process of turning a dissertation into a book was made possible by the generosity of many people at various institutions. First of all I wish to express my gratitude for a University of Akron Faculty Research Grant (2000), and a Miller Humanities Center Travel Grant (2001), which funded several months in the archives. I would also like to thank the caretakers and archivists at the Archivo General de Simancas, the Instituto de Valencia de Don Juan, and the Archivo de Zabálburu, particularly for all the photocopies they made for me.

Many scholars and friends contributed to and corrected my work. I would especially like to thank John Marino for the care and thoroughness with which he reviewed my manuscript. I would also like to thank Geoffrey Parker, Jim Boyden, Carlos Eire, and Ed Muir for their invaluable advice and support.

My colleagues in the History Department at the University of Akron have been extraordinarily generous with their time and patience. In particular, I wish to thank Kevin Kern, Michael Graham, Connie Bouchard, Walter Hixson, Michael Carley, and Elizabeth Mancke for their help proofreading and editing, as well as for their friendship.

Finally, I would like to thank my family. The love we share is beyond words. Mom, Dad, and Rachel, this book is for you.

Agents of Empire

Introduction

On August 22, 1560, Francisco de Vargas, the Spanish resident ambassador in Rome, wrote a cautionary letter to King Philip II. The political situation in Italy, he warned, was far from stable. To the contrary, "disquiet" loomed throughout the peninsula, in large part because the Italian princes were fickle and fond of change for its own sake (*amig[os] de novedades*). Vargas suspected that a number of the powers of Italy, including the pope himself, were plotting to drive out Spanish troops. For this reason, Vargas wrote, Philip and his ministers should be more fearful at that moment than ever before. "It has occurred to me to express these ideas to Your Majesty," Vargas concluded, "not because I thought to say something new, but only because I see it as my duty, seeing what happens in the world, which is filled with mutability and inconstancy, and there may be nothing in which one can trust, except in vigilance and power."[1]

This dispatch is one of many such expressions of anxiety by Spanish officials in sixteenth-century Italy, a region that was, supposedly, firmly under the thumb of the Spanish Crown. Modern historians have posited the idea that late Renaissance Italy experienced a period of absolute "domination" by Spain, starting in 1559. In that year, Spain and France signed the Treaty of Cateau-Cambrésis, in which the French monarchy formally renounced all dynastic claims on Italy. The peace treaty marked the end of the Italian Wars, sixty years of struggle between the Habsburgs

1. Archivo General de Simancas, Sección Estado (hereafter AGSE), 886 #59.

1

and the Valois over control of Italy. So complete was the Habsburg victory
that most modern historians designate 1559 as the beginning of a period
of uncontested Spanish hegemony in Italy. Fernand Braudel, the great
chronicler of the age of Philip II, writes that after 1559 Italy came under
a "pax hispanica" for at least the next century and a half.[2]

More recent studies echo this argument. Eric Cochrane, for example,
states that in the half-century after the treaty the Spanish Habsburgs
forged "a period of peace and stability" in Italy.[3] Thomas Dandelet similarly asserts that events of 1559 "left Spain virtually unchallenged in Italy,"
and that Spanish influence over the papacy "would not be seriously challenged" for the next sixty years.[4] Philip's modern biographers are equally
certain of Spanish control of Italy. Henry Kamen claims that the Treaty of
Cateau-Cambrésis "immeasurably strengthened Spain, which was confirmed in its domination of Italy," while Manuel Fernández Álvarez states
that through the treaty Spain's political aspirations "crystallized in the
dominion of Italy."[5] Geoffrey Parker, while he does not claim Spain had
uncontested hegemony in Italy, does suggest that only "minor disturbances" marred the "pax hispanica" in the fifty years following 1559.[6]
The great majority of historical studies in the last century thus contend
that from 1559, Spain's domination of Italy went virtually unchallenged
for the remainder of the sixteenth century.[7]

But a close examination of Spanish diplomatic correspondence suggests that the pacification of Italy never happened, and that there was no
sudden solidification of Spanish hegemony in 1559. Vargas, writing a year

2. "L'Italia fuori d'Italia: Due secoli e tre Italie," *Storia d'Italia: Dalla caduta dell'Impero romano
al secolo XVIII* (Turin, 1974), Vol. II, pp. 2156–57. Conversely, Braudel also saw a negative
side to the treaty, which, "by confirming the Spanish presence in Italy, helped to make
southern Europe the focus of the foreign policy of the Catholic King at the expense of more
urgent and possibly more fruitful endeavors." *The Mediterranean and the Mediterranean World
in the Age of Philip II*, trans. Siân Reynolds, 2 vols. (New York, 1973), Vol. II, p. 950. The idea
of Italy as a trouble spot for Spain is closer to my thesis.
3. *The Origins of the State in Italy 1530–1630*, ed. Julius Kirshner (London, 1988), p. 3.
4. *Spanish Rome 1500–1700* (New Haven, 2001), p. 57.
5. *Philip of Spain* (New Haven, 1997), p. 73; *Felipe II y su tiempo*, 10th ed. (Madrid, 2000), p.
340.
6. *The Grand Strategy of Philip II* (New Haven, 1998), p. 85.
7. In the late nineteenth and early twentieth centuries, in the wake of the creation of Italy
as a modern nation-state, Italian historians tended to view Renaissance Italy as the birth-
place of Italian nationalism. Benedetto Croce, in particular, described Italy in the early
modern period as being under foreign tyrannical rule—i.e., that of Spain. See Croce's work,
La Spagna nella vita italiana durante la Rinascenza (Bari, 1922); and Edmund E. Jacobitti,
"Hegemony before Gramsci: The Case of Benedetto Croce," *Journal of Modern History* 52
(1980), pp. 66–84. Christopher F. Black recently wrote that Spanish influence on sixteenth-
century Italy "has probably been exaggerated," although he focuses more on socio-cultural
issues than on political history. *Early Modern Italy: A Social History* (London, 2001), p.11.

after the Treaty of Cateau-Cambrésis, certainly does not seem confident about the political situation in Italy, and neither did any of his fellow ambassadors. As representatives of the power of Spain, the ambassadors sought to project a masterful image, but their letters reveal the hollowness of the façade. The fears, and the diplomatic failures, of Vargas and many other Spanish ambassadors in Italy should force us to reexamine the idea of a "Spanish peace."

Careful analysis of the inadequacies of Spanish diplomacy in Italy also reveals much about the weaknesses of the entire Habsburg imperial system in the early modern period. The Spanish ambassadors, as well as their masters, blundered in the classic way of the powerful: they assumed that their power represented the natural order of things, and that everyone would agree with this perception.[8] This study seeks to illuminate the limits of Spanish Habsburg imperialism, by focusing on the inability of Spanish diplomats to control Venice and Rome, the two most powerful states in Italy. Both the Venetians and the Papacy often defied Spanish power, confounding the Spaniards' belief in their own supremacy. Thus sixteenth-century Spanish-Italian relations serve as a microcosm of the wider struggle for hegemony in early modern Europe, which the Habsburgs would ultimately lose. The European continent never experienced a "pax hispanica" either, and an examination of the struggle for Italy helps to explain why. Furthermore, the Spanish experience in Italy highlights the dangers of imperialism in general: tremendous, even overwhelming power does not guarantee peace and security. Indeed, the paradox of such power is that the resentment it generates undermines the very peace it is supposed to enforce.

Clearly, both Charles V and Philip II sought control of Italy. Mercurino Gattinara, Charles's Grand Chancellor and one of his closest advisers early in his reign, convinced Charles that Italy should be the symbolic and strategic foundation of his empire.[9] In his famous "Political Instructions" to his son Philip (1548), Charles emphasized that the power and security of the Spanish empire depended on the ability to dominate the Italian peninsula.[10] When Charles abdicated his crowns between 1555 and 1558, he ceded Italy to his son Philip, the new king of Spain, rather than to his

---

8. Geoffrey Parker refers to this attitude of the Spaniards as "messianic imperialism." See *The Grand Strategy of Philip II,* and his essay "David or Goliath? Philip II and His World in the 1580s," in *Spain, Europe and the Atlantic World: Essays in Honour of J. H. Elliott,* ed. Richard Kagan and Geoffrey Parker (Cambridge, 1995), pp. 245–66.

9. John M. Headley, "The Habsburg World Empire and the Revival of Ghibellinism," in *Theories of Empire 1450–1800,* ed. David Armitage (Aldershot, 1998), pp. 45–79.

10. See Parker, *The Grand Strategy of Philip II,* pp. 80–83.

brother Ferdinand, the new Holy Roman Emperor. As J. H. Elliott writes, the Spaniards saw Iberia and Italy as a "logical unit."[11] Thus the Spanish Habsburgs envisioned Italy as integral to their imperial plans. Don Luis de Requeséns, who served as one of Philip's ministers in Italy, stated unequivocally, "the preservation, peace, and grandeur of Spain depend on the affairs of Italy being well ordered."[12]

Sixteenth-century Italy, however, was never unified or "well ordered." Instead, it consisted of a chaotic mixture of city-states, duchies, republics, and kingdoms, and all of these political entities had their own interests and agendas. Northern Italy alone contained hundreds of feudal territories, controlled by dozens of different noble Italian families. The one political point of view many Italian princes and states could agree on was that Italy suffered from oppression by foreign armies. Different Italian states may have hated each other, but they were even more contemptuous of non-Italians. Modern historians disagree on the strength of "Italianità" (Italian national identity) in the early modern period. By contrast, Spanish diplomats in Italy at the time were all too certain that Italians shared a common bond of resentment against the imperial power of Spain.[13]

On the surface, Habsburg hegemony in Italy seemed solid. Over the course of the sixteenth century the kings of Spain sought to win over or conquer as many of the individual territories of Italy as possible. In 1504, Charles's grandfather Ferdinand the Catholic incorporated the kingdoms of Naples and Sicily into the Spanish Crown, so southern Italy was relatively secure—although even here, resentment against foreign rule persisted throughout the sixteenth century.[14] During Charles's reign, northern Italy became one of the most important battlegrounds in the Habsburg-Valois struggle for European hegemony. Charles gained a great deal of ground: the Republic of Genoa made a decisive move into the Habsburg camp in 1528, and Charles annexed the key Duchy of Milan in 1535. The Republic of Florence resisted for a while, but it too fell to

11. *Imperial Spain 1469–1716* (reprint, 1990), p. 210.
12. Requeséns to Philip, November 7, 1574; quoted in Parker, *The Grand Strategy of Philip II*, p. 82. Requeséns served as ambassador to Rome from 1563 to 1568, lieutenant to Don Juan de Austria in Spain's Mediterranean fleet 1568–1571, and governor general of Milan 1571–1573; for his tenure as ambassador see chapter three.
13. For a description of Italian ideas of national identity, see Felix Gilbert, "Italy," in *National Consciousness, History, and Political Culture in Early-Modern Europe*, ed. Orest Ranum (Baltimore, 1975), pp. 21–42.
14. In 1536, for example, one of Charles's ministers in Italy warned that in Naples, the Spanish viceroy's "pacification" policies (which involved a "divide and conquer" approach toward the populace) had caused much unrest, and could lead to a revolt. John A. Marino, *Pastoral Economics in the Kingdom of Naples* (Baltimore, 1988), p. 175.

imperial troops in 1530, and the pro-imperial Medici family was restored to power.

Philip continued his father's work by wooing many of the great Italian noble families. With some he forged marriage alliances; the duke of Savoy for example (another key player in northern Italy) wedded Philip's younger daughter Catalina in 1585. To other Italian nobles Philip granted pensions or titles and feudal honors. At the same time, Philip fortified Spanish territories in Italy and quartered troops in strategic posts.[15] By the late sixteenth century, of all the Italian territories, only the Republic of Venice and the Papal States remained free of Spanish control.[16] But they represented potential threats to Spanish interests, and even some of Philip's Italian allies showed disturbing signs of independence. In 1569–1570, for example, Duke Cosimo de'Medici of Florence accepted the title "grand duke of Tuscany" from Pope Pius V. Cosimo technically owed feudal allegiance to both Philip and his cousin, Emperor Maximilian II of Austria, but he acted on his own, and against Habsburg wishes. Cosimo's son Ferdinando inherited the title of grand duke, and married a French princess (1589). So Venice, the Papal States, and to a lesser degree Tuscany, all remained islands of Italian power, and thus potential enemies of Spain.

The Spanish Habsburgs were uncomfortably aware that any Italian power could at any time jeopardize what control they had in Italy, simply by allying with one of Spain's enemies. After all, in 1494 the Italian Wars began when an Italian prince invited the French king Charles VIII into Italy, a scenario that haunted the Habsburgs throughout the sixteenth century and beyond. The Habsburgs also knew that the Italian princes did not necessarily perceive themselves as logically subordinate to Spain. Venice and the Papacy were particularly wary of Spanish domination, and had the ability to act on their anti-Spanish impulses. They represented the last stumbling blocks between the Habsburgs and total control of Italy, and thus had to be contained as far as possible. To accomplish this task, the Spanish crown depended on its resident ambassadors.

The office of resident ambassador developed in Italy during the fifteenth century, when permanent embassies and diplomatic channels of communication became instruments in maintaining the balance of

15. Milan, for example, became a bastion of Spanish power, anchoring the southern end of the "Spanish Road" to the Netherlands; see Geoffrey Parker, *The Army of Flanders and the Spanish Road 1567–1659*, (reprint, Cambridge, 1990).
16. Eladi Romero García, *El imperialismo hispánico en la Toscana durante el siglo XVI* (Lérida, 1986), p. 5

power in the peninsula.[17] The practice then spread throughout Europe. Generally, Renaissance princes appointed loyal nobles as ambassadors; envoys received detailed instructions, but little to no formal diplomatic training.[18] In the Middle Ages, ambassadors usually had very limited authority, but in the early modern period, as states established permanent embassies, the status of ambassadors increased. They became fixtures in the courts, and demanded recognition befitting the princes they represented. Diplomatic rituals became ever more elaborate, as ambassadors jealously guarded their rank and privileges. Ceremonies involving ambassadors transformed into political theater: where envoys stood or sat in relation to each other served as a barometer for relationships between states and rulers.[19] So in addition to negotiating state business in his prince's name, an ambassador also sought to burnish his prince's image—in fact, by the seventeenth century the projection of state power had become an ambassador's primary function.[20] And as we will see, no one understood this better than the Spaniards.

King Ferdinand the Catholic of Spain was one of the first Western European monarchs to adopt the Italian diplomatic system, and during the period 1480–1500 established resident embassies in Rome, Venice, London, Brussels, and the itinerant court of the Holy Roman Emperor.[21] Ferdinand envisioned these embassies, which encircled France, as a tool to help contain French expansion. A corps of Spanish diplomats formed, which would develop into what Garrett Mattingly called "the most impressive diplomatic service in Europe."[22] Charles V inherited this system from Ferdinand, and soon learned the benefits derived from having representatives in strategic posts, as well as having sources of accurate political information.[23]

17. The classic work on this topic is Garrett Mattingly, *Renaissance Diplomacy* (reprint, New York, 1988). For more recent work on Italian diplomacy, see *Politics and Diplomacy in Early Modern Italy: The Structure of Diplomatic Practice, 1450–1800*, ed. Daniela Frigo (Cambridge, 2000).

18. In the later sixteenth century, the English diplomatic corps was "professionalized," with more members coming from the gentry, and with greater emphasis on formal training. See Gary M. Bell, "Elizabethan Diplomacy: The Subtle Revolution," in *Politics, Religion and Diplomacy in Early Modern Europe: Essays in Honor of De Lamar Jensen*, ed. Malcolm R. Thorp and Arthur J. Slavin (Kirksville, 1994), pp. 267–88.

19. William Roosen, "Early Modern Diplomatic Ceremonial: A Systems Approach," *Journal of Modern History* 52 (1980), pp. 452–76.

20. See Charles H. Carter, "The Ambassadors of Early Modern Europe: Patterns of Diplomatic Representation in the Early Seventeenth Century," in *From the Renaissance to the Counter-Reformation: Essays in Honor of Garrett Mattingly*, ed. Charles H. Carter (New York, 1965), pp. 269–95.

21. Elliott, *Imperial Spain*, p. 132.

22. Mattingly, *Renaissance Diplomacy*, p. 129.

23. Ibid., p. 160.

This was especially critical in Italy, and in the 1520s Charles expanded the system there by establishing two additional embassies, in the Republic of Genoa and the Duchy of Savoy.[24] While Charles recruited men from many nations into his diplomatic service, reflecting the nature of his multinational empire, all of his ambassadors in Italy were Spaniards.[25] By the time Philip II inherited the throne, the embassies (along with the territories of Milan and Naples) had become anchors for the Spanish imperial system in Italy.[26]

The ambassadors functioned as representatives of the king of Spain, and their task, in the words of Francisco de Vargas, was to exercise "vigilance and power." As diplomats, they sought to influence the Italians according to Spanish interests. The ambassadors sometimes employed subtle methods, but more often they depended on bluster and brute force; they were not often "diplomatic" in the modern sense of the term. The Spaniards of early modern Europe developed a well-earned reputation for arrogance, and no one did more to perpetuate this image than Spain's ambassadors.[27] Time and again the ambassadors expressed frustration that the Italians refused to acknowledge the benefits of Spanish rule. Evidence suggests that the ambassadors honestly did not understand why this should be the case. Every time the Venetians or the Papacy acted against Spanish interests, which they often did, the ambassadors displayed shock and a sense of betrayal. Sometimes their frustration boiled over into fury; Requeséns once wrote that he abhorred Italians more than any other nation in the world, and "if God had not done me the favor of making me Spanish, I would wish to be a Tartar before being Italian."[28] With this kind of attitude it is not surprising that Spanish ambassadors were sometimes less than persuasive.

Nonetheless, the primary responsibility of the resident ambassadors in Rome and Venice was to convince those powers to aid Spain in its quest for hegemony in Italy and beyond—and conversely, they had to be prevented from abetting Spain's enemies.[29] This basic mission remained the

24. The Savoy embassy was expelled when the French invaded that state in 1536; it would be reestablished in 1570.

25. Mattingly, *Renaissance Diplomacy*, p. 160.

26. See *Nel sistema imperiale: L'Italia spagnola*, ed. Aurelio Musi (Naples, 1994).

27. For a recent description of European perceptions of Spain and the Spaniards, see J. N. Hillgarth, *The Mirror of Spain, 1500–1700: The Formation of a Myth* (Ann Arbor, 2000).

28. Requeséns to Gonzálo Pérez, March 3, 1565; AGSE 1394, #138.

29. Since Genoa was a firm ally during most of this period, the embassy there did not have quite the same function. Instead, it primarily acted as liaison between the Crown and the Genoese bankers who financed the empire. Yet here too the resident ambassador had to keep his eyes open (as any ambassador must). In his instructions to Antonio de Mendoza, a new ambassador to Genoa, Philip ordered Mendoza to "learn which of those people [in

same for all ambassadors throughout the sixteenth century. At various points the Habsburgs believed they had achieved these goals, only to be disappointed by a fresh crisis. This book begins, for example, with the events that led to the imperial coronation of Charles V in Bologna in 1530, a symbolic triumph that supposedly marked Charles's ascendancy in Italy.[30] But over the next few decades France invaded Italy repeatedly, often with the connivance of Italian states. Philip, of course, also thought he had established mastery of Italy in 1559, but for the rest of his reign Venice and the Papacy remained stubbornly independent. In 1598, the final year of Philip II's life, Pope Clement VIII seized the northern Italian city-state of Ferrara, with Venetian connivance. This move threatened the stability of the entire region, and demonstrated Philip's ultimate inability to control Italian power politics.[31]

Venice, one of the greatest military and commercial powers in the Mediterranean during the early modern period, figured heavily in Spain's imperial ambitions for that region. Spanish diplomacy in Venice focused on creating and sustaining a military alliance with the Republic against the Ottoman Turks. Twice, however, the Venetians abandoned Spain and signed a separate peace (in 1540 and in 1573), pursuing their own interests rather than Spanish strategic concerns. Venetian resentment of Spanish power, as well as the efforts of Turkish and French agents, often undermined the ambassadors' efforts. The Venetians thus remained beyond Spanish command: never openly hostile, but also rarely friendly, except when it suited them.

In Rome, Spanish ambassadors faced an even more critical task: ensuring that a friend (or at least not a foe) sat on the throne of St. Peter. All the Habsburgs' grand designs, including mounting a crusade against the Muslims, suppressing Protestant heresy, and defending their empire against all enemies (particularly France), depended on the spiritual, political, and financial support of the Papacy. But at several critical moments, the ambassadors failed. During Charles V's reign, imperial ambassadors bungled two papal elections. The worst disaster occurred at

---

Genoa] favor our affairs, which do not, and which are those who belong to France." October 1, 1570; AGSE 1401, #258.

30. See Bonner Mitchell, *The Majesty of the State: Triumphal Progresses of Foreign Sovereigns in Renaissance Italy (1494–1600)* (Florence, 1986), pp. 135–49; idem, "Carlos V como triunfador," in *Carolus V Imperator*, ed. Pedro Navascués Palacio (Madrid, 1999), pp. 213–51; and Marcello Fantoni, "Carlo V e l'Immagine dell'Imperatore," in *Carlo V e l'Italia*, ed. Marcello Fantoni (Rome, 2000), pp. 101–18.

31. For a description of the Ferrara crisis, see Ludwig von Pastor, *The History of the Popes from the Close of the Middle Ages*, trans. Ralph Francis Kerr, 40 vols. (London, 1891–1953), Vol. XXIV, pp. 367–416.

the end of Charles's reign, when Pope Paul IV came to power in 1555. A sworn enemy of Spain, Paul excommunicated both Charles and Philip, declared war on the Habsburgs, and tried to free Italy from their control. And even when the Spanish ambassadors successfully manipulated the Papacy, as they did with Julius III (1550–1555), their machinations often backfired. The War of Parma (1550–1552), a futile conflict provoked by the Spanish ambassador, exemplifies this type of failure. Throughout the first half of the sixteenth century, Charles's envoys proved remarkably unable to control the Papacy.

Under Philip II, Spanish ambassadors had much greater success at getting friendly popes elected, but even in the period directly following the Treaty of Cateau-Cambrésis, they experienced some painful setbacks. One of their most notable failures concerned the issue of precedence: in 1564, Pope Pius IV (1559–1566) confirmed France in its claim to diplomatic precedence over Spain.[32] This jarring propaganda defeat demonstrates that even after 1559, the Papacy could and did defy Spanish power. Pope Pius V (1566–1572) drove this point home when he awarded Cosimo de'Medici the title of "grand duke of Tuscany," against the Spaniards' strenuous objections. Spanish ambassadors did, however, succeed in crafting a military alliance or "Holy League" between Spain, the Papacy and Venice, which culminated in the great naval victory over the Ottoman Turks at Lepanto (1571). Yet the torturous negotiations over the terms of the alliance again demonstrated the limits of Spanish influence: the strategic aims of the league reflected Italian priorities, not those of the Spaniards. And two years after the league's victory, the Venetians defected from it, again testifying to the fragility of a "pax hispanica."

In the later decades of Philip's reign, the king's attentions turned away from the Mediterranean and toward the Atlantic. Spanish ambassadors tried to induce the Papacy to aid Spain's great military endeavors, including the defeat of the Dutch revolt and the invasion of England. Here, too, the ambassadors encountered more resistance than they expected. Pope Sixtus V (1585–1590) in particular had his own agendas and priorities, which often clashed with those of King Philip. Pope Clement VIII (1592–1605) proved even worse from the Spanish point of view: in 1595, he confirmed the ex-heretic Henry of Navarre as king of France, ignoring Spanish outrage. Three years later, as Philip lay dying, Clement seized the territory of Ferrara. This move threatened Spanish

---

32. See Michael J. Levin, "A New World Order: The Spanish Campaign for Precedence in Early Modern Europe," *Journal of Early Modern History* 6 (2002), pp. 233–64.

hegemony in northern Italy, because a war between Italian states might lure France into invading once again. The panic in the letters of all of Spain's ambassadors during this crisis testifies to their insecurity about their ability to maintain control of Italy.

The Spanish ambassadors in Rome also had various special responsibilities, which increased the difficulty of their task. For example, the ambassadors constantly worried about matters of Church finance, jurisdiction, and dispensations. Without money generated by Church revenues, the Spanish Crown would be severely hampered—a fact the Papacy well knew, and used to force concessions out of Spain's envoys. Conflicts over jurisdiction also indicate the limits of Spanish power: the Papacy often challenged the Crown over control of Church property in Spanish dominions. Finally, the Spanish Crown and nobility bombarded the ambassadors with requests for special favors from the Papacy, which annoyed both them and the popes. These small matters could add up, for the ambassadors had only so much time and energy, and the popes had only so much patience and goodwill.

While their mission required them to be diplomats first, the ambassadors also acted as intelligence officers, and all too often they did not like the information they uncovered. They perceived quite clearly the limits of Spanish power in Italy, and repeatedly warned their masters about this fact. To refer back to the words of Francisco de Vargas, their position required "vigilance": to be alert for any threats, either foreign or domestic, to Spanish hegemony. The ambassadors acted as spies, gathering information on what the Italians really thought about the Spaniards, as well as on external threats to Spanish power, particularly from France and the Ottoman Turks. The ambassadors collected much of this information themselves, but they also employed informants and ran intelligence networks.[33] Sometimes this work could be dangerous: a number of ambassadors instigated, or dodged, violence and assassination. Many ambassadors acted as if they were living in enemy territory, another indication of the limitations of the "pax hispanica."

Spanish ambassadors in Italy served another important function, that of conduit of Italian Renaissance culture to Spain. Besides its strategic importance, Italy also represented a storehouse of artistic and scholarly wealth. The ambassadors often acted as middlemen between the Spanish Crown and nobility, and the artists of the late Italian Renaissance. They

---

33. Early modern states and princes had an unspoken understanding that espionage was part of the duties of an ambassador; see Mattingly, *Renaissance Diplomacy*, pp. 207–19; Donald E. Queller, *The Office of Ambassador in the Middle Ages* (Princeton, 1967), chap. IV; and M. S. Anderson, *The Rise of Modern Diplomacy 1450–1919* (London, 1993), pp. 12–13.

also scoured Italy for books and manuscripts, many of which ended up in the Escorial library. In a similar vein, the ambassadors arranged for the transportation of large numbers of religious relics from Italy to Spain, again destined for Philip's palace/mausoleum.[34] Finally, the ambassadors tapped the human resources of Italy, recruiting soldiers, engineers, and others with skills the Habsburg empire needed. In all of these efforts the Spaniards exhibited little regard for Italian sensibilities.

The ambassadors did, however, worry quite a lot about Italian intentions, as revealed by their constant use of the word *novedades* (novelties, changes, upsets).[35] By the early sixteenth century, the necessity of avoiding instability had become a commonplace in political theory and discourse, particularly in Italy. Niccolò Machiavelli, for example, advised princes, especially those in newly conquered territories, to beware intervention by other powers. Such threats to stability, he warned, would always be encouraged by a subjugated populace, "either because their ambitions are unsatisfied, or because they are afraid of the dominant powers."[36] The Spaniards in Italy encountered exactly this problem. Similarly, Francesco Guicciardini traced the woes of Italy to the death of Lorenzo de'Medici, who had "preserved the peace" and had been "diligently on the watch against every incident, even the slightest."[37] From Guicciardini's perspective, which many of his countrymen shared, the "novelties" of 1494 marked the beginning of national humiliation. But for the Spanish invaders, *novedades* had a very different—and very specific—meaning.

In the letter quoted above, Vargas spoke of the Italians disparagingly as a people addicted to *novedades*. This sentiment echoes throughout Spanish diplomatic correspondence in this period. Vargas and his fellow ambassadors also stated repeatedly that *novedades* in Italy had to be prevented at all costs. The Spaniards feared any threat to the political status quo, or anything that could jeopardize their control of Italy. And yet, according to the ambassadors, the princes of Italy loved to plot just such events. This Spanish obsession with *novedades* should make us suspicious of an absolute "pax hispanica" in sixteenth-century Italy. The fear of *novedades* existed in 1529, where this book begins, and it had in no way

34. See Fernando Checa Cremades, *Felipe II: Mecenas de las artes* (Madrid, 1992).

35. For a description of the use of this word in seventeenth-century Spanish political thought, see José Antonio Maravall, *Culture of the Baroque: Analysis of a Historical Structure*, trans. Terry Cochran (Minneapolis, 1986), pp. 126–28.

36. *The Prince*, ed. and trans. David Wootton (Indianapolis, 1995), p. 10. It should also be noted that Machiavelli specifically refers to Naples as just such a newly conquered state.

37. *The History of Italy*, trans. Sidney Alexander (reprint, Princeton, NJ, 1984), p. 7.

dissipated in 1598, where it ends. Indeed, it would only increase in the seventeenth century, as Spanish imperial power visibly declined.[38] Spain's ambassadors in Italy, who were responsible for maintaining control of the peninsula, never felt confident of success—and therefore, we should not be too certain of it either. We should perceive Spanish hegemony in Italy as they did: as something contingent and often contested.

To be sure, Spain indisputably dominated Italy to a large degree. Habsburg military strength had no rival in the peninsula, and no major wars occurred there for sixty years. The picture of Italy as seen through the ambassadors' eyes is in some ways distorted: it was their job to look for and worry about potential problems, and so of course they found them. The utopian vision of total control could never be achieved. Yet the ambassadors' opinions, actions, and failures must be taken into account if we are to understand the nature of Spanish power in Italy. In the final analysis, Spanish imperialism produced ambiguous results. The Spaniards suffered from an arrogant belief in their own imperial ideology, and with such an attitude they were never going to win the hearts and minds of all Italians. Many Italians responded with resentment and fear, which became worse the more pressure the Spaniards applied—a fact that points to the fundamental paradox of the entire Spanish Habsburg empire in the early modern period. Habsburg hegemony in Europe, and indeed the world, slipped away at the very moment when triumph appeared to be within their grasp. The threat of Spanish domination created too many enemies, whose combined strength was too great to overcome. Scholars such as Pierre Vilar and J. H. Elliott have pointed out the significance of Don Quixote as a symbol of Spain at this moment of history.[39] Like the Knight of the Sorrowful Countenance, the Spaniards believed in themselves and their mission, but their attempt to establish world dominance proved as futile as tilting at windmills. The Spanish empire had undeniable might, but ultimately it went the way of all such constructions. By the seventeenth century, it had become clear that vigilance and power could not save an empire in decline.

---

38. J. H. Elliott, "Self-Perception and Decline in Early Seventeenth-Century Spain," in *Spain and Its World 1500–1700* (New Haven, 1989), pp. 257–58.
39. Pierre Vilar, "The Age of Don Quixote," trans. Richard Morris, in *Essays in European Economic History 1500–1800*, ed. Peter Earle (Oxford, 1974), pp. 100–112; J. H. Elliott, "The Decline of Spain," in *Spain and Its World*, p. 240.

CHAPTER ONE

Diplomacy in Venice

The Republic of Venice played an important part in the Spanish Habsburgs' imperial plans for Italy, and indeed for the entire Mediterranean. Venice lay in a key geographical position, at the crossroads between Central Europe and Italy, and between Western Europe and the Levant.[1] Spain thus needed the Venetians to counter its two greatest enemies, the Turks and the French. On land, Venice controlled a large corner of northeast Italy, but its real power was at sea. The Venetian fleets, both military and commercial, were among the most powerful in the world, in large part due to the city's tremendous shipyards (the famous Arsenal).[2] The Venetians also controlled a network of colonies that extended throughout the eastern Mediterranean, which served as military bases, trading posts, and spy centers. Venetian power peaked in the early sixteenth century, and then began to decline, but they remained a force in Italian politics and Mediterranean warfare. Both Charles V and Philip II sought alliances with Venice in the war against the Turks, and also hoped the Republic would act as a bulwark against French invasions into northern Italy. But the Venetians often disappointed, not to say defied, both Spanish monarchs. Twice, in 1540 and in 1573, the Venetians abandoned a military alliance with Spain and signed a separate peace with the Turks. They also remained friendly with France, much to the Spaniards' disgust. Spanish ambassadors in Venice

1. William H. McNeill, *Venice, the Hinge of Europe 1081–1797* (Chicago, 1974).
2. See the classic work by Frederic C. Lane, *Venice: A Maritime Republic* (Baltimore, 1973); and more recently, Robert C. Davis, *Shipbuilders of the Venetian Arsenal: Workers and Workplace in the Preindustrial City* (Baltimore, 1991).

sought to guide the Venetians toward pro-Spanish policies, but they often failed. Throughout the sixteenth century, Spanish diplomats tried to master the Republic of Venice, but the Venetians refused to be servants of Spain.

In Venice, the ambassadors faced entrenched fear and resentment of Habsburg imperial power. The Venetians were hemmed in by Habsburg territories: to the north, the Republic bordered the Holy Roman Empire, while to the west lay the Duchy of Milan, which after 1535 became one of Charles V's feudal holdings. In the War of the League of Cambrai (1509–1517), Spain and the Emperor had participated in the attempted dismantling of Venice's land-based empire, and the destruction of the Republic's pretensions to dominating northern Italy.[3] For the rest of the sixteenth century the Spanish ambassadors would wrestle with the problem of converting the Venetians from enemies to allies. Additionally, the complexities of Venetian politics compounded the difficulty of their task. The ambassadors had to negotiate with dozens of individual government officials, whose agendas often conflicted.

For the most part, the ambassadors dealt with the *Signoria* of Venice: the Doge, the Ducal Council, and the Senate. The *Signoria,* as the policy-making body of the Venetian government, was the center of attention for all diplomatic activity.[4] The Doge's position as head of state was in part ceremonial, so the ambassadors could not focus their energies exclusively on him; they also had to talk with various senators, councilors, and other officials. Sometimes they made official speeches to the assembled Venetian government, or had formal audiences with the Doge and his councilors, while at other times they met informally with individuals. The instructions to new ambassadors to Venice illustrate the combination of ritual solemnity and raw politicking that typified the diplomatic experience in "The Most Serene Republic."

In March 1530, a trio of imperial diplomats arrived in Venice: Marino Caracciolo, a churchman and notary; Jean de Memorancy, a member of Charles V's household; and Rodrigo Niño, the new resident ambassador. At this point in time, the Spaniards enjoyed a position of strength in Italy. That same year the Treaty of Bologna concluded the latest phase of the Wars of Italy in Charles's favor. The French had been crushed at Pavia in 1525, and defeated again in 1529, leading to the Peace of Cambrai and Francis I's renunciation of claims to Milan and Naples.[5] Imperial troops

---

3. See Felix Gilbert, "Venice and the Crisis of the League of Cambrai," in *Renaissance Venice,* ed. J. R. Hale (London, 1973), pp. 274–92.
4. For a description, see D. S. Chambers, *The Imperial Age of Venice 1380–1580* (London, 1970), pp. 73–108.
5. Manuel Fernández Álvarez, *Charles V: Elected Emperor and Hereditary Ruler* (London, 1975), chap. 6.

had humbled Pope Clement VII and sacked Rome in 1527, and Venice itself had been badly hurt in the last two decades of war.[6] Charles had arranged to be crowned Emperor by Pope Clement VII at Bologna, a brilliant piece of imperial propaganda, re-creating the coronation of his namesake Charlemagne seven centuries earlier. He was eager to follow up this climactic moment with an effort to cement alliances in northern Italy. The imagery of his triumphal entry and coronation at Bologna had emphasized his role as peacemaker, but Charles evidently worried that the Venetians (among others) had not been convinced.[7]

The Emperor's instructions to the ambassadors stated that after presenting their credentials to the *Signoria*, the first thing they should do was to explain Charles's reasons for coming to Italy: "we saw how mistaken everyone or almost everyone was there about our intentions, and we are certain that once they become better known and proven [the Italians] will be assured of our friendship, with which all Italy may live in peace and tranquility, and then we would have better opportunity to remedy the rest of Christendom, which is what we most desire in the world."[8]

This document illustrates several key points. First of all, it shows that one of Charles's priorities, and thus that of his ambassadors as well, was "the peace of Italy." The Emperor had to deal with Europe-wide conflicts: Lutheran heresy was on the rise in Germany and beyond, while the armies of the Ottoman Turks had advanced as far into Central Europe as the gates of Vienna. Neither of these crises could be solved without a solid Italian base of operations. Second, Italy could not be pacified unless imperial diplomacy convinced the Italians that peace through Habsburg domination was a good thing. Charles's hopeful prediction that the Venetians would cooperate with the imperial agenda once they understood his intentions illustrates the Habsburg mind-set. Italians constantly surprised the Spanish kings and their ambassadors by refusing to accept Iberian overlords.

Charles instructed his ambassadors to campaign to get the message across. He commanded the diplomats to "visit on our behalf with the

6. See André Chastel, *The Sack of Rome, 1527*, trans. Beth Archer (Princeton, 1983); and Elisabeth G. Gleason, "Confronting New Realities: Venice and the Peace of Bologna, 1530," in *Venice Reconsidered: the History and Civilization of an Italian City-State, 1297–1797*, ed. John Martin and Dennis Romano (Baltimore, 2000), pp. 168–84.

7. On the imagery of the coronation, see Bonner Mitchell, *The Majesty of the State: Triumphal Progresses of Foreign Sovereigns in Renaissance Italy (1494–1600)* (Florence, 1986), pp. 135–49; and Tiziana Bernardi, "Analisi di una cerimonia pubblica: L'incoronazione di Carlo V a Bologna," *Quaderni storici* 61 (1986), pp. 171–99.

8. Charles to ambassadors, February 17, 1530; Archivo General de Simancas, Sección Estado (hereafter cited as AGSE) 1308, #16.

Illustrious Doge of Venice our cousin and with other persons you deem appropriate, and tell them of our desire to pacify Italy." Thus Charles established the pattern of Spanish diplomacy in Venice, as in all of Italy: the Venetians had to be courted, and the resident ambassador was the principle courter/courtier. The last paragraph of Charles' instructions specifically ordered Niño, as the permanent ambassador, to maintain the "devotion and friendship" of the Venetians, and to "advise us very often of everything which may come to your attention and whatever seems to you fitting that we may be informed of." As we shall see, this too reflects the pattern of Spanish diplomacy: the ambassador must promote good relations, but also keep his eyes open.

The Venetians greeted the ambassadors with much pomp and circumstance, which they took as their due: "This morning we made our first entrance accompanied by the entire Senate, with no exceptions, and they performed the full complement of demonstrations which Your Majesty's good works for them obliged them to do. . . . [later] this morning we made our public declaration of friendship according to your will and instruction, and the Doge responded as is to be expected of him."[9] The ambassadors' arrogant tone reflected their sense of power and entitlement. The Venetians' eagerness to please them no doubt added to their confidence. The ambassadors boasted to Charles that the Venetians had feted them to an extent never before seen in that city, and that "all of the people here rejoice in our arrival, because Your Majesty is loved here today as if you were their natural lord, and they do not know how to say anything other than praise of your most holy person."[10]

Niño tried hard to follow up this apparent wave of pro-imperial sentiment with continuing promises of friendship and security under the Habsburg banner. In June 1530 he read aloud a letter from Charles to the assembled Venetian government, and received a highly favorable response from Doge Andrea Gritti, who "gave thanks to Our Lord for having given us peace with his Imperial Majesty, which is the greatest gift he could give us."[11] Such votes of confidence were few and far between, however, as the Venetians remained jittery about the Emperor's intentions, as well as the continuing possibility of war in northern Italy over possession of Milan. A year after the coronation Niño had to again reassure the Venetian Senate that "what mattered most to [Charles] was the tranquility of Italy because then everyone would live in peace and each

---

9. Ambassadors to Charles, March 12, 1530; AGSE 1308, #20.
10. Ambassadors to Charles, March 19, 1530; AGSE 1308, #21.
11. Niño to Charles, June 2, 1530; AGSE 1308 #45.

would enjoy what God has given them."[12] The implication that Venice should be happy with its lot was surely not accidental, coming from the imperial ambassador.

The effort to keep Venice friendly with the emperor was only half the battle; Niño also sought to turn Venice into an enemy of Charles's enemies. Peace in Italy meant opportunities for war elsewhere, and the infidel Turk topped the list as potential target. Charles was eager to turn his attentions toward the Moslem threat, especially after a humiliating raid by the infamous corsair Barbarossa on the coast of Spain itself.[13] The Venetians, however, feared to become involved in open warfare against Suleiman. Indeed, they had sent messages of peace to Constantinople even as Charles's coronation was taking place.[14] Through most of the sixteenth century, Venice attempted to keep a foot in both the Habsburg and the Turkish camps. Many Venetian nobles had personal or commercial ties with Constantinople: Doge Andrea Gritti, for example, had lived there for many years in his early career as merchant and ambassador.[15] Spanish ambassadors never seemed able to accept the fact of Venice's interrelationship with the Ottoman Empire, or to empathize with the Venetian point of view. Instead, they accused the Venetians of greed, cowardice, or sheer perversity. Niño's reports on Venetian-Turkish relations demonstrated this typically narrow and self-righteous attitude.

The arrival of a Turkish ambassador in Venice in early June 1530 occasioned much speculation about the Republic's foreign policy. Rumors of a huge fleet being prepared for war in Constantinople had circulated in Venice for months, so the Turkish representative's appearance caused no little trepidation. The official reason for this visit was to inform the Republic of a major celebration in Constantinople in honor of the circumcision of Suleiman's sons, and to invite the participation of Venetian officials. Niño observed the rival ambassador's movements with extreme care, and noted how the Venetians honored him, in order to ascertain the real purpose of the meeting. Venetian diplomatic protocol was highly ritualized, and every element imbued with symbolic meaning. Who greeted a foreign dignitary, where they met, and how they proceeded to the audience chamber at the Ducal Palace, all indicated the importance

12. Niño to Charles, February 2, 1531; AGSE 1308 #128–31.
13. R. B. Merriman, *The Rise of the Spanish Empire in the Old World and in the New*, Vol. III, *The Emperor* (New York, 1925), pp. 294–301.
14. John Julius Norwich, *A History of Venice* (reprint, New York, 1982), p. 449.
15. During his time there he also fathered three illegitimate children; see James C. Davis, "Shipping and Spying in the Early Career of a Venetian Doge, 1496–1502," *Studi veneziani* 16 (1974), pp. 97–108.

of a visitor and the probable outcome of his mission.[16] The great honor done to this Turkish ambassador boded ill in Niño's eyes:

> [The Turkish ambassador] went to the Palace, they say accompanied from his residence by principle members of the College, and among them two of the most important on either side of him. The Doge descended his stairs and came halfway across the chamber to receive him, and there did him all the honors possible. He took him by the right hand and set him in the place reserved for the papal legate, or me in his absence. [The ambassador] gave his letter of credential, written on paper, which they say was an arm and a half long. . . . it came rolled in a container of brocade, sealed with white wax, and the seal was covered with a layer of gold. . . . he gave it to the Doge who broke the seal and gave it to a secretary of the Turkish language who read it. He read that the ambassador proposed his embassy and in effect it was for no other purpose but to announce that the Turk would circumcise his sons on the 8th of July, for which he would have the greatest celebration ever seen in his lands.[17]

Niño was clearly suspicious and resentful of the elaborate honors given to this representative of the infidel, particularly when the Turk usurped Niño's own position. But he dissimulated his anxiety with the Venetians. On Easter Day, with all of the ambassadors gathered together to celebrate Mass with the Doge, Niño joked with Gritti that if the Doge planned to leave for Constantinople, now would be a good time. The subtext of the joke is clear: how subservient toward the Turks did the Doge want to appear? The conversation turned serious, as Niño questioned the Doge closely about what the Turkish envoy was really doing in Venice. Gritti swore that there was no hidden agenda, but Niño obviously did not believe him.

Throughout the Turkish envoy's stay in Venice, Niño argued with Gritti about declaring war against Suleiman. Gritti maintained that it was important not to provoke the Turks just now, "because if they were to send out their armada it would be in order to destroy the world."[18] Niño assured the Doge that Charles stood ready to fight, but the Venetians remained unconvinced.[19] A week after the departure of the Turkish

---

16. See Edward Muir, *Civic Ritual in Renaissance Venice* (Princeton, 1981).
17. Niño to Charles, June 10, 1530; AGSE 1308 #52.
18. Ibid.
19. In 1533 Charles sent an envoy to Constantinople with an offer of peace; see Robert Finlay, "Prophecy and Politics in Istanbul: Charles V, Sultan Süleyman, and the Habsburg Embassy of 1533–1534," *Journal of Early Modern History* 2 (1998), pp. 249–72.

embassy Niño reported that the Venetians had given the ambassador costly gifts of clothing, and had sent to Suleiman a jeweled vase said to be worth ten thousand ducats.[20] If Niño had hoped to turn Venice into a staunch ally against the Turks, he clearly failed. Even in this period of Habsburg imperial might, the Venetians did not necessarily do what the imperial ambassador wanted.

Over the next few years, political and strategic circumstances—particularly Charles's growing power in Italy—helped push Venice further into the imperial camp. The death of Francesco Sforza, duke of Milan, in 1535 resulted in that state reverting to the Emperor's feudal overlordship, strengthening his hold on northern Italy. Charles installed the Marquis del Vasto, one of a number of "Hispanicized" Italian nobles who served the imperial cause, as governor of Milan.[21] Meanwhile, the Turkish threat in the Mediterranean grew worse. In 1537 they besieged the island of Corfu, key to many of Venice's trading colonies, which impelled the Republic to enter a military alliance or Holy League with Charles and Pope Paul III. But the League suffered a humiliating defeat the following year at the battle of Prevesa, in large part because the imperial commander Andrea Doria, admiral of the Genoese fleet (and thus no friend of the rival maritime power of Venice) had secret orders not to engage the enemy.[22] Not surprisingly, Venetian support for Charles took a drastic downturn. It was up to the resident ambassador to try to repair the damage.

In 1539, a new ambassador arrived in Venice named Don Diego Hurtado de Mendoza. He was an experienced diplomat, having already served as ambassador to England and as a soldier in France and northern Africa.[23] Mendoza was also one of Spain's leading humanists, and he brought his classical education and training as a rhetorician to bear on his new job as propagandist for the Emperor.[24] He came with favorable references from Alvise Mocenigo, Venice's ambassador to Charles, who remarked on his learning and "pleasant conversation," as well as his apparent goodwill towards the Republic.[25] He used all his skills to try to maintain the Venetians as military allies, but he too would ultimately fail.

20. Niño to Charles, June 28, 1530; AGSE 1308, #62.

21. Manuel Rivero Rodríguez, *Felipe II y el gobierno de Italia* (Madrid, 1998), pp. 31–35.

22. Gaetano Cozzi, ed., *Storia d'Italia*, Vol. XII, *La Repubblica di Venezia nell'età moderna: Dal 1517 alla fine della Repubblicà* (Turin, 1992), pp. 40–45.

23. Erica Spivakovsky, *Son of the Alhambra: Don Diego Hurtado de Mendoza, 1504–1575* (Austin, 1970), chap. 3.

24. Helen Nader, *The Mendoza Family in the Spanish Renaissance, 1350–1550* (New Brunswick, 1979), pp. 199–200.

25. Spivakovsky, *Son of the Alhambra*, p. 71.

FIGURE 1. Portrait of Don Diego Hurtado de Mendoza, by Titian (1540). Pitti Gallery, Florence. Courtesy of Alinari/Art Resource, NY.

Charles's initial instructions to Mendoza made clear the importance of holding together the Holy League.[26] Mendoza was first to consult with the outgoing ambassador, Lope de Soria, about the current state of Venetian morale, which he then had to bolster in any way possible. Charles expressed concern that the Republic's recent pledges of support lacked both enthusiasm and specific details. He commanded Mendoza to make public declarations of the Emperor's continuing friendship and support, and then to personally lobby the recently elected Doge, Pietro Lando, as well as other "principal persons of the Republic." He also told Mendoza to do his best to ascertain Venice's true state of war readiness, and to use "dexterity" in discovering whether the Venetians were talking with the Turks. Mendoza thus had to negotiate with Venice as a presumed partner, while simultaneously spying on them as a potential liability.

Mendoza arrived in Venice on July 25, 1539, and received a magnificent welcome, although he noted that the city had clearly suffered economically from loss of trade during the recent wars, as well as from several failed grain crops.[27] The following day Mendoza and Soria went together to appear before the *Signoria*, accompanied "by many Venetian gentleman."[28] Mendoza there launched his first verbal assault.[29] He began by summarizing Venice's current political and military options, from war through neutrality to peace with the Turk. He then stated his opinion on each alternative, stressing that the Holy League and war against the infidel represented the Venetians' only viable choice. He dismissed the idea of a separate peace with the Turk with scorn and mockery, suggesting that even to speak of such a possibility was absurd. He then addressed the issue of anti-imperial sentiment directly:

> You should not and cannot doubt the goodwill and friendship of His Majesty
> [Charles], because he is, always has been, and always will be a sure ally, as has
> been seen by experience and there is no reason to think otherwise. . . .
> Although there are some people who either feel or feign fear of His Majesty's
> power, and [fear] the office of Emperor which was always opposed to the liberty of republics, who may talk of the advantage of breaking the Holy League
> . . . [and] who may say that if the Turk makes war on His Majesty this *Signoria*
> will not be in any danger? . . . [I would say to them that] I do not wish to deny

26. Charles to Mendoza, April 19, 1539; Archivo General de Simancas, Patronato Real 45, #21. Published in Angel González Palencia and Eugenio Mele, *Vida y obras de Don Diego Hurtado de Mendoza*, 3 vols. (Madrid, 1941–1943), Vol. I, pp. 89–97.

27. Spivakovsky, *Son of the Alhambra*, pp. 71–72.

28. Lope de Soria to Charles; AGSE 1315, #156.

29. Mendoza's speech is reproduced in a document entitled "What Don Diego de Mendoza proposed and declared to the *Signoria* of Venice," n.d., AGSE 1315, #135–38.

the greatness and power of His Majesty which is very great and extends from Messina to the Low Countries . . . but this power and empire is like a weapon which is put in the hands of a prudent, just and Christian man, for use in the aid of Christendom, and the preservation of his friends and defense against his enemies, as we have seen that he has done [in the past].

In addition to this long sermon in defense of imperial power, Mendoza tacked on a little flattery. The Republic had nothing to fear from the Emperor, he suggested, for so great was the power of Venice, how could Charles wish to be its enemy? Here we see Mendoza's humanist rhetorical skills put to good use.

But the Venetians did not respond as Mendoza hoped.[30] They ignored Mendoza's rhetoric and asked for immediate proof of the Emperor's support, in the form of food. As they said, "without bread one cannot live," and they hinted at certain "inconveniences" if aid was not forthcoming. Mendoza understood this to be a reference to peace negotiations with the Turk, and urged Charles to expedite grain shipments from Naples and Sicily. For as he suspected, the Venetians were indeed trying to negotiate with Suleiman; in the summer of 1539 the sultan in fact rejected a peace offer, saying he feared no one and needed no one's friendship.[31]

Another obstacle facing Mendoza was the Venetians' concern that Charles would never devote his full attention to the Mediterranean because of his constant wars with France.[32] Nominally Charles and Francis I were at peace, but the Venetians wisely doubted the longevity of this accord between lifelong enemies. In November 1539 Mendoza could display some proof of good relations with France: Charles had visited France and publicly displayed his unity with His Most Christian Majesty.[33] Charles tried to take advantage of this new atmosphere by arranging for the Marquis del Vasto to appear before the Venetian Senate accompanied by the Marshal d'Annébaut, governor of Piedmont.

The envoys arrived in December 1539, and the Venetians arranged "the most sumptuous reception which has ever been seen here up to

---

30. Reproduced in a document entitled "The response which the *Signoria* of Venice gave to Don Diego de Mendoza," n.d., AGSE 1315 #139.

31. Kenneth M. Setton, *The Papacy and the Levant (1204–1571)*, 4 vols. (Philadelphia, 1976–1984), Vol. III, p. 448.

32. In fact, Charles's sister Mary of Hungary pushed Charles to concentrate on improving relations with France rather than embarking on another campaign against the Turks. Manuel Fernández Álvarez, *Carlos V, el césar y el hombre*, 4th ed. (Madrid, 2000), pp. 586–87.

33. This famous meeting was more notable for its jousts and pageants than for any real effort to promote peace or political unity. Karl Brandi, *The Emperor Charles V*, trans. C. V. Wedgwood (London, 1939), pp. 421–25.

now."[34] The marquis spoke to a huge crowd, followed by the Frenchman who testified to the friendship between Francis and the Emperor. Doge Pietro Lando then gave thanks to both for their evident concern for "the defense and unity of Christendom, and for the conservation and growth of this Republic." This show of goodwill, however, masked a grimmer reality for Mendoza. In the same letter that described Vasto's speech, the ambassador informed Charles that Cesare Fregoso, an agent of the French king in Venice, had informed the *Signoria* that the supposed friendship between Charles and Francis was a sham.[35] French diplomacy had bested the imperials, and by the end of December Venetian negotiations with the Turk were again moving forward. It thus came as no surprise when in October 1540 Venice signed a peace treaty with the Turks on humiliating terms.[36]

Even in the face of diplomatic failure, however, Mendoza never relented. In September 1541 he was back in Council, exhorting the Venetians to join a "defensive Italian league" in expectation of a Turkish attack.[37] He argued that such an alliance would "benefit all of Christendom, and particularly the members [of the League], and especially yourselves." Unfortunately, later that year Charles suffered a disastrous defeat in Algiers. Despite Mendoza's efforts to assure the Republic of the Emperor's prowess, the Venetians drew their own conclusions, and declined to join the league.[38] Yet Mendoza still persisted. As late as May 1546, only months before he left Venice to take up a new appointment as ambassador to Rome, Mendoza was still sending shrill letters to the Doge. He thundered at the Venetians for "placing the yoke of the enemy around your neck," and warned them that their actions would bring harm to themselves and all of Christendom.[39] But all such words were empty, as Mendoza well knew. During the last few years of his tenure in Venice he constantly asked to be transferred, ostensibly for health reasons, but also out of frustration.[40]

34. Mendoza to Charles, December 4, 1539; AGSE 1315, #158–61.
35. R. J. Knecht claims that d'Annébaut might also have sought to undermine Mendoza's efforts to convince the Venetians of Franco-Imperial friendship, but there is no evidence for this. *Renaissance Warrior and Patron: the Reign of Francis I* (Cambridge, 1984), p. 389.
36. Cozzi, *Storia d'Italia*, Vol. XII, *La Repubblica di Venezia nell'età moderna*, pp. 44–45.
37. Mendoza to Francisco de los Cobos, September 13, 1541; AGSE 1317, #22–23.
38. Spivakovsky, *Son of the Alhambra*, pp. 112–13.
39. AGSE 1316, #164–67.
40. In December 1545, for example, he wrote to Charles that "what I most desire is that Your Majesty name someone else for this [post] in Venice, which in truth is very harmful to my health, and I have served here for seven years." (AGSE 1318, #83–88.) Actually it had been six years, but perhaps it seemed longer.

The fact that French diplomacy in Venice had undermined his efforts particularly galled Mendoza. Whatever the current status of imperial-French relations, the resident ambassador in Venice had to be alert for French plots to weaken the Republic's ties with Charles. France played a devious game in the Mediterranean, allying with the Turks and encouraging the Venetians to abandon the Holy League. As early as 1530, Rodrigo Niño warned Charles of an agent for Francis I in Venice named Antonio Rincón.[41] A renegade Spaniard and fugitive from the 1520 Comunero Revolt, Rincón now served as a French spy and middleman between France, Venice, and the Turks. Niño learned that he had recently passed through Venice on his way to deliver an alliance proposal to the sultan. According to Niño, Rincón was also said to be fomenting sedition in Naples and Sicily, but to know the truth of this report "it would be most necessary to spy on this traitor, and on his leaving France he should be captured and examined and punished as his traitorousness and wickedness deserves." Niño's words were prophetic, as we shall see.

Mendoza's task in Venice involved keeping the Republic out of French clutches.[42] Even in times of peace with France, an atmosphere of distrust pervaded the ambassador's work. In October 1539, for example, just before the Marquis del Vasto and Marshal d'Annébaut appeared before the Senate, Mendoza received instructions from Charles that he should "always be vigilant [regarding the French], and always seek to learn what you can [about their actions], but with dissimulation and great show and demonstration that we have total confidence [in them]."[43] Charles indicated that he hoped the French would act honorably, but prudence suggested that precautions were necessary. His command to "dissimulate" is extremely interesting: he did not want to jeopardize the slender peace, or give the French a reason to declare war, so he called on his ambassador to practice the time-honored diplomatic art of lying.[44]

Mendoza's encounters with the French would take a darker turn in the next few years. Like Niño before him, Mendoza reported on the activities of Antonio Rincón, who along with an exiled Genoese named Cesare Fregoso often consorted with the French resident ambassador in Venice.[45]

41. Niño to Charles, May 18, 1530; AGSE 1308, #59.

42. *Algunas Cartas de Don Diego Hurtado de Mendoza, escritos 1538–1552*, ed. Alberto Vázquez and R. Selden Rose (New Haven, 1935), p. xii.

43. Charles to Mendoza, October 4, 1539; AGSE 1315, #232.

44. "Dissimulation" was an accepted practice in Renaissance diplomacy; see J. R. Woodhouse, "Honorable Dissimulation: Some Italian Advice for the Renaissance Diplomat," *Proceedings of the British Academy* No. 84 (Oxford, 1993), pp. 25–50.

45. Spivakovsky, *Son of the Alhambra*, pp. 75, 110; for French efforts to lure the Venetians into an alliance with the Turks, see *Négociations de la France dans le Levant*, ed. E. Charrière, 4 vols. (reprint, New York, 1966), Vol. III, pp. 363–554.

In early 1541 rumors circulated around Venice that the Emperor had marked Rincón and Fregoso for assassination, but Mendoza tried to convince everyone that the French had started these rumors. In early February he reported that the two French agents had requested, and received, an escort of fifty cavalry from the Venetian government, supposedly to protect them from imperial agents while in Venetian territory.[46] Mendoza complained to the *Signoria* that they were accessories in a publicity stunt and a smear campaign against Charles, and that the French sought to make people believe "that in its [the Republic's] territories ambassadors are not safe from the servants and ministers of [the Emperor]." He reminded the Venetians of Rincón's suspicious character, and insisted that the man was beneath the Emperor's notice. He also argued that giving Rincón a bodyguard reflected badly on the Venetian authorities: either they demeaned themselves by honoring such a lowlife, or they implied that they could not maintain order in their own territories. None of his arguments had any effect. Then the issue became moot: in early July imperial soldiers waylaid the two agents just outside of Pavia, and their corpses turned up a few months later.

The Marquis del Vasto, who commanded the soldiers in question, denied any knowledge of the murders, as did Charles.[47] Mendoza, meanwhile, found himself in an awkward position. The assassinations made both him and the Emperor look like liars. A week after the disappearance of the agents Mendoza showed the *Signoria* a letter from Charles, ordering him not to interfere with Rincón while the truce with France lasted. Whether he knew of the impending attack or not, he could at least claim he had no direct involvement.[48] But the affair of the slain diplomats had wide-ranging political consequences. Francis I seized on it as a reason to break the peace treaty with Charles.[49] The murders also affected Mendoza personally, as he began to fear for his own safety.

The French embassy and its supporters in Venice, angered by the death of their associates, sought revenge on the imperial ministers in Italy. Mendoza survived an attempt on his life, and the assailant admitted to working under orders from the French ambassador.[50] Mendoza also reported that "a certain crazy negro, who speaks Spanish and is Sicilian, [has] said that it would be easy to kill the Marquis [del Vasto] with an arquebus," and this individual had been observed being conducted to a personal

46. Mendoza to Charles, February 8, 1541; AGSE 1317, #109–10.
47. Setton, *The Papacy and the* Levant, Vol. III, pp. 457–58.
48. Spivakovsky, *Son of the Alhambra*, p. 111.
49. Fernández Álvarez. *Charles V,* pp. 124–25.
50. Spivakovsky, *Son of the Alhambra*, p. 116.

interview at the French embassy.[51] By late 1542 the situation had become
so tense that Mendoza wrote to Francisco de los Cobos, Charles's secretary of state, asking for a bodyguard of twenty-five to thirty men "for my
security and for the dispatches."[52] He complained about his "ruined life,"
and about being surrounded by enemies.

Soon afterwards, however, Mendoza turned the tables on the French in
a totally unexpected manner. Through a series of double dealings, Mendoza learned that two secretaries inside the Senate had been spying for
France, and managed to get one of them arrested.[53] The secretary
revealed that his information had been passed on to the Turks, which had
helped the sultan during the negotiation of the 1540 peace treaty. The
ensuing scandal forced several French officials, including the ambassador, to vacate the city. In December 1542 Mendoza had the pleasure of
reporting that the replacement French ambassador had received a very
cool reception from the *Signoria*.[54] The French had suffered a terrible
blow to their prestige; the English ambassador in Venice wrote to King
Henry VIII, "The French are now incredibly detestable here. They are
considered dogs . . . and monsters."[55] One can imagine Mendoza's glee.
Such victories were rare, however, and Mendoza left Venice for Rome
without a backward glance.

Sometimes political change caught the ambassadors unprepared, particularly when it happened back home. Charles V's abdication of his
thrones in 1555–1558, for example, surprised all of Europe, and shook
international diplomacy in unexpected ways. For one thing, precedence
of kings and their ambassadors suddenly became a burning issue.[56] As
representatives of the Holy Roman Emperor, Charles's ambassadors had
enjoyed diplomatic privileges for the last forty years, including walking
ahead of all other ambassadors in processions and sitting close to the
altar during church services.[57] Early modern diplomats took such marks
of rank and importance very seriously, and any change in the accepted

51. Mendoza to Charles, September 27, 1542; AGSE 1497, Libro 66, 60r–61v.
52. Document dated August 12, 1542; *Algunas Cartas*, p. 102.
53. Spivakovsky, *Son of the Alhambra*, pp. 117–19.
54. Mendoza to Charles, December 14, 1542; AGSE 1497, Libro 66, 60r–61v.
55. *Letters and Papers, Foreign and Domestic, of the Reign of Henry VIII*, ed. James Gairdner and
R. H. Brodie, Vol. XVII (reprint, Vadus, 1965), p. 384.
56. See Michael J. Levin, "A New World Order: The Spanish Campaign for Precedence in
Early Modern Europe," *Journal of Early Modern History* 6 (2002), pp. 233–64.
57. During the Middle Ages, an unofficial diplomatic hierarchy had developed for the representatives of the various kingdoms, with the Emperor at the top, followed by the king of
the Romans and the king of France. Garrett Mattingly, *Renaissance Diplomacy* (reprint, New
York, 1988), chap. 25; and Donald E. Queller, *The Office of Ambassador in the Middle Ages*
(Princeton, 1967), chap. 7.

order could be interpreted as a slight to national honor.[58] When Charles abdicated, it raised uncomfortable questions about the status of Spanish ambassadors. Charles divided his patrimony between his son Philip, who inherited the Spanish kingdoms, and his brother Ferdinand, who became Emperor.[59] This left Philip II in the strange position of possessing an empire but not an imperial title. His diplomatic representatives soon felt the consequences of this unprecedented problem.

In early 1557, Francisco de Vargas returned to his post as resident ambassador to Venice after witnessing Charles's abdication ceremonies. When he left Venice he had been the imperial ambassador, but on his return his status had become ambiguous. The French embassy claimed that Vargas had lost his previous rank as the Emperor's envoy, and now merely represented the king of Spain, and thus should be accorded secondary diplomatic honors behind those of the French king.[60] Vargas objected strenuously, and began a months-long campaign to maintain his accustomed position. Oddly, Philip initially reacted to this situation by suggesting that the transition from Charles to himself had not really changed anything. As he wrote to Vargas,

> I have seen everything that has occurred concerning the pretension of the French ambassador and it greatly amazes me, since it is such an obvious matter that [precedence] belongs to you as the ambassador of the Emperor my lord, and having returned to continue at your post in his name, there should not be any doubt, nor should it be placed in dispute. You should not be satisfied with the place you were given, as it would not be right for you to be content if you were solely my ambassador, much less that of his imperial majesty, whose preeminence is so well known.[61]

The king then instructed Vargas to do whatever he saw fit to rectify the situation, and not to allow either the French or the Venetians to "force this novelty" on him. His letter implied that from the Spanish point of

---

58. See WIlliam Roosen, "Early Modern Diplomatic Ceremonial: A Systems Approach," *Journal of Modern History* 52 (September 1980), pp. 452–76; and Maria Antonietta Visceglia, "Il ceremoniale come linguaggio politico: Su alcuni conflitti di precedenza alla corte di Roma tra Cinquecento e Seicento," in *Cérémonial et rituel à Rome (XVI–XIX siècle)* ed. Maria Antonietta Visceglia and Catherine Brice (Rome, 1997), pp. 117–76.
59. For a full description of this division and its consequences, see M. J. Rodríguez-Salgado, *The Changing Face of Empire: Charles V, Philip II and the Habsburg Authority, 1551–1559* (Cambridge, 1988).
60. Abraham van de Wiquefort, *The Embassador and his Functions*, trans. John Digby (London, 1716), pp. 209–10.
61. Philip to Vargas, May 26 1557; AGSE 1323, #198.

view, the change of monarchs had not altered the situation at all. We also
see that Philip had not yet escaped the shadow of his father; he clearly
still thought of Vargas as Charles's ambassador rather than his own. But
any anger he might have felt he kept hidden from the Venetians. He
wrote directly to Doge Lorenzo Priuli, offering a carrot rather than a
stick: he asked the Doge to be reasonable, and make the decision he
ought to make, and promised that he, the king, would be the very dear
friend of Venice if they did the right thing.[62]

Vargas, as Philip's representative, fought much more forcefully for his
king's honor than the king himself. A crisis came in May 1558, at the celebration of Ascension Day, during which all the ambassadors in Venice
participated in processions and rituals.[63] The French ambassador, under
instructions from King Henri II and the powerful Cardinal Tournon,
made a speech before the Senate demanding a position in front of the
Spanish envoy during the procession and subsequent church ceremonies.
According to Vargas, the Frenchman declared that he would take his
rightful place no matter what, and "with many noises of pride and insolence he finished his speech, and began to gather armed men, and make
no small fuss."[64] Not to be outdone, Vargas made a similar speech before
the Venetian lords the next day. He "marveled at the insolence of the
French ambassador," as well as the possibility that the Venetians might be
swayed by such odious tactics. Unlike the French, who threatened the
peace of Venice, he had done his best to "contain his household and keep
them disciplined." After ridiculing the French, and chastising the *Signoria*
for even listening to their arguments, Vargas announced that nothing
would prevent him from marching at the front of the line. "It is necessary
for me to act thus," he concluded, "and to employ a thousand lives if I
had them." Interestingly, Vargas seems to have reacted with more outrage
to French demands than Philip did. The ambassador suggested that it
might prove necessary to withdraw the embassy from Venice rather than
suffer a loss of reputation—a solution we will see used again in Rome.

Vargas described the resolution of the crisis in a letter to Philip's sister
Juana, Princess of Portugal and Philip's regent in Spain during his absence.
After summing up the state of affairs, he noted how the French claimed
that their king should be given precedence "over all kings in the world,
always and in all places," to which he responded that "my legation in the
name of the Emperor still endured as the Empire has not ceased to exist,
and besides this I would still have to have precedence as the ambassador of

62. AGSE 1323, #197.
63. Muir, pp. 119–134 and 232–37.
64. Vargas to Philip, May 26, 1558; AGSE 1323, #214.

his Catholic Majesty for evident reasons and causes."[65] He did not specify those reasons, but it is interesting that he had begun to make the mental transition from being imperial ambassador to being representative of an exclusively Spanish monarch. In any case, after numerous efforts to get the ambassadors to soften their positions, the Venetians "resolved that neither of us should go any longer to the festival." Vargas initially refused even to discuss this possibility, but eventually he agreed that if the French ambassador stayed home so would he. He regarded this compromise as a defeat, as the Venetians evidently agreed with the French argument that Philip's envoy should not be granted the privileges of an imperial ambassador. After much deliberation, the Senate had refused to acknowledge Spain's supremacy over France in the diplomatic hierarchy.[66]

In protest of the *Signoria*'s decision, Philip ordered Vargas not to appear before the Senate without a direct order.[67] When this move had no effect on the situation, the king decided to take his ambassador's advice and withdraw his envoy from Venice. Vargas made his dramatic exit on July 29, 1558, when he announced to the "aghast" Venetians that Philip had ordered him out of the city.[68] With much ceremony he packed up his entire household and staff, leaving only a secretary behind to administer to necessary business. He left Venice for good in early September; as he wrote to Princess Juana, "I do not wish to remain here or to die in such an ungrateful place, as I have been grateful [to the Venetians] and done them more service than any of those who preceded me." The pique in his tone is obvious: he clearly felt that the Venetians had insulted him personally as well as the King. Philip transferred him to the more prestigious post at the Roman embassy, but he left for his new assignment with a bitter taste in his mouth—exactly like Mendoza twelve years earlier. Unfortunately, as we will see in the next chapter, affairs in Rome would not fare much better, as the precedence dispute raged on.

Meanwhile, the Venetians continued to refuse to fight in the Habsburg's struggle with the Turks. In 1555 Vargas reported that the French were again trying to lure Venice into an alliance with them and the Turks against Charles, but the *Signoria* was divided and took no action.[69] Their

65. Vargas to Juana, May 27, 1558; AGSE 1323, #217.
66. Louis Paris, *Négociations, lettres, et pièces diverses relatives au règne de Francois II, tireés du portefeuille de Sébastien de l'Aubespine* (Paris, 1841), pp. 505–6 n. 1.
67. Muir writes that after the Venetian decision to support French claims, "the Spanish envoy refused to participate in any procession where the French ambassador appeared." *Civic Ritual*, p. 236 n. 34. We should note, however, that it was the Venetians who first suggested this solution.
68. Vargas to Juana, September 4, 1558; AGSE 1323, #222.
69. Vargas to Charles, January 31 and February 4, 1555; AGSE 1323, #57–58.

neutral stance, established in the 1540 peace treaty, would hold for thirty years. In the 1560s, however, the Turks again became aggressive and started to encroach on Venetian colonies in the eastern Mediterranean. In 1565 they besieged the strategically important island of Malta, alarming all of Europe. The imminent threat to Italy prompted Pope Pius IV to call for a new Holy League. His death put a halt to negotiations, but in 1566 the election of the zealous crusader Pope Pius V renewed interest in a military alliance.[70] The Venetians still hoped to avoid involvement in the war, but then in 1570 the Turks invaded Cyprus, their key outpost in the eastern Mediterranean. This threat to their economic survival shook the Republic out of its malaise. Diego Guzmán de Silva, who took up the post of resident ambassador to Venice in 1571, thus entered the scene at a time of great anxiety. Yet he too would have limited success in his efforts to create and sustain a military alliance with the Republic.

Like Mendoza, Guzmán had served as ambassador in England before his assignment to Venice.[71] He was an ecclesiastic rather than a soldier, however, and performed his duties with much less flamboyance than either Mendoza or Vargas. Yet he displayed dedication and a clear sense of mission in his attempts to maintain Venice as an ally in the war with the infidel. He would know both triumph and humiliation in that task. The year he arrived saw the tremendous victory of the Holy League over the Turks at Lepanto; a mere two years later Venice would once again sign a separate peace with the Turks. Like Mendoza, Guzmán had to work for a monarch whose worldwide military commitments often prevented him from delivering much needed aid to the city of Venice.[72] But his real problem was that Venetian interests simply did not parallel those of Spain, much as he tried to convince them otherwise.

Guzmán was assigned to Venice in 1569, but the sudden death of the resident ambassador in Genoa caused Philip to divert Guzmán to that post on a temporary basis.[73] In February 1570 Guzmán wrote to Doge Pietro Loredan apologizing for the delay, and indicated that he hoped to serve the interests of the Republic as soon as possible.[74] He finally arrived in Venice in March 1571, where he received the usual honors, and apparently made a good first impression. The Spanish secretary who had been

70. Fernand Braudel, *The Mediterranean and the Mediterranean World in the Age of Philip II*, trans. Siân Reynolds, 2 vols. (New York, 1973), Vol. II, pp. 1027–29.

71. Manuel Fernández Álvarez, *Tres embajadores de Felipe II en Inglaterra* (Madrid, 1951), pp. 132–90.

72. Geoffrey Parker, "Spain, her Enemies, and the Revolt of the Netherlands, 1559–1648," *Spain and the Netherlands 1559–1659* (reprint, London, 1979), pp. 17–42.

73. Philip to Guzmán, November 26, 1569; AGSE 1398, #253.

74. Archivio di Stato di Venezia, Collegio, Lettere Principi, Filza 35 (unfoliated).

manning the embassy wrote that Guzmán was "very well received," and that upon his visiting the *Signoria* the second day, "they showed much contentment and satisfaction with his person. And I have no doubt that according to the skill with which he proceeds he will gain more goodwill every day."[75] Guzmán wrote much the same thing in his account of the initial encounter. He said "what seemed appropriate" to the Doge, "to which the Doge responded with many fine words and great eloquence, stressing the esteem he held for what Your Majesty had conveyed to them."[76]

As may be noted from these letters, the Venetian government's reception of the new ambassador was positive, but not overwhelmingly so. Guzmán arrived in the middle of delicate negotiations over the Holy League, and his relationship with the *Signoria* quickly became strained. The Venetians were hardly committed to the League—in fact, they secretly sent an envoy to the Turks even as they discussed an alliance with Spain and the Papacy.[77] The Spanish ambassador to the Papacy, Don Juan de Zúñiga, wrote to Guzmán that Venetian envoys had stalled the League negotiations by arguing about how many ships each of the allies was to commit to the summer campaign.[78] Together, Guzmán and Zúñiga wheedled and swore at the Venetians to get them to commit. The primary negotiations took place in Rome, but Guzmán did what he could to keep things moving. In April 1571 he reported a meeting with the Doge and the Senate, in which he conveyed "the necessity of making haste, and the great inconveniences which result from being irresolute, [such as] animating the spirits of the enemy while weakening those of their friends and troubling their subjects."[79] The Doge answered that he was in fact prepared to set out, and had 27,000 men ready to sail; he blamed Philip's ministers of state for not gathering forces together in a timely fashion. Guzmán, no doubt gritting his teeth, responded that the king's half-brother Don Juan de Austria, commander of the Spanish fleet, had no less than eighty galleys waiting for orders. And so the conversations went round and round, as the weeks trickled by.

Much of the delay resulted from mutual suspicions and memories from the last Holy League. The Venetians still harbored resentment about Andrea Doria's abandonment at the battle of Prevesa, while many

75. Julián López to Philip, March 16, 1571; AGSE 1329, #23.
76. Guzmán to Philip, March 16, 1571; AGSE 1329, #24.
77. Gaetano Cozzi, "Venezia dal Rinascimento all'Età barocca," *Storia di Venezia*, Vol. VI, *Dal Rinascimento al Barocco*, ed. Gaetano Cozzi and Paolo Prodi (Rome,1994), p. 52.
78. Guzmán to Philip, March 16, 1571; AGSE 1329, #24.
79. Guzmán to Philip, April 7, 1571; AGSE 1329, #25.

Spaniards believed the Republic would abandon the alliance as soon as the Turks offered reasonable terms.[80] Guzmán urged Philip to hasten negotiations, since delays (and the appearance of irresolution) played into the hands of those Venetians who argued against entering the League.[81] A mere two weeks before the official proclamation of the signing of the League treaty, Guzmán reported being summoned to appear before an unhappy Senate. He tried to be as pleasant as possible, claiming that he "had here no other occupation other than to give [the Venetians] contentment, and for this [purpose] Your Majesty sent me here."[82] The Senate was in no mood to hear such sentiments, however, and castigated Philip and his ministers for blocking the success of the alliance.

Yet Guzmán himself evidently maintained good relations with the *Signoria*. When the envoys finally agreed on terms for a League, the Doge had the news publicly proclaimed, and the Spanish ambassador played a significant role in the celebrations that followed. As he wrote to Philip,

> Their Lordships determined yesterday to announce [the signing] of the League with great solemnity and demonstration of contentment. . . . two days earlier His Holiness's Nuncio came to talk to me, saying that he understood from [the Venetians] that because this proclamation was to be done with great authority, all of the princes' ambassadors who are here would take part, and that they had determined to send to me to ask if I would do them the honor of celebrating the mass that day, being certain that my assistance would be very appropriate.[83]

That Guzmán, a mere canon, should perform this rite, rather than the patriarch of Venice or any of a number of bishops, was a singular sign of official approval and favor. Guzmán perhaps returned the favor by hosting eight days' worth of festivals and feasting in his residence.[84] This however only foreshadowed an even more public role he would play later that year.

The great battle of Lepanto took place on October 7, 1571; the news of the Christian victory reached Venice on the eighteenth, prompting

80. Cozzi, *Storia d'Italia*, Vol. XII, *La Repubblica di Venezia nell'età moderna*, p. 55.
81. Guzmán to Philip, April 24, 1571; AGSE 1329, #34.
82. Guzmán to Philip, May 10, 1571; AGSE 1329, #44.
83. Guzmán to Philip, July 3, 1571; AGSE 1329, #67.
84. Iain Fenlon, "Lepanto: Le arti della celebrazione nella Venezia del Rinascimento," in *Crisi e rinnovamenti nell'autumno del Rinascimento a Venezia*, ed. Vittore Branca and Carlo Ossola (Florence, 1991), p. 377.

jubilation on a scale rarely seen before, lasting for days.[85] And Guzmán was right in the middle of it. The Venetians again asked him to celebrate the mass during the celebrations, and he was clearly moved by their expressions of devotion. He even reported that during a routine visit to the *Signoria,* the Doge spontaneously asked Guzmán to give him and the entire Senate communion, as well as to celebrate a mass in memory of those killed in battle. As he wrote, "I accepted it all with the goodwill and grace which was appropriate, so that in everything they would know the honor which Your Majesty wishes to do them."[86] This statement is significant. No doubt it pleased the devout Guzmán to perform this service, but he also perceived his actions as a diplomatic gesture. As Philip's representative, his participation in these ceremonies expressed the king's benevolence and protection. His celebration of the mass also underlined the religious significance of a Spanish-led triumph. Philip II promoted himself as the secular champion of Counter-Reformation Catholicism, and in this moment of victory over the infidel, his ambassador performed a Catholic rite that demonstrated that God fought for Spain. But Venice of course had also struggled and sacrificed in the battle, and so the Spaniards wished to "honor" the Venetians for the part they played. Guzmán was careful to "gracefully" accept the compliments of the Venetians, in the manner of a senior partner; his air of superiority is evident.

Guzmán had yet another opportunity to strike a public pose a few days later, during a grand celebratory procession down the canals of Venice. At one point he addressed the Doge and the crowds in a short Latin oration: "Serenissime Principe, concordia parve res crescunt, discordia maxime dilabuntur; et dux noster Jesus Christo dixit, Hoc est preceptum meum, ut diligatis invicem, sicut dilexi vos." (Most Serene Prince: small things grow great on concord, great things are destroyed by discord; and our lord Jesus Christ said, this is my commandment, that you love one another, as I have loved you.)[87] Here Guzmán displayed both religious and Renaissance humanist training, by combining a passage from the Gospels (John 15:12) with a quote from Sallust (a favorite among Renaissance diplomats).[88] Again, as an ecclesiastic/ambassador, he represented perfectly His Catholic Majesty Philip II, the defender of the faith and the greatest power

85. Ibid., and see also E. H. Gombrich, "Celebrations in Venice of the Holy League and of the Victory of Lepanto," in *Studies in Renaissance and Baroque Art Presented to Anthony Blunt on His Sixtieth Birthday* (London, n.d.), pp. 62–68.
86. Guzmán to Philip, October 22, 1571; AGSE 1329, #106.
87. Guzmán to Philip, October 31, 1571; AGSE 1329, #112.
88. Joycelyne G. Russell, *Diplomats at Work: Three Renaissance Studies* (Wolfeboro Falls, 1992), p. 81.

in Western Europe. After the procession, Guzmán returned to his residence accompanied by the Doge and other Venetian notables, where they feasted together. "They say it has been the day of greatest joy and devotion together that has been seen in this city," he stated proudly.[89] It would be the climax of his tenure in Venice.

The period directly after Lepanto, however, saw a rapid deterioration of Venetian-Spanish relations.[90] The League members almost immediately began to squabble over what the next step should be. Don Juan, under orders from Philip, withdrew the Spanish squadron, despite Pope Pius's eagerness to follow up the League's victory.[91] Philip had several reasons for this move: first, he hoped to mount an attack on North Africa, a more important target for Spanish interests than the Levant; second, he feared a French offensive against Italy or the Netherlands, which would require all available forces to counteract.[92] These reasonable strategic decisions, however, did not help Guzmán justify to the Venetians why they could expect no military support from Spain. The official explanation from Madrid was that with the destruction of the Turkish fleet at Lepanto, the purpose of the League had been fulfilled. Guzmán echoed this argument in his discussions with the *Signoria*, and defended the actions of his king and his ministers in Italy, but he sounded increasingly glum.[93] Then in May news arrived that Pope Pius V, the driving force behind the League, was on his deathbed. Guzmán told the Venetians "that I greatly sorrowed for the loss of his person, especially at this time. But when God saw fit to gather up [his soul], I was certain that the general business of the League . . . would continue without fail."[94] It would be an empty promise.

During this time of strained relations, it is clear that Guzmán disagreed with his king's policy decisions. He knew about the revolt of the Netherlands, which erupted in 1572 and would obsess Philip for decades, but he believed that the unfinished business with the Turks should be a priority.[95] In one of his conversations with the Doge, he revealed his true feelings:

89. Guzmán to Philip, October 31, 1571; AGSE 1329, #112.
90. Alberto Tenenti, "La Repubblica di Venezia e la Spagna di Filippo II e Filippo III," *Studi veneziani* 30 (1995), pp. 115–17.
91. Braudel, *The Mediterranean and the Mediterranean World*, Vol. II, pp. 1103–04.
92. Ibid., pp. 1114–1118. France would in fact have launched an attack in the early summer of 1572 if not for internal chaos. See N. M. Sutherland, "The Massacre of St. Bartholomew and the Problem of Spain," in *Princes, Politics and Religion 1547–1589* (London, 1984), pp. 173–82.
93. Guzmán to Philip, February 23, 1572; AGSE 1331, #19.
94. Guzmán to Philip, May 2, 1572; AGSE 1331, #40.
95. Luciano Serrano, *La Liga de Lepanto entre España, Venecia y la Santa Sede (1570–1573)*, 2 vols. (Madrid, 1918–1919), Vol. I, p. 236.

The Doge said to me that I was very right to say that [continuing the League] was very desirable, and thus it should be pursued, because if this year we do not take advantage of [the opportunity to] engineer the destruction of the Turkish fleet, while the League is more powerful, it is understood that next year they will be prepared, making resistance more difficult. . . . He showed great disgust in general, and particularly at this news of the states of Flanders; and [the Venetians] show extremely little satisfaction with [the situation], as is right.[96]

Guzmán was in a bind: he sympathized with the Venetians, and shared their irritation with the situation, but he could not openly criticize his own king.

If he could not directly express his disapproval to Philip, however, he could report on the growing anger at Spain in Venice. "Many speeches are being made here," he wrote, "everyone judging matters in his own way without knowing fact or cause, because Your Majesty had decided to order [our] fleet not to proceed. But this is an ancient malady of Italy, which cannot be cured."[97] Guzmán then goes on to give a curious account of what he has heard on the streets. "They say" that perhaps Spain is not as powerful as everyone believes, and that its forces are incapable of action. Philip also seems to have broken his promises, "which have been inviolable up to now, and thus most princes have had faith in Your Majesty." The Venetians are extremely suspicious, Guzmán says, "and they will not have faith [in us] from now on, which greatly hurts them, but is even more damaging to Christendom, for whose defense Your Majesty is more responsible than others. And the princes of Italy will be more hesitant, it seeming to them that when Your Majesty has time to consider your affairs you care more for [your] particular concerns than for the common good." At this point we have to ask, whose opinion is Guzmán really expressing? He never identifies the speakers or the audience, and the entire speech seems artificial. Which Venetians truly believed that Philip's word had been inviolable up to now? What Italian prince was actually shocked that Philip acted in his own self-interest? It seems possible we are hearing Guzmán's disillusionment, or an attempt to indirectly chastise the king.

Nonetheless, Guzmán went on to describe how he answered these charges. The response is as odd as the indictment, and deserves to be quoted at some length.

96. Guzmán to Philip, June 14, 1572; quoted ibid., p. 236.
97. Guzmán to Philip, July 2, 1572; AGSE 1331, #69.

In the state the world is in today, one cannot and ought not live without prudence and caution; and the greatest, best, most holy and most healthy princes had better be even more so, in order to serve and respond to their obligation to God. Reputation is not acquired or conserved with words or good intentions, but with deeds, and the execution of them; and princes do not have to live according to the judgment of all who wish to discuss them, but only in conformity with necessity, and to their primary obligations, which is what they have promised to God, sworn to their subjects, and ordered for their honor, valor, and estimation, trusting in their prudence, which places health and truth before the vain and baseless rumors of men. And for these reasons and many others, which have been pointed out to [those who speak ill of Philip] at length, they ought to be silent, and to think that what Your Majesty commanded of Don Juan ought to be more widely accepted. . . . It is temerity and an indefensible matter to condemn anyone without [first] listening to him, and much more so Your Majesty, who from birth until today has governed your lands in such manner as to gain much credit . . . [so] that it would be great stupidity and daring to wish to judge your actions.[98]

It is perhaps a sign of the difficulty of Guzmán's situation that he resorted to arguing that Philip answered only to God. Diego Hurtado de Mendoza had portrayed Charles as Venice's best friend and only hope; Guzmán told the Venetians that Philip knew best, and they should stop whining.[99] But he did not say this to all Venetians. In a coded addendum, Guzmán noted that he used this argument with "people of quality" (*personas de calidad*), but not before the entire Senate. With them, he planned only to reiterate Philip's "concern for the common good and theirs in particular," in order not to engender any more distrust. So Guzmán argued for the divine right of kings with the nobility, but with others he tried to be conciliatory. Thus do diplomats tailor their words for their audience.

In the end, Philip did in fact bow to pressure from his allies and allow Don Juan to join other League forces in a Levantine campaign in the late summer of 1572. Unfortunately the long delay and bickering among the allies (particularly between Don Juan and the Venetian general Sebastiano Venier) prevented any real accomplishments.[100] With the League

98. Ibid.
99. The "Black Legend" of Spain, which portrayed Spaniards as arrogant, originated in Italy. See Sverker Arnoldsson, "La Leyenda Negra: Estudios sobre sus origines," *Goteborg Universitets Arsskrift* 66 (1960), pp. 11–103; and more recently, J. N. Hillgarth, *The Mirror of Spain, 1500–1700: The Formation of a Myth* (Ann Arbor, 2000).
100. Setton, *The Papacy and the Levant*, Vol. IV, pp. 1081–84.

threatening to disintegrate, Guzmán sent a rather desperate letter to the *Signoria,* suggesting it would be blind, stupid, and wicked of the Republic to abandon its allies.[101] He begged them in the name of God, Philip, and "the particular love I bear for this Most Serene Dominion" to act in the common interest. Yet it was all for naught. By this point the Venetians had had enough: they had lost many of their colonies in the Mediterranean, spent huge sums of money, suspected their ally of using them, and still faced a powerful foe. On March 3, 1573, Venice once again signed a separate peace with the Turks. Like Mendoza before him, Guzmán had failed in his primary mission.

He did not give up immediately, however, any more than Mendoza had. For months after the announcement of the peace treaty, Guzmán tried to shame the Venetians into reconsidering their decision.[102] In April 1573, for example, he reported an exchange between himself and the Doge in front of the Doge's councilors and the papal nuncio.[103] The Doge began by making a long speech justifying the decision to make peace. He stated that Philip, whose "desire for the common good and [ours] in particular" was well known, should accept the peace treaty with the "benevolence, prudence, modesty, and goodwill that he has always shown in our affairs." It is difficult to know if the Doge was being sarcastic, but the ambassador certainly took it that way, and angrily answered in the same mode. After once again championing Philip's actions, including the aid he had given Venice against the Turks before the League ever existed, he sneered that "If this peace which they have made was useful for the service of God and the common good, and for the conservation and growth of this Republic, then I certainly believed that Your Majesty would indeed receive the news with the goodwill and love which [the Doge] alluded to." But of course Guzmán made it clear that the peace treaty was anything but in the interests of Christendom or of Venice itself. Indeed, he suggested, the Venetians had better look to the defenses of the lands bordering those of their "new friend."

Guzmán's anger was genuine, yet part of it may have been directed at himself. Despite the ominous signs, the actual announcement of a peace treaty seems to have caught him by surprise. Only a week before the declaration of peace, the Doge had assured both Guzmán and the papal nuncio that Venice would stay in the League, a story which had been

101. February 1573; AGSE 1332, #21.
102. There were quite a few Venetians who did indeed feel shame at how low the Republic's fortunes had ebbed, including Leonardo Dona, the ambassador to Spain. Cozzi, "Venezia dal Rinascimento all'Età barocca," pp. 53–54.
103. Guzmán to Philip, April 4, 1573; AGSE 1332, #38.

confirmed by other sources.[104] Afterwards, Guzmán sent Philip a coded, apologetic note: "These past days I have been deceived in this business by the notices I received from good people. . . . I could not on my part have made greater efforts [than what] I have described to Your Majesty in my previous letters. I have told you of what I did here, which was much less than I wished. . . . I confess some fault in this [failure] more than in my will and desire to serve Your Majesty."[105] Guzmán had been hoodwinked, to his evident embarrassment. Yet again the Spanish embassy had failed to bend the Venetians to Spain's needs.

To add insult to injury, Guzmán knew perfectly well that French agents had facilitated the Venetian-Turkish peace negotiations, just as they had thirty years earlier.[106] At this point, sabotage of Spanish diplomacy was the most France could do in Italy. During the late 1570s and 1580s, religious turmoil in France kept it on the sidelines of Mediterranean politics. In 1594, however, with the ascent of Henry IV to the throne, France again began to assert its power throughout Europe. Venice took notice, and sent ambassadors to Paris with offers of friendship.[107] By the end of Philip's reign in the late 1590s, Spanish ambassadors in Italy had once again grown insecure about their hold on the peninsula. Their reaction to a crisis in the Duchy of Ferrara in 1597–1598 illustrates how jittery they could be.

In October 1597, Alfonso d'Este, duke of Ferrara, died without a legitimate heir. According to a papal bull of 1567, Ferrara ought to have devolved to Pope Clement VIII as the duke's feudal overlord, but Alfonso's cousin Cesare d'Este claimed the duchy and seized power.[108] Clement quickly formed an army in order to enforce his right of possession, and the ensuing conflict threatened to destabilize all of northern Italy, as both sides called on other European powers for help. Neither Spain nor Venice was eager to see an expansion of the Papal States, but war with the papacy lacked appeal as well. The timing was particularly bad from the Spanish point of view: Philip II had fallen into his final illness,

104. Guzmán to Philip, February 25, 1573; AGSE 1332, #23. For more on intelligence sources in Venice, see chapter 6.

105. Guzmán to Philip, April 4, 1573; AGSE 1332, #38.

106. See Alberto Tenenti, "Francia, Venezia, e la Sacra Lega," in *Il Mediterraneo nella seconda metà del '500 alla luce di Lepanto,* ed. Gino Benzoni (Florence, 1976); and the correspondence of the bishop of Aix, France's chief agent in the Mediterranean, in Charrière, *Négociations de la France dans le Levant,* Vol. III, pp. 195–511.

107. Cozzi, *Storia d'Italia,* Vol. XII, *La Repubblica di Venezia nell'età moderna,* pp. 63–67.

108. See Bonner Mitchell, *1598: A Year of Pageantry in Late Renaissance Ferrara* (Binghamton, 1990), pp. 18–22; and Ludwig von Pastor, *The History of the Popes from the Close of the Middle Ages,* trans. Ralph Francis Kerr, 40 vols. (London, 1891–1953), Vol. XXIV, pp. 382–401.

while his ministers struggled to extract Spain from a war with France. A new battlefront in Italy was the last thing the Spaniards needed. The resident ambassador in Venice, Iñigo de Mendoza, sent a flurry of letters to Madrid during this period that clearly demonstrate his fear that a new political upheaval could have serious consequences for Spanish interests.

Mendoza's first warning about the impending crisis came on November 8, 1597, when he informed the secretary of state Juan de Idiáquez that the king "needed to be advised" about the "pretender" Cesare d'Este's coup.[109] Cesare had sent an envoy to Venice seeking aid, and the Spanish ambassador watched the Venetians intently to see what they would do. To his disappointment the Republic did not immediately bar the messenger from the door, but instead accorded him the usual honors for a foreign ambassador. Cesare's man was escorted by several high-ranking members of the *Signoria* into the Senate, where "they listened to him and gave him the ambassador's place which is as Your Excellency knows at the Doge's right hand." That Mendoza noted these details implies his disapproval: treating Cesare's ambassador with respect gave legitimacy to his claims.[110] In any case the *Signoria* received Cesare's message, and according to Mendoza "their response was polite and very general, and did not obligate them to do anything." Evidently the Venetians meant to temporize while they studied their options. Meanwhile Cesare's envoy also tried to approach Mendoza, but when he came to the Spaniard's residence Mendoza ducked him by claiming to be sick in bed. Until he got instructions, he wanted nothing to do with Cesare.

Those instructions were not immediately forthcoming, however, and Mendoza grew panicky. The various Spanish officials in Italy, including the governor of Milan and the duke of Sessa in the Roman embassy, were paralyzed with indecision. "I supplicate Your Lordship most urgently," Mendoza wrote to Idiáquez, "that you speak to His Majesty to have him command someone to write to us on how we should proceed and what we ought to say and do, because I see that we [in Italy] are totally divided. The Constable [in Milan] is involved with Cesare up to his eyeballs, I support the pope, and every minister does what is necessary in his opinion."[111] If this were merely a matter of a breakdown in the chain of

---

109. AGSE 1676, unfoliated. Mendoza sent almost all of his correspondence to Idiaquez rather than Philip, perhaps reflecting his awareness of the king's weakened condition.

110. According to Pastor, the Venetian ambassador in Rome "worked zealously on behalf of Cesare" and his claims to the duchy (*History of the Popes*, Vol. XXIV, p. 387). But this did not mean the Republic was willing to go to war against the pope.

111. Mendoza to Idiáquez, November 19, 1597; AGSE 1676, unfoliated. The governor of Milan whom Mendoza mentions offered Cesare the use of Spanish soldiers to garrison his fortresses, but he apparently did this on his own.

command, it would have been bad enough, but Mendoza made it clear that in his opinion, much more was at stake: "The obligation I have forces me to say that Italy will burn and be consumed if His Majesty does not support the pope, and the same if he remains neutral, because he who is neutral does not head off the war before the explosion." The Ferrara affair, in other words, could threaten Spain's control of Italy if it was not dealt with quickly. As with all Italian conflicts in the sixteenth century, the specter of French involvement and invasion haunted Spanish officials—and King Henry IV did in fact offer military assistance to the pope, in hopes of weakening Spain.[112]

Unfortunately for Mendoza, Philip II rarely did anything quickly, even in the prime of his life, let alone now in his painful last year. The king favored the pope less than Mendoza seems to have done, mostly because of Clement's absolution of the ex-Protestant king of France, so he was not inclined to take Mendoza's advice. On the other hand he had no wish to fan the flames of war in Italy by supporting Cesare's claim.[113] So in the end, no official action came out of Madrid. Cesare's hopes for aid from the Venetians also came to nothing; they may have preferred him to the pope as a neighbor on their southern border, but they were not going to risk too much. As Mendoza wrote in a short note to Philip, "Everything which I can tell Your Majesty on the subject of Ferrara is that the Venetians prepare themselves [for war] in secret, that their preference is for Cesare, that they will comply with the pope with most beautiful words, and that they will openly aid no one until they see how things go."[114] A week later Mendoza reported that Cesare still had envoys in Venice pleading for help, and the Venetians were still raising troops in case of war, but nothing else had happened.[115]

Pope Clement acted much more decisively. Besides raising a large army, on December 23 he excommunicated Cesare and threatened to put his entire city under interdict. The cowed citizens of Ferrara turned against Cesare, leaving him little choice but to negotiate surrender. A representative of the pope entered Ferrara to much fanfare in late January 1598, to be followed by Clement himself that May.[116] The swiftness of events caught everyone by surprise, including Mendoza. In early January he was still sending urgent dispatches to Madrid calling for Philip to aid the pope against Cesare, "the causer of chaos"

112. Mitchell, *1598*, p. 21.
113. Pastor, *History of the Popes*, Vol. XXIV, p. 389.
114. Mendoza to Philip, November 20, 1597; AGSE 1676, unfoliated.
115. Mendoza to Idiáquez, November 29, 1597; AGSE 1676, unfoliated.
116. Mitchell, *1598*, pp. 22–30.

in Italy.[117] When the crisis suddenly resolved itself, everyone scrambled to join the winning side. As Mendoza wrote, "There is great controversy in Italy about who is responsible for His Holiness having proceeded so well and so quickly with his designs, because there is no one who in the current state of affairs does not wish to take credit for much of the honor of this business."[118] The Venetians, for example, claimed credit for not accepting any of Cesare's bribes in order to help him, but Mendoza noted that some in Venice realized that Philip's noninvolvement was also a factor. In this case Mendoza's fears of political upheaval in Italy proved ungrounded.

But why should Mendoza have shown such concern in the first place? By all modern accounts, Spanish hegemony in Italy was well established by the end of Philip II's reign.[119] Yet Mendoza, like all of the other ambassadors we have looked at, greatly feared threats against the status quo in Italian politics. The word they all used to refer to such upsets was *novedades,* meaning changes or anything new being introduced into the volatile Italian political scene.[120] The turmoil in Ferrara in 1598 represented just such an event, which clearly alarmed the resident ambassador in Venice. Diego Hurtado de Mendoza, Francisco de Vargas, and Diego Guzmán de Silva likewise all spoke of "novelties" as something to avoid at all costs.[121]

The Spanish ambassadors' fear of *novedades* in Italy tells us much about their insecurity inspired in them the entire political situation. Spain wielded a great deal of power in the Mediterranean, but Spanish ambassadors displayed neither complacency nor confidence in their dominion. And as we have seen, the resident ambassadors in Venice had nothing like total control over the Republic. Twice the Venetians abandoned military alliances with Spain, and the ambassadors often cited the Venetians' fear and resentment of Habsburg power as a reason for their

---

117. Mendoza to Idiáquez, January 3, 1598; AGSE 1676, unfoliated.
118. Mendoza to Idiáquez, January 24, 1598; AGSE 1676, unfoliated.
119. See for example Manuel Rivero Rodríguez, "Felipe II y los 'Potentados de Italia,'" in *La dimensione europea dei Farnese, Bulletin de l'Institut Historique Belge de Rome* 63 (1993), pp. 337–70; and Gregory Hanlon, *The Twilight of a Military Tradition: Italian Aristocrats and European Conflicts, 1560–1800* (New York, 1998), chap. 2.
120. For a discussion of the Spanish fear of *novedades* in the seventeenth century, see José Antonio Maravall, *Culture of the Baroque: Analysis of a Historical Structure,* trans. Terry Cochran (Minneapolis, 1986), pp. 126–28.
121. To cite one example, Mendoza demanded that the Venetians expel certain political elements in their city who tried to "engineer *novedades* in Italy unfavorable to the Emperor." Mendoza to Charles, June 1544; "Cartas de Don Diego Hurtado de Mendoza," ed. R. Foulché-Delbosc, *Archivo de Investigaciones Históricas* 2 (1911), pp. 155–62. The Venetians ignored him.

defection. The ambassadors themselves demonstrated considerable skill and devotion, but not enough to compensate for the basic conflicts between Spanish and Venetian interests. Furthermore, the ambassadors' own arrogance and inability to understand the Venetians often undermined their efforts. This pattern also appears in Spanish diplomatic relations with the papacy. Like their colleagues in Venice, the Spanish resident ambassadors in Rome may have been vigilant and powerful, but they enjoyed very little peace.

CHAPTER TWO

Diplomacy in Rome under Charles V

As vexing as the situation in Venice was for the Spanish ambassadors, conditions in Rome proved even more difficult to control. The Spanish Habsburgs needed a friendly papacy: its moral authority made it a key player in both local Italian politics and the wider European geopolitical world. Charles V well understood this; indeed, he emphasized the critical importance of good relations with the papacy in his famous political instructions to his son in 1548.[1] The papacy's own political ambitions, however, potentially endangered Spanish hegemony in Italy, especially if it allied with France. The Holy See also played a crucial role in all of the emperor's most cherished dreams, including the defeat of the Ottoman Turks and the extirpation of Lutheran heresy. The first order of business for imperial ambassadors in Rome, therefore, was to get pro-imperial popes elected. Yet several of the papal conclaves during Charles's reign, most notably in 1549–1550 (the election of Julius III) and in 1555 (Paul IV), went against imperial wishes. In addition, every pope Charles dealt with had his own agenda, which usually involved counteracting imperial power in Italy. And even when Charles did successfully manipulate the pope, his policies sometimes backfired, as they did when papal and imperial forces got caught in the unwinnable War of Parma (1550–1552). As hard as they tried, Charles and his ambassadors never fully succeeded in bending the papacy to their will, or in ensuring the pacification of Italy.

1. Geoffrey Parker, *The Grand Strategy of Philip II* (New Haven, 1998), pp. 80–81.

Early in Charles's career, he came tantalizingly close to securing the
Italian peninsula. The three greatest obstacles between him and total
hegemony in Italy were France, Venice, and the papacy. The War of the
League of Cambrai (1509–1517) brought Venice low.[2] At the battle of
Pavia in 1525, Charles's armies smashed those of his rival, King Francis I
of France, and captured the king himself. As part of the agreement that
set him free, Francis relinquished dynastic claims on Italy. Two years later
imperial troops committed the Sack of Rome, a terrible event that nevertheless underlined imperial power in Italy and humbled the papacy.[3]
Thus in 1528, when this chapter begins, Spanish domination of Italy
seemed assured. But Charles would be frustrated for the next thirty years
by repeated French incursions into Italy, abetted by papal machinations.
The worst blow came in the final years of Charles's reign, when Pope Paul
IV invited French troops into Italy for the express purpose of ending
Spanish hegemony in the peninsula (the "Carafa War," 1556–1557).
When Charles abdicated his thrones in the period 1555–1558, Habsburg
control of Italy still seemed precarious at best.

Throughout Charles's reign, his resident ambassadors in Rome fought
to advance their master's interests. The papal court functioned as the
stage on which the rivals for hegemony in western Europe acted out their
struggle, and so the resident ambassador in Rome shouldered a great
deal of responsibility.[4] They felt this burden keenly, and often despaired
of getting better results. Much like in Venice, the ambassadors in Rome
faced entrenched jealousy and resentment of Habsburg power in Italy.
The papacy and the citizens of the Papal States never completely forgave
or forgot the Sack of Rome, nor were papal dreams of driving the barbarian foreigners from Italy ever totally forsaken.[5] Spanish ambassadors to
the Holy See also faced a particular challenge because they dealt with an
ever-changing cast of characters. Each new conclave and papal election
set all the dials back to zero, and a whole new campaign would have to

---

2. See chapter 1.
3. See Judith Hook, *The Sack of Rome 1527* (London, 1972); and André Chastel, *The Sack of Rome, 1527* trans. Beth Archer (Princeton, 1983).
4. For more on early modern Rome as a "world stage," see Mario Rosa, "The 'World's Theatre': The Court of Rome and Politics in the First Half of the Seventeenth Century," in *Court and Politics in Papal Rome, 1492–1700.* ed. Gianvittorio Signorotto and Maria Antonietta Visceglia (Cambridge, 2002), pp. 78–98. One mark of the importance the Habsburgs placed on the Roman embassy (as well as the higher expenses incurred there) is that the salary for that post was the highest in the Spanish diplomatic system: twelve thousand ducats, as opposed to the second highest, eight thousand for the embassy in Vienna. Manuel Fernández Álvarez and Ana Díaz Medina, *Los Austrias mayores y la culminación del imperio (1516–1598)* (Madrid, 1987), p. 240.
5. See Denys Hay, "Italy and Barbarian Europe," in *Italian Renaissance Studies,* ed. E. F. Jacob (London, 1960), pp. 48–68.

begin to establish a working relationship with the pope, his councilors, and his favorites. But of course the Spanish representatives planned ahead of time for these events, by carefully recruiting and grooming cardinals for the papacy. The ambassadors enjoyed a good deal of success in creating a Spanish faction, or "party," among the College of Cardinals and the Roman nobility.[6] But few if any of the sixteenth-century Spanish ambassadors in Rome ever felt secure about who the next pope would be, or what the papacy might do next.

The adventures of Miguel Mai, the imperial ambassador to Pope Clement VII from 1529 to 1532, provide an excellent example of the difficulties inherent to his post. An Aragonese noble, Mai is described by a number of historians as a man totally dedicated to the imperial cause.[7] He certainly displayed the zeal and the impatience that seemed to be the hallmarks of Spanish diplomacy.[8] His correspondence also reveals insecurity, bordering on paranoia, about the political situation in Italy. He constantly complained about the slippery character of the Italian princes, the pope included, and the difficulties he faced gauging the true status of shifting political allegiances. In March 1529, for instance, he wrote to Charles a long apology for the "confused" nature of his reports, which he blamed on the perplexing negotiations he had plunged into. "Please God from here forward I will write to you clearly and in detail about everything," he wrote, "because [hopefully] the negotiations will be sincere whereas up to now they have been a fantasy."[9] This uncertainty might be attributed to Mai's lack of experience, but three years later he was still expressing the same insecurities.

Mai arrived in Rome in December 1528, accompanied by Francisco de Quiñones, the Franciscan General, who had for some time served as special envoy from Charles to Pope Clement VII. Clement had recently made Quiñones Cardinal of Santa Croce, which perhaps made him more

6. For recent descriptions of the Spanish faction in Rome, see Thomas James Dandelet, *Spanish Rome 1500–1700* (New Haven, 2001); and Maria Antonietta Visceglia, "Factions in the Sacred College in the Sixteenth and Seventeenth Centuries," in Signorotto and Visceglia, *Court and Politics in Papal Rome*, pp. 99–131.
7. The great nineteenth-century historian of the papacy, Ludwig von Pastor, wrote about Mai with some suspicion, as he did about most Spaniards; *The History of the Popes from the Close of the Middle Ages*, trans. Ralph Francis Kerr, 40 vols. (London, 1891–1953), Vol. X, p. 38. Charles's biographer Karl Brandi seems more sympathetic: *The Emperor Charles V*, trans. C. V. Wedgwood (London, 1939), p. 275.
8. Miguel Angel Ochoa Brun notes that Mai displayed impatience with his own colleagues as often as with the Italians. *Historia de la diplomacia española*, 5 vols. (Madrid, 1991–1999), Vol. V, p. 208.
9. Mai to Charles, March 23, 1529; Archivo General de Simancas, Sección Estado (hereafter AGSE) 848, #25.

beholden to the pope than the emperor would like for his representative.[10] Mai stepped in as a zealous advocate for his lord's affairs. The first
order of business was to get Clement to commit to an alliance with
Charles, which meant persuading the Pope to abandon his former allies
in the anti-imperial League of Cognac. The League, formed in 1526 and
spearheaded by France, England, and the pope, had contested Charles's
hegemony in Italy, and the imperials knew that until its power could be
permanently broken there would be no peace in the peninsula. Rome
was the key: if Clement's spiritual leadership could be removed from the
anti-imperial forces, the League would be seriously weakened. But
Clement had long resented imperial power in Italy, and he had been subjected to a humiliating imprisonment at the hands of Charles's soldiers
after the Sack of Rome. How could Charles and Clement ever trust one
another? Charles desperately wanted to travel to Italy to receive an imperial coronation at the pope's hands, and to be acknowledged as the
"peacemaker of Italy."[11] Mai had to find a way to make this happen.

Unfortunately for Mai, during his first two months in Rome the pope
suffered serious illness, and some even despaired of his life.[12] Mai
haunted the papal palace, hoping for an audience, but had to be contented with conversations with various cardinals and papal advisors. Many
of them argued that the pope would and should remain neutral.[13] He
answered that "neutrality" would only mean a loss of reputation for the
pope, implying that it would be perceived as cowardice; he also said if
Clement thought he could be neutral and a peacemaker at the same
time, he was deceiving himself. Furthermore, if the pope truly wanted
peace he had best be friends with the more powerful side, which was certainly the emperor, whatever his enemies might say.[14] Thus Mai's initial
encounters in Rome established his belligerent position. Charles wanted
to portray himself as the peacemaker of Italy, but his representative made
it clear that peace depended on the side with the biggest armies.

10. Brandi, *Emperor Charles V,* p. 275.
11. Manuel Fernández Álvarez, *Charles V: Elected Emperor and Hereditary Ruler* (London, 1975), chap. 6.
12. Pastor, *History of the Popes,* Vol. X, pp. 39–43.
13. Gasparo Contarini, the Venetian ambassador in Rome, told Clement that he must remain neutral to counteract imperial power; otherwise Charles would render everyone "subservient to his wishes," to the harm of all. Contarini to Lodovico Falier, Venetian ambassador in London, January 26, 1529; *Calendar of State Papers and Manuscripts, Relating to English Affairs, Existing in the Archives and Collections of Venice,* ed. Rawdon Brown and G. Cavendish Bentinck, Vols. IV–VII (reprint, Nendeln, 1970), Vol. IV, p. 194 (hereafter *Calendar of State Papers Venetian*).
14. Mai to Charles, March 6, 1529; AGSE 848, #30.

Mai labored to convey a sense of the emperor's strength at every opportunity. Upon hearing that "those devils of the League [of Cognac]" had started a rumor that Charles and his brother Ferdinand, King of Bohemia and Hungary, were at odds with each other, Mai immediately sought to counteract it, by arranging for a show of solidarity with Andrea del Burgo, Ferdinand's ambassador to Rome.[15] The ambassador would not allow any cracks to appear in the Habsburg defenses. But would the pope be reassured by displays of imperial power? Mai was not certain. After finally getting in to see Clement, Mai reported that the pope expressed ambivalence about Charles's imminent arrival in Italy. "I cannot say that I do not recognize in the pope some good will toward Your Majesty," Mai wrote, "because he well knows Your Majesty's virtues, power, and prudence, and their opposites in everyone else . . . but he also wants to see all the foreigners out of Italy."[16] Here we have the dilemma in a nutshell. Mai does say that if Clement had to choose between France and the emperor, he would side with the latter, but the pope clearly perceived such a decision as the lesser evil—which did not bode well for a solid alliance with Clement.

The prospects for improvement did not please Mai either. Along with constant updates on the pope's health, Mai also sent a gloomy assessment of political allegiances in the College of Cardinals. "I have said it a thousand times," he wrote with a certain degree of hyperbole, "and now with Your Majesty's permission I will repeat it, that Your Majesty has very few servants in this College."[17] As he explained, this was a serious matter, for Mai suffered from a lack of friends in Rome; worse, if "by some disgrace" a Frenchman or an ally of the League of Cognac were to be elected as the next pope, "we would be in deep trouble" (*terniamos harto trabajo*).[18] Mai warned Charles of the explosiveness of the political situation: all of the Italian powers were up in arms. The pope feared being overwhelmed by foreign armies, the duke of Ferrara had been seen talking with the Venetians and other members of the League, the Sienese were said to be plotting with the Florentines, and as Mai said, "I don't trust any of them."[19] Mai clearly felt surrounded by enemies. He urged Charles to hasten to Italy and force peace on the peninsula.

15. Mai to Charles, March 22, 1529; AGSE 848, #24.
16. Mai to Charles, March 16, 1529; AGSE 848, #26.
17. Mai to Charles, May 11, 1529; AGSE 848, #36.
18. Ibid. Mai sent a similar warning a year later to Francisco de los Cobos, Charles's minister of state. He begged Cobos, "for the love of God," not to let Charles neglect this critical problem. Mai to Cobos, August 10, 1530; AGSE 851, #66.
19. Ibid.

The first step toward pacification came in the early summer of 1529, with the Treaty of Barcelona between Charles and Clement. Both men wanted to solve the problems of Christian Europe in order to focus on the Turkish threat in Austria.[20] They also agreed to help each other in Italy, primarily by installing friendly regimes in Milan and Florence and reinforcing Charles's rights in Naples.[21] Interestingly, Mai seemed to participate only minimally in the conclusion of this treaty. Clement sent a special envoy to Spain to negotiate terms on May 9, 1529.[22] The pope's friendship seemed to be assured, but in early June Mai still sounded suspicious. As he wrote,

> I spoke [to Clement] about the pacification of Italy as Your Majesty commanded me, although it seems impossible, as [the Italians] are united [against us] by fear. This is a very important matter, because this past winter [Clement] disappointed Andrea del Burgo and me a thousand times by saying he did not want to discuss Italian peace treaties, but only a peace treaty with France, because [only] from the latter would the former happen; this manifestly had to do with the obviating of Your Majesty's power, because [the Italians] clearly say that if the peace of Italy [came first] you would overcome France, and then them, and all the world.[23]

Mai did not trust the pope, and believed the feeling was mutual. Mai admitted that the pope had recently claimed to have changed his mind, and now thought the reverse of what he had earlier believed, but Mai had little faith in him. He recommended pursuing alliance negotiations cautiously, because a hostile pope would be a dangerous enemy. Mai seems to have been much more negative or cynical about the pope, and the political situation in general, than Charles's ministers. Mercurino Gattinara, Charles's Grand Chancellor, for example, so pleased Clement by his efforts to engineer the Treaty of Barcelona that the pope rewarded him with a cardinal's hat.[24] Mai, however, often expressed doubts about the pope's motives, and warned that the "whole world" opposed the emperor.[25]

---

20. Kenneth M. Setton, *The Papacy and the Levant (1204–1571)*, 4 vols. (Philadelphia, 1976–1984), Vol. III, p. 327.

21. Pastor, *History of the Popes*, Vol. X, pp. 55–58; Brandi, *Emperor Charles V,* pp. 274–77.

22. Pastor, *History of the Popes*, Vol. X, p. 55.

23. Mai to Charles, June 5, 1529; AGSE 848, #45.

24. Pastor, *History of the Popes*, Vol. X, pp. 66–67. On the other hand, according to John H. Headley, Gattinara, Charles's other ministers, and the imperial agents in Italy all agreed that "the political pretensions of the papacy must be annihilated" for true peace to be established. *The Emperor and His Chancellor: A Study of the Imperial Chancellery under Gattinara* (Cambridge, 1983), p. 98.

25. Mai to Charles, June 7, 1529; AGSE 848, #15.

Despite the ambassador's fears, however, events continued to favor the emperor. In July 1529 Charles and Francis I concluded the Treaty of Cambrai (the "Ladies' Peace" negotiated by the emperor's aunt Margaret of Austria and the queen mother of France, Louise of Savoy), in which the French king renounced his dynastic claims on Naples and Milan. The way now lay open for Charles to make his triumphal entry into Italy, and receive the imperial crown from the pope's hands. Charles had long wanted to march into Italy as a conquering hero, and the pope had long feared the same thing.[26] Now that Charles had made peace with France, Clement hoped to turn the emperor's wrath against the Turks and the Lutherans. This goal, the pope told a Venetian ambassador, justified "dissembling" friendship with Charles, "even were we to know for certain that he bears the Italians ill will."[27] (Clearly Mai was not the only one to distrust his allies, nor were his suspicions of the pope unjustified.) Whatever the rationale, planning for the coronation could proceed, which became the next big headache for the resident ambassador.

Over a period of three months Mai and Louis de Praet, a special imperial envoy, conducted a series of negotiations with the pope over the details of the coronation ceremony.[28] Clement argued repeatedly that the ceremony should be held in Rome.[29] The emperor, however, was anxious to counter the Turkish offensive in central Europe, and felt that Rome was too distant; he suggested Bologna as a more tactically convenient place to be crowned.[30] Clement delayed making a decision, greatly irritating the imperial representatives. They reported much grumbling among the cardinals and courtiers of Rome about the expense of traveling to Bologna, which elicited little sympathy from the imperials.[31]

In late August the ambassadors were still complaining to Charles about "how many times we have begged His Holiness to tell us what he is going to do about Your Majesty's arrival in Italy," but also reported that they had finally pried something out of him.[32] What Clement had to say was somewhat surprising: according to Mai and Praet, the pope wanted Charles

26. Manuel Fernández Álvarez, *Carlos V, el césar y el hombre*, 4th ed. (Madrid, 2000), pp. 389–91.
27. Gasparo Contarini to the Signory of Venice, August 10, 1529; *Calendar of State Papers Venetian*, Vol. IV, p. 227.
28. Praet, a high-ranking diplomat, arrived in Rome on July 22, 1529, with a copy of the Treaty of Barcelona; Pastor, *History of the Popes*, Vol. X, pp. 62–63. He remained in Rome until the coronation, and shared ambassadorial duties with Mai.
29. One example among many: Mai and Praet to Charles, September 11, 1529; AGSE 848, #77.
30. Fernández Álvarez, *Charles V*, p. 83.
31. Mai and Praet to Charles, September 24, 1529; AGSE 848, #72.
32. Mai and Praet to Charles, August 24, 1529; AGSE 848, #66.

to remain in Italy with peace and gentleness, because then the Italians will
be more content, seeing that you will not do them the harm they feared,
and you have even greater reason to do so seeing that [the Italians] are
unhappy with the French, who left them stuck in a war . . . and Your Majesty
will give them peace and quiet, which he thinks will give them great satisfaction, and that it will last a fair time [although] only God could give them
perpetual peace and repose.[33]

It is difficult to know what to make of this statement, given Clement's
evident uneasiness with the idea of Charles coming to Italy in the first
place. Certainly Clement stood to gain from Habsburg victory in Italy: in
the Treaty of Barcelona Charles promised to restore a number of northern Italian cities to papal control, and to return Clement's Medici relatives to power in Florence.[34] But here the pope seems to be asking that
the emperor impose a "pax hispanica" on Italy, which would be a radically
altered position for him to take. The rest of the pope's reported conversation is also remarkably humble in tone. He says that if Charles should
wish to come to Rome, he will do his best to honor him, "although Rome
is in poor condition as is His Holiness"; or if Charles preferred Bologna,
Clement "hoped with God's help" that he could manage to make the trip.
The imperial ambassadors suspected the pope of negotiating with a
politic meekness.

French diplomatic activity added to Mai's feelings of insecurity.
Although the Treaty of Cambrai would seem to have ended the French
threat in Italy, Francis I had hardly distinguished himself as trustworthy
over the years. The pope himself warned the imperials that the French
intended to renew their Italian campaigns in the near future.[35] Mai also
knew that the French had not given up their attempts to win back the
papacy's friendship, even as Charles embarked for Italy. The emperor
landed in Genoa on August 12, 1529; on August 20, Praet and Mai wrote
that the French ambassador in Rome had warned Clement that "popes
and emperors have never gotten along," that "friendship" with Charles
really meant enslavement, and that the pope would be better off in a new
anti-imperial league.[36] The pope reportedly mocked the Frenchman for

---

33. Ibid.
34. Setton, *The Papacy and the Levant,* Vol. III, p. 327; Brandi, *Emperor Charles V,* pp. 274–76.
The Medici had been thrown out of Florence in 1527 and replaced by a republican government, but with Charles's help the Medici would be restored to power in 1530. See J. R. Hale,
Florence and the Medici: The Pattern of Control (London, 1977).
35. Praet and Mai to Charles, August 24, 1529; AGSE 848, #66.
36. Praet and Mai to Charles, August 20, 1529; AGSE 848, #79–80.

making such a suggestion, but Mai and Praet still felt compelled to inform Charles about this possible treachery. As late as September 4, with the emperor waiting in Genoa and imperial troops closing in on Florence, the French ambassador was still offering a military alliance to Clement.[37] The pope again rejected the proposal, but the imperial ambassadors noted ominously that the French agent needed to be watched, and that the pope had a "restless spirit." Even with the emperor on the pope's doorstep, Praet and Mai still did not express confidence about Clement's intentions.[38]

Nevertheless, the imperial coronation went forward more or less as planned, and made a great impression on the Italian audience.[39] Charles made his triumphal entry into Bologna on November 5, 1529, accompanied by a large number of troops and artillery. The emperor came to Italy as a peacemaker, but he clearly demonstrated his ability to impose peace on anyone who opposed him.[40] Over the next few months Charles sat down with Clement and negotiated settlements for most of the outstanding political conflicts plaguing the Italian peninsula. One of the emperor's greatest concerns was to allay Italian fears, and particularly those of the pope, about his ambitions for "universal empire."[41] In this project he appeared to be successful. Most of the members of the old League of Cognac, including the pope, Venice, and Francesco Sforza (newly invested with the Duchy of Milan), now entered into a new alliance with the Habsburgs. This realignment of powers was announced with much fanfare on New Year's Day, 1530.[42] The actual coronation ceremonies occurred the following month, in which ambassadors from France, England, and the various Italian princes participated.[43] The world seemed to acknowledge Charles's mastery of Italy, if not of all of Europe.

37. Praet and Mai to Charles, September 4, 1529; AGSE 848, #87.

38. Ibid. Praet and Mai also urged Charles to hasten his efforts to restore the Medici to power in Florence, because the current Florentine government was pro-French. As they wrote, "there is an Italian proverb that when a Florentine is born, so is a Frenchman."

39. For a recent description of the impact of imperial propaganda used during the coronation on Italian culture, see Marcello Fantoni, "Carlo V e l'Immagine dell'Imperator," in *Carlo V e l'Italia*, ed. Marcello Fantoni (Rome, 2000), pp. 101–18. For an alternative view (emphasizing the financial aspects of Charles's Italian journey), see Guido Guerzoni, "Di alcune ignote e poco nobili cause del soggiorno bolognese di Kaiser Karl V," ibid., pp. 197–217.

40. Bonner Mitchell, *The Majesty of the State: Triumphal Progresses of Foreign Sovereigns in Renaissance Italy (1494–1600)* (Florence, 1986), pp. 139–40.

41. Peter Pierson, "Carlos V, gobernante," in *Carolus V Imperator*, ed. Pedro Navascués Palacio (Madrid, 1999), pp. 130–36.

42. Pastor, *History of the Popes*, Vol. X, pp. 84–88.

43. Mitchell, *The Majesty of the State*, p. 145.

Mai witnessed the ceremonies, and before departing for Germany the emperor renewed Mai's appointment as resident ambassador in Rome.[44] One would think that at this point Mai should have felt considerably more confident. And many of the ambassador's letters in the following months did indeed reflect an unaccustomed tranquility. As Mai wrote in July 1530, "Affairs in Italy by God's grace are well quieted, thanks to Your Majesty's good works and the good impression you left behind here."[45] Yet a mere two weeks later Mai warned that

> As Rome is the vortex for all the world's affairs, and the Italians catch fire at the least spark, those who are partisan [against us] and even more those who have been ruined [by recent events] are stirring up trouble here, because they always want *novedades,* and [the bishop of] Tarbes [the French ambassador], either because of his nature or because he hopes for some advantage, is closeted with the pope even more than usual, shamelessly [lobbying him].[46]

We have seen Spanish preoccupation with *novedades* before, in the correspondence of the ambassadors in Venice. Here we see it again, expressed at a time and place when all such concerns should have been assuaged.

Mai was perhaps more paranoid and irritable than most of his fellow diplomats; in fact, he became involved in a serious feud with some of his Spanish colleagues in Rome, over whether to trust the pope.[47] Yet his fears should not be automatically dismissed, nor his distrust of mercurial Italians, since similar sentiments can be found throughout Spanish diplomatic correspondence. Nor were his fears without justification. Individual Italian princes and noble families still harbored resentments against imperial power, even in territories directly ruled from Spain; Naples, for example, seethed with discontent.[48] Nor had France given up its Italian designs. In March 1532, towards the end of his tenure in Rome, Mai reported that the French might be plotting some *novedad,* specifically a military venture in Italy, and that neither the pope nor the Venetians

---

44. Mai to Empress Isabella, May 27, 1530; AGSE 849, #93.
45. Mai to Charles, July 19, 1530; AGSE 850, #79.
46. Mai to Charles, July 31, 1530; AGSE 851, #52–53.
47. Pastor, *History of the Popes,* Vol. X, pp. 209–10.
48. Giuseppe Galasso, "Trends and Problems in Neapolitan History in the Age of Charles V," in *Good Government in Spanish Naples,* ed. Antonio Calabria and John A. Marino (New York, 1990), pp. 40–42. Galasso points out that in 1531 Charles appointed the Castilian Don Pedro de Toledo as viceroy of Naples, specifically to bring that territory more firmly under control.

were likely to oppose them.[49] And in fact Antonio Rincón, that thorn in the imperial side, was at that moment trying to coordinate a Turkish-French offensive in Italy, with the possible connivance of Venice.[50]

Charles shared his ambassador's concerns, and felt obliged to return to Bologna in the winter of 1532, to try to settle the peninsula down. He appointed Mai to a commission of his top advisors to negotiate with the pope's men.[51] After three months of discussions, this group finagled an agreement with the pope and most of the major powers of Italy to form yet another alliance or "defensive league"—but immediately afterwards Clement accepted a marriage alliance between his niece Catherine de'Medici and Prince Henry of France.[52] Spanish diplomacy never really won over Clement VII, who after all had been humiliated in the Sack of Rome.

Matters would improve somewhat under the next pope, Paul III (Alessandro Farnese). Paul had many of the same goals as the emperor, including a crusade against the Ottoman Turks and the calling of a general Church council to heal the religious schism caused by Luther and his followers. It was also under Paul III that the Habsburgs would begin to build up a Spanish faction of cardinals and Roman nobles, which greatly enhanced their control of papal politics.[53] But this did not mean that Paul always obeyed imperial wishes. Diego Hurtado de Mendoza, who served in Rome from 1547 to 1552, discovered this fairly quickly. Fresh from his less than successful tenure in Venice, Mendoza faced another challenge: besides acting as resident ambassador to the Holy See, he was also appointed as governor of Siena, a position which ultimately cost him his diplomatic career.[54] His tenure in Rome proved to be no easy task either.

Like Miguel Mai, Mendoza arrived at his post at what seemed to be an opportune moment; 1547 was a good year for the imperial cause. Charles V won a major battle at Mühlberg against the German Protestants, and his greatest personal rival, Francis I, died. Mendoza and his Spanish colleagues in Rome hoped that their position of strength would

49. Mai to Charles, March 12, 1532; AGSE 857, #59.

50. Setton, *The Papacy and the Levant*, Vol. III, pp. 360–66. Setton also notes that in the fall of 1532 "Clement was again moving toward an entente with France."

51. Hayward Keniston, *Francisco de los Cobos, Secretary of the Emperor Charles V* (Pittsburgh, 1960), p. 154.

52. Geoffrey Parker, "The Political World of Charles V," in *Charles V 1500–1558 and His Times*, ed. Hugo Soly (Antwerp, 1999), pp. 162–63.

53. Dandelet, *Spanish Rome*, pp. 45–48.

54. Erica Spivakovsky, *Son of the Alhambra: Don Diego Hurtado de Mendoza, 1504–1575* (Austin, 1970), pp. 249–67.

make it easier to manage the pope.[55] Mendoza's initial attitude seems to have been hopeful, if cautious. In November 1546 he promised the emperor that "in this position [of ambassador] which is so honorable and important, as in whatever matter I may serve Your Majesty, I will do the best I can with God's help, and I will seek to compensate with fidelity and diligence for what I lack in ability."[56] He would need all three qualities.

When Mendoza arrived in Rome, he faced a number of difficult issues. As in Venice, his primary concern was foiling the aims of French diplomacy, but the problems related to the recently opened Council of Trent had become even more pressing. Mendoza had in fact already become intimately involved with the council before his appointment to Rome; for the last two years he had made periodic appearances as an imperial envoy to the council.[57] In 1547 Pope Paul III moved the council from Trent to Bologna (inside the Papal States), much to Charles's annoyance, as this move threatened to further alienate the German Protestants. He ordered Mendoza to convince Paul to reverse his decision. Mendoza thus expected a tense first meeting with the pontiff, but it went better than he had feared. The new ambassador expressed his wish that he might have the close relationship with His Holiness that "the service of God, the benefit of the Christendom and the inclination and will of His Imperial Majesty would require."[58] Paul responded positively, adding that he had known Mendoza's father and grandfather, both of whom had served as diplomats in Rome.

Despite the cordiality of this first meeting, within a week the pope and the ambassador had begun to argue. When Mendoza tried to raise objections to the transferring of the council to Bologna, the pope interjected that "he had double the years of Your Majesty and fifty-four years of experience in the governing of ecclesiastical matters," and so knew what he was doing.[59] Mendoza replied that experience was one thing, common sense another. Paul also argued that Bologna was a more "neutral" location than Trent, but Mendoza insisted that neutrality should not be the pope's position toward the German Protestants. Indeed the pope's stated desire for "neutrality" often incensed Mendoza.

55. Pastor, *History of the Popes*, Vol. XII, p. 360.

56. Mendoza to Charles, November 12, 1546; AGSE 1461 (Estados Pequeños), #140–41.

57. Spivakovsky, *Son of the Alhambra*, pp. 127–55; and see also C. Gutiérrez, *Españoles en Trento* (Valladolid, 1951), pp. 265–71.

58. Mendoza to Charles, May 3, 1547; AGSE 874, #56. This document describes the first few weeks of Mendoza's tenure in Rome; sections are quoted in Ángel González Palencia and Eugenio Mele, *Vida y obras de Don Diego Hurtado de Mendoza*, 3 vols. (Madrid, 1941–1943), Vol. II, pp. 23–40.

59. Ibid.

Mendoza tried to remedy his antagonistic relations with the pope by winning friends and influencing people around His Holiness. The same day as his first papal audience, he met with Cardinal Sfondrato, who had just received a commission as a special papal envoy to Charles. Sfondrato asked how best to ease the current tensions between pope and emperor; Mendoza answered that everything depended on Paul, and that his inconsistent policies were the cause of the trouble.[60] Next Mendoza encountered Cardinal Alessandro Farnese, the pope's grandson, who often acted as liaison with the pontiff.[61] Again the discussion centered on improving relations between Charles and Paul, although this time the ambassador focused on their conflicting claims on the northern Italian territories of Parma and Piacenza. Mendoza criticized Paul for sending troops into what was "clearly" an imperial fief, and wondered aloud if the pope was just trying to make trouble (*si se intentasse alguna novedad*).[62] Mendoza obviously hoped to influence papal policy through the pope's councilors, a strategy he would pursue throughout his tenure in Rome.

His relationship with Paul, however, continued to be strained over the next few years. In addition to Church reform and European power politics, they also argued over money: Charles wanted permission to draw large sums from the Spanish Church, and Paul stalled giving it. At one point Mendoza exclaimed to Charles that the pope "says that I, Don Diego, have acted like a gypsy and like a Venetian *meriol*, which means pickpocket."[63] Mendoza claimed that the insult did not bother him, but certainly it did. Like many of his fellow ambassadors, he defended his honor and his public image fiercely. When he arrived at chapel for Christmas mass in 1547, he discovered someone sitting in his seat: Orazio Farnese, another of the pope's grandsons, who had recently married a French princess. Enraged by this public snubbing by the pope, Mendoza forcibly ejected Orazio from his seat, shouting that that place had always belonged to the imperial ambassador, and that nobody would remove him from it alive.[64] As we will see, the issue of ambassadorial precedence would long be a point of conflict for Spanish diplomats.

Mendoza's behavior may seem undiplomatic, to say the least, but he had explicit permission from Charles to be blunt with the pope. In January 1548 Charles sent his ambassador instructions on how to conduct

60. Ibid.
61. See the recent biography of Farnese, Clare Robertson, *Il gran cardenale: Alessandro Farnese, Patron of the Arts* (New Haven, 1992).
62. Mendoza to Charles, May 3, 1547; AGSE 874, #56.
63. Spivakovsky, *Son of the Alhambra*, p. 206.
64. Ibid., p. 207.

negotiations.[65] He emphasized that Paul must be made to understand the emperor's unhappiness with papal policy, especially concerning Parma and Piacenza, to the point of possibly causing a rupture in papal-imperial relations. Further, Mendoza should say that

> Since not only in Rome but also in all of Italy and in these parts it is said that His Holiness has made or discussed some alliances in order to disturb the peace of Italy, and to make war against us, and to steal our lands. . . . we wish to advise him and his [councilors] that if they make some move, we will come to blows in such manner and so hotly and suddenly [that the Pope would quickly regret his actions].

The message was clear: do what we want or else. In addition to this belligerent declaration, Charles also ordered his ambassador to deliver a formal protest against the transference of the council to Bologna. Mendoza did so in late January, and reported that the pope, while furious, "did not say a word, because his councilors had told him to be quiet."[66]

If Charles and Mendoza hoped to cow the pope into submission, they were disappointed. Paul if anything became more defiant and resentful of imperial power. In July 1549 the pope complained to the Venetian ambassador in Rome that Charles was "unable to slake his thirst for universal empire, which he seeks to obtain by all possible means, so that all powers should take warning."[67] Imperial diplomacy had apparently backfired, but Mendoza did not soften his approach—although he did use mockery rather than open threats. According to tradition, once a year the Kingdom of Naples (a Spanish territory since 1504) sent a symbolic gift of a white horse dressed in costly trappings to the pope, its feudal overlord.[68] Mendoza arranged for the pope to be presented with a brokendown nag. When Paul refused to leave his palace to receive the "gift," Mendoza walked the horse right into the building.[69] Mendoza may have been arrogant, but he did not lack a sense of humor.

Mendoza's relationship with the pope continued to be prickly up to Paul's death in November 1549. Mendoza saw the ensuing conclave as an opportunity to improve the situation, although, like every papal election,

65. Charles to Mendoza, January 16, 1548; AGSE 875, #18. Printed in González Palencia and Mele, *Vida y obras de Don Diego Hurtado de Mendoza*, Vol. III, pp. 342–45.

66. Spivakovsky, *Son of the Alhambra*, pp. 213–14.

67. Matteo Dandolo to the Signory of Venice, July 6, 1549; *Calendar of State Papers Venetian*, Vol. V, p. 236.

68. See Dandelet, *Spanish Rome*, pp. 55–57.

69. Spivakovsky, *Son of the Alhambra*, pp. 221–23; and González Palencia and Mele, *Vida y obras de Don Diego Hurtado de Mendoza*, Vol. II, pp. 119–20.

it also represented a potential disaster. A pro-imperial pope would of course be extremely welcome, while a hostile one could be catastrophic. Naturally, the French had the direct opposite view. The conclave of 1549–1550 would be one of the most bitterly contested papal elections of the sixteenth century. Henry II of France brought a great deal of political pressure to bear on the College of Cardinals, in an attempt to break the perceived Habsburg influence on the papacy.[70] Meanwhile Charles made clear the importance of this election in his instructions to his ambassador:

> Our intention . . . is that as dignified and accommodating a pope as possible be elected for the service of God and the good of his Church . . . and although we may be entirely confident that this is also your goal, still, because this business is so grave and important, we charge you as far as is possible to guide [the conclave] by every method and means you know to use with your prudence, dexterity, and good manner, keeping in mind the damage and great inconveniences to God's Church which could result from [the election of] the wrong pope.[71]

We should note, of course, the assumption that only a pro-imperial pope could truly be beneficial for Christendom. The emperor also explained in detail which cardinals he saw as "wrong" for the job: any Frenchman, and any Italian "who could be pernicious and whose [anti-imperial] intentions and actions are known." He mentioned several by name, and stressed that Mendoza must at all costs prevent their election. Charles then listed the cardinals he approved of, including Sfondrato and the English reform cardinal, Reginald Pole.[72] Interestingly, Charles suggested promoting a Spanish or German candidate only as a last resort, if all other choices failed; perhaps he felt that any cardinal closely associated with Habsburg territories would have difficulties gaining support.

The emperor's instructions proved difficult for Mendoza to follow, partly because the ambassador did not agree with all of them. Charles had specifically excluded the Florentine cardinal Jacopo Salviati, a

70. See Frederic Baumgartner, "Henry II and the Papal Conclave of 1549," *Sixteenth Century Journal* 16 (1985), pp. 301–14.

71. Charles to Mendoza, November 20, 1549; AGSE 875, #95. Printed in González Palencia and Mele, *Vida y obras de Don Diego Hurtado de Mendoza*, Vol. II, pp. 129–32.

72. Pole enjoyed the support of many of the pro-imperial cardinals, and came within one vote of being elected, but in the end suspicions of unorthodoxy sabotaged his candidacy. See Dermot Fenlon, *Heresy and Obedience in Tridentine Italy: Cardinal Pole and the Counter Reformation* (Cambridge, 1972), pp. 226–32; and Thomas F. Mayer, "The War of the Two Saints: The Conclave of Julius III and Cardinal Pole," in *Cardinal Pole in European Context* (Aldershot, 2000), chap. 4.

nephew of Pope Leo X and a popular figure in the College. Salviati had known French ties, but Mendoza initially favored his candidacy for personal reasons. Salviati and Mendoza shared a common enemy: Juan Alvarez de Toledo, bishop of Burgos. The rival Spanish noble houses of Mendoza and Toledo traditionally hated each other. Salviati, meanwhile, opposed the Toledo family because they were related by marriage to his greatest rival, duke Cosimo de'Medici.[73] The conclave became a battleground of opposing factions. Salviati enjoyed the support of the Gonzagas, the pro-imperial rulers of Mantua, but was opposed by the Farnese of Parma, who favored the emperor but also supported Cosimo. Mendoza had all he could manage negotiating this minefield of alliances and counter-alliances—and then he had to reverse his position to fulfill his master's orders. His maneuvers give us an insight into the Byzantine world of Roman politics.

Mendoza's first task was to block Salviati's election, as Charles had ordered, but to do it in secret. He thus set out to weaken Salviati's support in the College. To begin with, he made a tricky deal with the Farnese: he pretended to do them a favor by promising not to support Salviati.[74] The Farnese faction had no way to know that Mendoza had been commanded to oppose Salviati, and in return for this "concession," they agreed to withdraw their support for Cardinal Santa Croce, one of their top choices, who had also been on Charles's list of unacceptable candidates. But this double-dealing only hinted at what was to come. In a letter to Antoine Perrenot de Granvelle, bishop of Arras and one of Charles's ministers of state, Mendoza described the "great artifice" he used to block Salviati's candidacy.[75] First, he made Salviati "suspect to the French," by hinting to certain people that the emperor favored the cardinal, or at least did not oppose him—thus ensuring that the French would vote against him. Then Mendoza indirectly discouraged pro-imperial cardinals from voting for Salviati by publicly declaring an alliance with the duke of Florence.[76] Next, he told both Salviati and Santa Croce that he

73. See Spivakovsky, *Son of the Alhambra*, pp. 225–36; and Carlos José Hernando Sánchez, *Castilla y Nápoles en el siglo XVI: El Virrey Pedro de Toledo* (Salamanca, 1994), pp. 105–7. Pedro de Toledo, nephew of the bishop of Burgos, was the viceroy of Naples (1532–1553); his sister Leonora de Toledo married Cosimo de Medici.

74. Spivakovsky, *Son of the Alhambra*, pp. 234–35.

75. December 1, 1549; *Algunas Cartas de Don Diego Hurtado de Mendoza, escritas 1538–1552*, ed. Alberto Vazquez and R. Selden Rose (New Haven, 1935), pp. 136–40.

76. This declaration of friendship was a sham; Cosimo and the Toledo clan waged a propaganda war against Mendoza throughout the conclave, trying to get him in trouble with the emperor by accusing him of incompetence. Mendoza to Granvelle, December 31, 1549; *Algunas Cartas*, pp. 156–60.

would support the one against the other, in order to make them vote against each other. Finally, Mendoza labored to hasten the calling of a vote, so that not all of the French cardinals would arrive in time to participate. With these tactics, Mendoza assured Granvelle, Salviati's candidacy "will certainly be impeded," and so it was. Mendoza sometimes complained about the twisted world of Church politics, but he obviously knew how to work the system.

Or at least he thought he did. The final result of the conclave, the election of Giovan Maria del Monte as Pope Julius III, initially horrified Mendoza. Del Monte had been on the emperor's list of unacceptable candidates, and Mendoza had written that although he liked the cardinal personally, he believed he would make a terrible pope from the imperial point of view.[77] Del Monte had supported the transfer of the council from Trent to Bologna, and had voiced a number of anti-imperial opinions. In France, news of the election was greeted with joy.[78] On the morning after the election, Mendoza's face must have reflected his dismay; the Venetian ambassador reported that Don Diego "did not appear very joyful."[79] The new pope noticed and laughed, calling out "Do not be so afraid, Don Diego!"[80] Over the next few days, however, Mendoza's worst fears were allayed, as Julius seemed surprisingly eager to please the emperor. He promised to open a new council in Trent, and to settle the dispute over Parma in Charles's favor.[81] In return, Charles instructed Mendoza to assure Julius of his goodwill, and sent a high dignitary to Rome to perform the ceremonial oath of obedience to the new pontiff.[82]

During the first year of Julius's papacy, Mendoza enjoyed an excellent working relationship with the pope. At the ambassador's suggestion, Charles, Prince Philip, and Ferdinand of Austria all sent special envoys to Julius, congratulating him on his election and covering him with praise.[83] Julius responded well to flattery; Prince Philip held a large feast in Brussels in honor of the pope, and Mendoza reported that "His Holiness is very content and well-disposed toward [us after] the demonstration

77. Mendoza to Granvelle, December 21, 1549; *Algunas Cartas*, pp. 155–56.
78. Baumgartner, "Henry II and the Papal Conclave of 1549," p. 312.
79. Matteo Dandolo to the Signory of Venice, February 9, 1550; *Calendar of State Papers Venetian*, Vol. V, p. 309.
80. Spivakovsky, *Son of the Alhambra*, p. 244; and Pastor, *History of the Popes*, Vol. XIII, p. 78.
81. Spivakovsky, *Son of the Alhambra*, p. 247.
82. Charles to Mendoza, February 27, 1550; AGSE 875, #119. For a description of the elaborate rituals of Rome, see Pio Pecchiai, *Roma nel Cinquecento* (Bologna, 1948), pp. 321–60; and more recently, Peter Burke, "Sacred Rulers, Royal Priests: Rituals of the Early Modern Popes," in *The Historical Anthropology of Early Modern Italy* (Cambridge, 1987), pp. 168–82.
83. Spivakovsky, *Son of the Alhambra*, pp. 268–69.

which Your Highness made in celebration of his election, and neither he nor his supporters stop talking about how Your Highness spent twenty thousand escudos on the feast."[84] Mendoza also predicted that such displays would make Julius malleable to imperial wishes, "because he is a vainglorious man and likely to please his friends." Conversely, the pope understood that those who crossed the emperor "do not always do well." The Habsburg campaign to turn the pope's head worked so well that an alarmed King Henry II of France felt it necessary to send a special emissary of his own. During an audience with this envoy, Julius thanked the Frenchman, and then turned to Mendoza and explained that it was necessary to appear grateful in order to appease French jealousy.[85] Mendoza must have felt smug at this point.

All of this goodwill, however, would be lost in the War of Parma.[86] Charles, who had been plotting the acquisition of Parma for years, thought he saw his chance now that he had a pope who could be manipulated. In February 1550, Julius invested Ottavio Farnese, grandson of Pope Paul III, with Parma. Ottavio was married to Margaret of Austria, the emperor's natural daughter, but Charles still wanted more direct control of the city. The Farnese family knew this, and began negotiating with King Henry II of France for military support against Charles, which he granted. Charles, for his part, saw an opportunity to eliminate one of the last remaining Italian allies of France.[87] Once again a local Italian conflict became a focus of European power politics, and Mendoza became a key player in the ensuing conflagration. Charles ordered him to play a dangerous game: maneuver Julius into declaring war against Ottavio, to give the emperor an excuse to invade Parma in "aid" of the pope. As Charles wrote to Mendoza, "Always persist in stirring things up . . . so that we can make use of [the result]."[88] Unfortunately for both Charles and his ambassador, they would end up reaping the whirlwind. A war over Parma did indeed occur, but it did not go as the imperials planned.

Mendoza had his doubts about this affair from the beginning. He worried that unless victory came quickly, political chaos in Italy could jeopardize the success of the Council of Trent.[89] Nonetheless he did his best to ensnare the pope in a war against Ottavio. A series of small incidents

84. Mendoza to Philip, March 18, 1550; AGSE 876, #54. Printed in González Palencia and Mele, *Vida y obras de Don Diego Hurtado de Mendoza*, Vol. III, pp. 382–83.
85. Spivakovsky, *Son of the Alhambra*, p. 269.
86. For a summary of the War of Parma, see Setton, *The Papacy and the Levant*, Vol. III, pp. 548–64.
87. James D. Tracy, *Emperor Charles V, Impresario of War* (Cambridge, 2002), p. 6.
88. Charles to Mendoza, April 20, 1551; quoted in Spivakovsky, *Son of the Alhambra*, p. 277.
89. Mendoza to Granvelle, February 20, 1551; *Algunas Cartas*, pp. 207–8.

between Farnese's troops and papal soldiers, in part incited by imperial plotting, led to a growing rift. Mendoza urged Julius to take harsh action, promising imperial assistance if Ottavio resisted.[90] Eventually Farnese formally broke ties with the pope and allied himself with France. In March 1551 Mendoza composed a long letter to Julius exhorting him to take up arms, in much the same way he had orated to the Venetians against the Turks.[91] With "total humility and submission and the love of a true servant," Mendoza carefully laid out the moral, legal, and practical reasons why the pope could not let Ottavio remain unpunished. Farnese had risen up against his feudal overlord as well as his spiritual father. Even worse, however, Ottavio had invited the French into Italy. While Charles "does not intend anything except the defense and protection of Your Holiness's honor, authority, and states," Mendoza claimed, the King of France interferes only "in order to disturb Italy." The letter made it clear that by taking action against Ottavio, Julius would not only be defending his rights, he would also be defending Italy against wicked French plots. Of course, Mendoza lied about Charles's intentions, but his fear of upset in Italy was genuine; he dissimulated in a good cause.

The War of Parma quickly degenerated into a war of attrition, and Mendoza's unhappiness grew. The imperial siege of Parma cost Charles almost 800,000 ducats, with nothing to show for it.[92] Relations between Charles and Julius became increasingly strained, placing the imperial ambassador in a painful dilemma. As he wrote to Granvelle,

> I am certain that although His Majesty and His Holiness are trying hard to preserve their friendship, all things grow, peak, and decline; and if at some point this friendship should weaken . . . it will be the worst break there has ever been between pope and emperor. I do not wish to be caught in this scenario, which may happen in my time, because I am a servant of the emperor and I love the pope like my own life.[93]

Mendoza felt torn between his master and his spiritual father. Mendoza also faced professional and personal disaster: in addition to the potential failure of his ambassadorship in Rome, he encountered growing unrest in Siena.[94] To crown it all, by the spring of 1552, Charles had begun to

---

90. Spivakovsky, *Son of the Alhambra,* pp. 272–73.
91. "Cartas de Don Diego Hurtado de Mendoza," ed. R. Foulché-Delbosc, *Archivo de Investigaciones Históricas* 2 (1911), pp. 469–74.
92. Tracy, *Emperor Charles V,* pp. 232–41.
93. May 4, 1551; *Algunas Cartas,* p. 230.
94. Spivakovsky, *Son of the Alhambra,* chap. 13.

blame Mendoza for getting him involved in this costly war, which instead of strengthening the imperial hold on Italy, had ended up jeopardizing it. The emperor charged his envoy with finding an exit strategy—only now, Mendoza had to feign eagerness to continue the fight, and then "reluctantly" agree to peace negotiations. In other words, Mendoza had to reverse his previous arguments, and persuade Julius to end the war the imperials had incited in the first place!

Mendoza wearily complied with his new instructions. He advised Julius "not as a minister but as a friend" to start pulling his troops out of battle.[95] The pope naturally proved reluctant, and expressed doubts about the emperor's intentions as well as whether the French or the Farnese would be willing to talk peace. Julius also claimed to have planned a battle strategy worthy of Scipio or Hannibal, a dubious assertion at best. Nevertheless Julius began to see the advantages of peace; indeed he soon alarmed Mendoza by going too far in the opposite direction. King Henry II of France sent Cardinal François de Tournon to Rome with enticing new proposals.[96] Mendoza suddenly found himself struggling to prevent Julius from becoming too friendly with the French. The pope spoke of his wish to be "neutral," an idea Mendoza ridiculed. At one point Mendoza demanded of Julius "how it is possible that His Holiness wanted to be neutral between Your Majesty and the King of France, having received good works from the former and disrespect from the latter."[97] The pope answered that according to Cardinal Tournon, King Henry had not disturbed the Papal States or any client state of Rome. He also insisted that while he wanted to remain a friend of the emperor, he also did not want to be an enemy of the king of France. This evidence of French influence on Julius must have infuriated Mendoza, but he hid it well, only repeating that he wished to advise Julius as a friend.

The summer of 1552 represented the nadir of Mendoza's career. The War of Parma had failed, and French troops remained in Italy. The pope was furious with the imperials; as the ambassador wrote to Granvelle, "The pope almost never mentions the emperor, and when he does it is with a terrible expression."[98] The emperor blamed his ambassador for this fiasco, a charge Mendoza vigorously denied, even daring to declare, with "all fitting humility and veneration, that His Majesty bears the guilt he imputes to me."[99] But the worst blow came in July, when the city-state

95. Mendoza to Charles, April 4, 1552; AGSE 878, #10.
96. Gladys Dickinson, *Du Bellay in Rome* (Leiden, 1960), pp. 112–13.
97. Mendoza to Charles, April 13, 1552; AGSE 878, #14.
98. Mendoza to Granvelle, April 15, 1552; *Algunas Cartas*, p. 356.
99. Quoted in Spivakovsky, *Son of the Alhambra*, p. 282.

of Siena revolted against imperial rule.[100] For years, Mendoza had been trying to build a castle to guard the city, but had experienced endless financial delays. When he tried to make the Sienese pay for the new fortifications, they threw out the Spanish garrison and invited in French troops for protection.[101] Mendoza, the governor general of this rebellious territory, rushed to Florence to plead for Cosimo de Medici's aid in retrieving the situation, but his old rival denied him any help. Siena would remain outside of imperial control for three years. This humiliation was the final straw; in August 1552 Charles recalled Mendoza to Spain.[102] Although he would later enter the service of Prince Philip, Mendoza's diplomatic career was over. His failure to pacify Italy greatly depressed him; as he wrote to Granvelle, "I beg you to remember my honor. I would have picked up a pike and served in battle [myself], rather than be given the whole world, if it would have solved [the Italian problems]."[103]

The fall of Mendoza coincided with a change in imperial policy toward Italy.[104] During the 1540s several of Charles's ministers of state, led by Mendoza's patron Granvelle, had advocated a policy of forcibly integrating the Italian states into the imperial system. The War of Parma demonstrated that this approach did not work. A new faction of ministers, closely associated with Prince Philip, advanced a new plan, based on the power of patronage. If the princes of Italy could be bought with money, titles, and honors, Spanish influence could be spread indirectly. One of the ministers who supported this strategy was Fernando Alvarez de Toledo, the duke of Alba (a member of the Toledo clan hated by Diego de Mendoza).[105] In 1554 Alba became captain general of Italy, a mark of his new power and prestige. But efforts to spread Spanish bounty around Italy would be interrupted in the spring of 1555 with the death of Pope Julius. Alba, along with the other Spanish ministers in Italy, again emphasized in his letters the importance of electing a pope who would not "light the fires" of political unrest in the peninsula.[106] But the fates would turn

---

100. See ibid., chap. 13.
101. Eric Cochrane, *Italy 1530–1630*, ed. Julius Kirshner (London, 1988), p. 40.
102. *Algunas Cartas*, p. xliii.
103. Mendoza to Granvelle, August 20, 1552; *Algunas Cartas*, p. 392. Mendoza had been a soldier in imperial service, and had seen action in Africa, but by now he was almost fifty years old.
104. See Manuel Rivero Rodríguez, *Felipe II y el gobierno de Italia* (Madrid 1998), pp. 44–48.
105. For a full description, see William S. Maltby, *Alba: A Biography of Fernando Alvarez de Toledo, Third Duke of Alba 1507–1582* (Berkeley, 1983).
106. Quoted by Gianvittorio Signorotto, "Note sulla politica e la diplomazia dei pontifici (da Paolo III a Pio IV)," in Fantoni, *Carlo V e l'Italia*, p. 48.

against the Habsburgs. In April 1555 Marcello Cervini was elected as Pope Marcellus II, to universal acclaim, but he would die a mere two months later.[107] He would be followed, to the great consternation of the imperials, by Gian Pietro Carafa, Pope Paul IV.

Paul IV, a native of Naples, was driven by a lifelong desire to free his homeland, and indeed all of Italy, from Spanish rule. His election came as a nasty surprise for the Spaniards; Charles had ordered his exclusion, but the pro-imperial candidates failed to coordinate their efforts.[108] Conversely, on hearing that Spain opposed Carafa, Henry II of France threw him all of his support.[109] Paul soon proved to be the nightmare the Spaniards feared: in December 1555 he signed a secret pact with Henry, promising him Naples in return for military assistance against the Habsburgs.[110] So once again an Italian prince invited a French invasion of Italy, the scenario that haunted Spanish diplomacy ever since the beginning of the Italian Wars in 1494. In fact, the threat to Naples now carried even greater consequences, because of that territory's increasingly critical role in Spanish imperial finances.[111] The imperial diplomats and ministers in Italy saw the disaster develop, but they could only watch helplessly. The imperial ambassador in Rome in this period, Fernando Ruiz de Castro, the Marques de Sarria, had little political experience. He arrived in Rome in July 1555, but was denied a papal audience; Paul seized on trivial Spanish transgressions in Italy as a reason to ignore Charles's ambassador.[112] For the next year the pope subjected Sarria to increasingly blatant insults of this kind, until Habsburg-papal relations broke down altogether.

Most of the letters written by Sarria during his short tenure in Rome were terse and gloomy. In January 1556 he reported that Paul, together with several French cardinals, was definitely plotting war against Spain.[113] According to the ambassador's sources, both the pope and the French had made overtures to various Italian powers, including Venice, in order to form a general league. Sarria, meanwhile, apparently did little to appease the pope. In February Bernardo Navagero, the Venetian ambassador in Rome, reported a conversation with Sarria which made the

107. Pastor, *History of the Popes*, Vol. XIV, pp. 33–53.
108. Ibid., pp. 56–62.
109. Frederic J. Baumgartner, *Henry II, King of France 1547–1559* (Durham, 1988), p. 172.
110. Brandi, *Emperor Charles V*, pp. 632–33.
111. See Antonio Calabria, *The Cost of Empire: The Finances of the Kingdom of Naples in the Time of Spanish Rule* (Cambridge, 1991).
112. Pastor, *History of the Popes*, Vol. XIV, pp. 92–96.
113. Sarria to Princess Juana (Philip's sister, regent in Spain), January 23, 1556; AGSE 883, #9–10.

Spaniard sound like the aggressor.[114] According to what Sarria told Navagero, the pope tried to discuss peace with the imperial ambassador, but he had thrown this peaceful gesture back in Paul's face, telling him that "by treating us so badly as you do, you give us small cause to trust you entirely." Sarria also declared to Navagero that

> Had there been anybody but myself at this court, a total rupture would have taken place many months ago; what has not been said about me here? What sort of injury have they abstained from doing to the honor of my masters? Yet it has been tolerated, and this our toleration will serve as testimony to the world that we, on our part, shall not have recourse to arms, save from compulsion.

This dramatic declaration, of course, is reported to us second-hand, but it rings true with the sense of righteous anger often displayed by Spanish diplomats. In any event it is clear that the antagonism was mutual.

Then a trivial incident occurred which triggered an open break. On the evening of March 25, Sarria returned to Rome after a day of hunting in the countryside, only the guard at the gate did not recognize him and refused him entrance into the city. In a fit of rage Sarria and his entourage broke the gate and forced their way in.[115] Paul perceived this as an insult to his authority and sought to institute legal proceedings against Sarria. The Spanish Cardinal Siguenza, who shared diplomatic duties with the ambassador, wrote an indignant letter back to Spain complaining that the pope had barred Sarria from attending chapel because of this uproar.[116] Sarria made some feeble gestures of reconciliation, but it was too late. From this point on the pope and the Spanish ambassador stopped speaking to each other. In May 1556 Sarria reported that his relations with Paul were beyond hope of repair, and that matters would improve only if major change came to Rome—which could only mean a new pope.[117] The following month Cardinal Siguenza wrote that "His Holiness is still angry at the marquis, and seeing that he could not talk to [Paul] or negotiate in any way, [Sarria] asked for permission to leave here, which the pope promptly gave him."[118] What would later be called the "Carafa War" was about to begin.

114. Navagero to the Doge and Senate, February 1, 1556; *Calendar of State Papers Venetian,* Vol. VI, Part I, pp. 333–34.
115. Pastor, *History of the Popes,* Vol. XIV, pp. 118–19.
116. Siguenza to Princess Juana, April 9, 1556; AGSE 883, #17.
117. Sarria to Princess Juana, May 21, 1556; AGSE 883, #22–24.
118. Siguenza to Princess Juana, June 4, 1556; AGSE 883, #25. Sarria did not actually leave until August 7; according to Pastor, Pope Paul tried to prevent the ambassador's departure up to the last minute. *History of the Popes,* Vol. XIV, pp. 133–34.

The conflict of 1556–1557 marked a major transitional period for Habsburg relations with Rome. Change started at the top: in this same period, Charles shocked Europe by abdicating his crowns.[119] Philip II, the new king of Spain, was thus just adjusting to his role when the political situation in Italy exploded. The pope declared war on Spain, excommunicated Philip, and invited French troops into the peninsula. Philip responded with decisive, if restrained, action. The duke of Alba led a powerful army from Naples into the Papal States and besieged Rome, but without causing great damage. The threat of a repeat of the 1527 Sack of Rome was enough to make Paul capitulate. The Spaniards designed the peace treaty to smooth out relations as quickly as possible, although Paul did swear never again to make war on Spain or assist those who did. Philip's instructions to a new ambassador to Rome, Juan de Figueroa, referred delicately to the "differences" which had recently occurred between himself and the pope, which the king hoped could be quickly forgotten.[120]

But Philip would not forget. When Paul died in 1559, Philip determined that there would never be a recurrence of this kind of opposition in Rome.[121] He began to pour money into pensions for cardinals at a greater rate than Charles had ever managed, and instructed his ambassadors to spend more effort than ever on manipulating conclaves to Spain's advantage. In many ways he was successful: there would be no rabidly anti-Spanish popes for the next sixty years. But the open war between Spain and the papacy at the end of Charles V's reign underscores the weaknesses of Habsburg diplomacy. Throughout the first half of the sixteenth century Charles sought control of Italy, but his successes themselves caused concern and resentment in every pope he faced. The papacy, just as much as any of Charles's open enemies, feared Habsburg hegemony in Italy or in Europe in general. As one of Charles's biographers recently wrote, "as temporal rulers the popes were no less anxious about Habsburg 'tyranny' than other Italian potentates—especially at moments of Habsburg triumph."[122] When Charles accepted the imperial crown from Pope Clement VII in 1530, he imagined that he had become the master of Italy, with the papacy's blessing. Bitter experience proved him wrong. When Charles resigned his crown, he passed on the tasks of taming the papacy and pacifying Italy to his son Philip. Philip, and his ambassadors, would suffer their own frustrations as a result.

119. For a full description of the transition of power in the Habsburg ranks, see M. J. Rodríguez-Salgado, *The Changing Face of Empire: Charles V, Philip II and Habsburg Authority, 1551–1559* (Cambridge, 1988).
120. Philip to Figueroa, September 25, 1558; AGSE 883, #104.
121. Dandelet, *Spanish Rome*, pp. 53–57; and Parker, *The Grand Strategy of Philip II*, pp. 80–81.
122. Tracy, *Emperor Charles V*, p. 306.

CHAPTER THREE

Philip II and the Papacy, 1556–1573

Throughout the reign of Philip II, his relationship with the papacy was a source of aggravation. As the co-leaders of the Counter-Reformation, Philip and the papacy were natural allies, and yet individual popes had an irritating tendency to have their own agendas. As Geoffrey Parker writes, "The king was almost always disappointed in his popes."[1] On the larger scale of European politics, the papacy often annoyed Philip by not actively assisting his efforts to combat heresy in the Netherlands and England, or to keep France in check. On a more local level, popes continued to act as Italian princes, often asserting their authority in the peninsula, which the Spaniards perceived as a threat to Italy's fragile stability. All of these issues boil down to one problem: the Spanish Habsburg assumption that the interests of the papacy, Italy, and indeed all of Christendom mirrored their own, and the papacy's refusal to acknowledge this idea. Recent historiography has stressed the close relations between Philip II and the papacy, which helped establish Spanish domination in Italy.[2] A close examination of Philip's ambassadors in Rome, however, reveals a different story.

During the first twenty years of Philip's reign, Spanish diplomats in Rome experienced a number of significant failures. These failures are the more remarkable because they happened just after the Treaty of

1. Geoffrey Parker, *Philip II,* 3d ed. (Chicago, 1995), p. 57.
2. See for example Thomas Dandelet: "By keeping Rome closely allied with them, Spanish monarchs kept their Italian possessions at peace." *Spanish Rome 1500–1700* (New Haven, 2001), p. 218.

Cateau-Cambrésis, the supposed turning point for Spanish domination of Italy. For example, the first ambassador I will examine, Francisco de Vargas, so antagonized Pope Pius IV that Philip had to replace him as resident ambassador. The next ambassador, Luis de Requeséns, lost a bid for precedence over the French ambassador to the papacy, and stormed out of Rome in protest. Yet another ambassador, Requeséns' younger brother Juan de Zúñiga, could only object ineffectually while Pope Pius V nearly started several wars in Italy. Finally, what should have been a great triumph of Spanish diplomacy, a military alliance with Rome and Venice against the Turks, proved to be impossible to manipulate, and ended in impotent futility when the Republic of Venice defected. Each of these mishaps occurred at least in part because of the ambassadors' arrogance and presumption; together, they indicate Spain's inability to control the papacy, even after 1559.

As we have seen, Philip's reign began with a war against the papacy. Obviously, Philip hoped that the next pope would look more kindly on Spanish affairs. Even before Paul IV's death, Philip instructed his new ambassador to Rome, Juan de Figueroa, to start the process of getting the right man elected. Tellingly, Philip emphasized the next pope's role in Italian affairs over whether he favored Spain per se. According to Philip, the next pope should serve God and the Church, and most importantly he should "preserve Christendom, and especially Italy, which had been so sorely tried by the [Carafa] war, in peace and unity."[3] So four months after signing the Treaty of Cateau-Cambrésis Philip still worried that the wrong pope could jeopardize the hard-won peace of Italy. He listed five cardinals who would be acceptable candidates (including Gianangelo Medici, who would in fact be elected), and urged Figueroa to exclude all French cardinals and their allies.

Unfortunately, Figueroa never had an opportunity to carry out his instructions. Pope Paul refused to accept him as ambassador because of a perceived slight to papal jurisdiction by Figueroa in the past.[4] Figueroa retreated to Gaeta, in the Kingdom of Naples, where Philip told him to wait until he could find a way to placate the pope.[5] The king wrote directly to Paul, asking for forgiveness on behalf of his ambassador.[6] Considering that Philip had just won a war against the pope, this was a

3. Philip to Figueroa, September 25, 1558; quoted in Ludwig von Pastor, *The History of the Popes from the Close of the Middle Ages*, trans. Ralph Francis Kerr, 40 vols. (London, 1891–1953), Vol. XV, pp. 10–11. Note that Pastor mistakenly dates the letter from 1559.
4. Ibid, p. 11.
5. Philip to Figueroa, January 20, 1559; Archivo General de Simancas, Sección Estado (hereafter AGSE) 885, #226.
6. June 30, 1559; AGSE 885, #206.

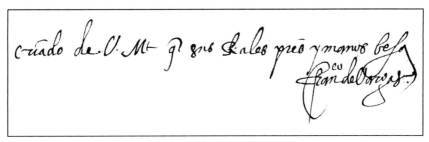

FIGURE 2. Signature of Francisco de Vargas, with phrase "Your Majesty's servant who kisses your royal hands and feet." (March 14, 1561).

remarkable move, but Figueroa's death in July 1559 made the issue moot. Philip now had to find a replacement, and he made an interesting choice: Francisco de Vargas, the ex-ambassador to Venice.[7]

Vargas, after storming out of Venice in September 1558 following the precedence dispute, had been residing in Antwerp. In August 1559 Philip wrote to him there, informing him of his new assignment. His instructions stressed two things: the necessity of maintaining the intelligence network between Rome and the other Spanish embassies throughout Europe; and most critically, "staying in the good graces of His Holiness."[8] Vargas had already spent a number of years in Italy, so he understood the complexities and the importance of Italian politics. As a man who could keep a watchful eye on Italian affairs, he was well qualified for the posting in Rome. But if Philip wanted a smooth diplomat who could soothe a hostile pope, Vargas seems like an odd choice. He had already shown himself to be irritable and irritating in Venice, and he would do no better in Rome. Nonetheless he got the call, and immediately found himself in the midst of a crisis. Almost simultaneously with his new instructions, Vargas received word that Pope Paul had died. He vowed to Philip that he would "make all the effort my age allows and more" to hasten to Rome, and throw himself into the fray of a papal election.[9]

The conclave opened on September 5, 1559. It turned into one of the most hotly contested papal elections of the century, and dragged on until late December. During this election various secular envoys flouted the Church's strict rules against outside interference, and none more so than Vargas. His complete disregard for propriety outraged many of the other

7. See chapter 1.
8. Philip to Vargas, August 22, 1559; AGSE 885, #249.
9. Vargas to Philip, August 31, 1559; AGSE 885, #24. Vargas's age in 1559 is not certain, but he was at least in his sixties.

participants.[10] For months, Vargas bullied cardinals and shamelessly campaigned for pro-Spanish candidates. Philip several times instructed Vargas to be discreet, and to "dissimulate" his true preferences, so as not to make enemies.[11] Vargas totally ignored these orders. Alvise Mocenigo, the Venetian ambassador in Rome, described Vargas's actions during the conclave as "hateful and nearly indefensible."[12] Here again we have an example of a Spaniard's arrogant assertion of power, which generated resentment among Italians.

Yet in Vargas's letters to Philip, he often blamed the various cardinals in the Spanish faction for causing trouble in the conclave, and usually portrayed himself as a peacemaker. According to Vargas, the worst offender was Guido Ascanio Sforza, the *camerlengo* or chief treasurer of the apostolic household, who presided over the conclave. Sforza led the Spanish faction, and received a pension from Philip, but this did not mean he always did the king's bidding. As one modern historian writes, "Italian cardinals [even if they received pensions] . . . continued to act and react as Italians, and as Italian princes at that."[13] Sforza and all of the other cardinals had their own agendas, and sought favors in return for their votes. They also often hated each other. A week after arriving in Rome, Vargas reported great discord between Sforza, Cardinal Alessandro Farnese (also a member of the Spanish faction), and Cardinal Carlo Carafa (nephew of the late Pope Paul), which threatened to disrupt the entire conclave.[14] Vargas attempted to pacify them, but weeks of labor brought them no closer to cooperation. "You would not believe the rancor and dissidence which exists between [these cardinals]," Vargas complained later that month, "from which comes all of [our] problems in this [election]." Thus Vargas blamed the cardinals for the Spanish faction's inability to get a pro-Spanish pope elected quickly. "I don't know what will happen," he concluded, "as every hour there are a thousand *novedades*."[15]

Throughout the conclave Vargas castigated the Italian cardinals for their hostility, but he was to blame for much of their antagonism. He alienated the powerful Cardinal of Mantua (Ercole Gonzaga), for exam-

10. Kenneth M. Setton, *The Papacy and the Levant (1204–1571)*, 4 vols. (Philadelphia, 1976–1984), Vol. IV, p. 727.

11. For example, on November 16, Philip wrote that Cardinal Cesis's election should be blocked, but it should be done with "such dissimulation and dexterity" that Cesis would not be angered or antagonized. AGSE 885, #246.

12. Quoted in Setton, *The Papacy and the Levant*, Vol. IV, p. 727.

13. Barbara McClung Hallman, *Italian Cardinals, Reform, and the Church as Property* (Berkeley, 1985), p. 58.

14. Vargas to Philip, October 3, 1559; AGSE 885, #31.

15. Vargas to Philip, October 28, 1559; AGSE 885, #45.

ple, despite Philip's instructions to block his candidacy "in such a way and with such dexterity that everyone with whom you speak of the cardinal thinks we have great confidence in him."[16] The Gonzaga family supported Spain, but Philip worried that their power and connections in Italy could threaten Spanish hegemony if Ercole should become pope.[17] The king thus wanted Ercole excluded discreetly, but evidently Vargas did not lie very well. He initially told Ercole that he had Philip's support, but then Vargas made obvious moves to block his election. Paolo Tiepolo, the Venetian ambassador in Spain, reported that the duke of Urbino (an important ally) believed that Vargas had "failed in his duty," because he had insulted Gonzaga with his clumsy maneuvers. According to the duke, Vargas had pretended to the conclave that he supported Gonzaga, but he spoke with such little enthusiasm that everyone knew he was lying. Presumably Vargas had been trying to block Gonzaga's candidacy indirectly, but the ruse was so transparent that it backfired. By his ineptitude Vargas had "set a bad example to the king's servants," and offended Philip's allies.[18] Vargas, meanwhile, blamed Gonzaga for causing discord in the conclave.[19] Either Vargas was covering up his incompetence, or he did not recognize how badly he had erred.

Throughout the conclave Vargas had great difficulty scraping together votes. The French faction successfully blocked the Spaniards' first choice, Rodolfo Pio of Carpi. The two factions also tangled over the support of Carlo Carafa. Carafa, an unscrupulous character, had been absolved of rape, sacrilege, and murder by his uncle Pope Paul IV on becoming a cardinal.[20] He now tried to sell his vote to the highest bidder. Vargas dangled money in front of Carafa's nose, assuring him that Philip was "the best and greatest prince of the world, and the most generous."[21] The ambassador even promised a large increase in the pension Carafa received from Spain, an offer he had no authorization to make.[22] The bribe worked: Carafa joined the Spanish faction. The cardinal's blatant corruption, however, disgusted many of his peers, canceling any gains for the Spanish

16. Philip to Vargas, October 20, 1559; AGSE 885, #243.
17. Setton, *The Papacy and the Levant,* Vol. IV, pp. 725–26.
18. Tiepolo to the Doge and Senate, December 11, 1559; *Calendar of State Papers and Manuscripts, Relating to English affairs, Existing in the Archives and Collections of Venice,* ed. Rawdon Brown and G. Cavendish Bentinck, Vols. IV–VII (reprint, Nendeln, 1970), Vol. VII, p. 137.
19. Vargas to Philip, October 13, 1559; AGSE 885, #36.
20. Massimo Firpo, "The Cardinal," in *Renaissance Characters,* ed. Eugenio Garin, trans. Lydia G. Cochrane (Chicago, 1991), p. 70.
21. Vargas to Philip, November 5, 1559; AGSE 885, #52.
22. Pastor, *History of the Popes,* Vol. XV, p. 39. In fact, Vargas forged a letter from Philip promising Carafa a large reward; Setton, *The Papacy and the Levant,* Vol. IV, p. 731.

cause.[23] Through it all Vargas clearly felt justified in doing whatever it took to get a pro-Spanish pope elected. As he wrote to Philip, "I certify to Your Majesty that not since I was born, nor in any other endeavor, have I worked so hard . . . as in this [election], and thus I will work to the end. And I believe that if in the end our hopes fail (may God not allow it), my life may end with them."[24] As usual, Vargas overdramatized, but his ideological devotion was genuine.

In the end, Vargas could breathe easy, for the conclave elected Gianangelo Medici as Pope Pius IV.[25] Vargas described Medici, a native of the Spanish-controlled territory of Milan, as a "much-loved and dignified and deserving subject of Your Majesty," and predicted that he would do well by Philip.[26] Vargas gave himself a great deal of credit for this victory, particularly for having successfully maneuvered around "the dissensions and hostilities and extravagant humors of our own people [in the Spanish faction]."[27] Evidence suggests, however, that the conclave elected Pius because he had few enemies, and was fairly old and sickly (so his papacy would not last long), rather than because of anything Vargas did.[28] A month after the election several cardinals were still grousing about Vargas's strong-arm tactics during the conclave.[29] The Spanish ambassador may have helped get a friendly pope elected, but he did not win many friends for Spain doing so.

At first, Pius appeared to be everything the Spanish ambassador could hope for. The new pope assured Vargas that he would dedicate himself to God's service and the peace of Christendom; even better, as one of Philip's Milanese "vassals," he swore to love and to serve the king.[30] If Vargas hoped for a pliant pope, however, he soon became disillusioned. Pius, while certainly less hostile toward Spain than Paul IV had been, had a strong will in his own right. Like most Renaissance popes, he used the power of his office primarily to benefit his family and his countrymen.[31] He also quickly displayed independence from Spanish influence. Pius put on trial Carlo Carafa, the cardinal Vargas had tried so hard to recruit, and

23. Setton, *The Papacy and the Levant*, Vol. IV, pp. 731–33.

24. Vargas to Philip, November 5, 1559; AGSE 885, #52.

25. Gianangelo was not related to the famous Florentine Medicis; see Pastor, *History of the Popes*, Vol. XV, pp. 66–68.

26. Vargas to Philip, December 25, 1559; AGSE 885, #74.

27. Vargas to Philip, December 29, 1559; AGSE 885, #79.

28. Setton, *The Papacy and the Levant*, Vol. IV, p. 736.

29. Paolo Tiepolo to the Doge and Senate, January 30, 1560; *Calendar of State Papers Venetian*, Vol. VII, p. 149.

30. Vargas to Philip, December 29, 1559; AGSE 885, #79.

31. A. V. Antonovics, "Counter-Reformation Cardinals: 1534–90," *European Studies Review* 2 (1972), pp. 310–11.

executed him for his many crimes.[32] By August 1560 Vargas had begun suspecting Pius of plotting with other Italian powers against Spain— although it seems likely that he was misinterpreting the pope's personal distaste for Vargas himself. "Italy is nothing but disquiet and a friend of *novedades*," Vargas grumbled in the middle of a long diatribe against the pope, "and totally full of old and new humors."[33] Just when Vargas thought he had procured a friendly pope, and stabilized the political situation in Italy, the Italian pontiff remained independent and unpredictable.

Vargas's worst disappointment during his tenure in Rome concerned another old nemesis, the issue of precedence. The conflict that had driven Vargas out of Venice in 1558 had continued to simmer for the next several years. The French and Spanish ambassadors at the imperial court quarreled for months, and in September 1560 the French king sent a formal protest through his ambassador in Madrid, accusing Philip of usurping the ancient rights of France.[34] French ambassadors in Rome also began agitating for the pope to pronounce judgment on the issue. The uproar over precedence coincided with increasing political and religious tension in France. In 1559 King Henry II died in a freak jousting accident, leaving a sickly fifteen-year-old boy on the French throne. At the same time bloody conflicts between Catholics and Protestants erupted throughout the country. Pope Pius grew increasingly alarmed about the religious health of France, and in November 1560 called for the reconvening of the Council of Trent (the second session had closed in April 1552). The previous March the French Cardinal of Lorraine had urged Pius to allow France to convene a national Church council to heal itself, but Pius feared this would lead to the loss of the French Church.[35] Pius desperately wanted to convene a Church council to stop the rise of heresy. A conflict over ceremonial protocol was the last thing the pope needed at this dangerous moment—and yet that is what he got.

Through 1561 Spanish-papal relations worsened. Vargas harangued Pius that his financial support for Spanish military efforts was insufficient, especially considering that the Holy See had "no other defender."[36] Meanwhile, Philip and his bishops quibbled with Pius about whether the Church council would be a continuation of previous meetings (thus confirming the legality of the council's edicts) or would be entirely new

32. Setton, *The Papacy and the Levant*, Vol. IV, pp. 742–53.
33. Vargas to Philip, August 22, 1560; AGSE 886, #59.
34. Blas Casado Quintanilla, "La cuestión de la precedencia España-Francia en la tercera asamblea del Concilio de Trento," *Hispania Sacra* 36 (1984), pp. 199–201.
35. R. J. Knecht, *Catherine de'Medici* (London, 1998), p. 66.
36. Vargas to Philip, January 3, 1561; AGSE 889, #83.

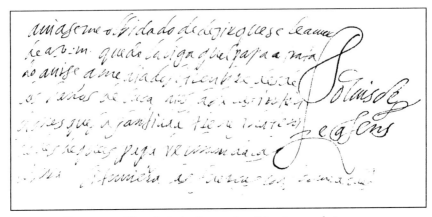

FIGURE 3. Signature of Don Luis de Requeséns (March 3, 1565).

(which would mean arguing every point as if starting from scratch).[37] And on top of everything, Vargas continued to press the precedence question. He enlisted several cardinals to campaign for him, and gave the pope no peace. Uncharacteristically, Vargas asked Philip's permission to pressure Pius harder; he acknowledged that the negotiations were risky, and the stakes were high.[38] His unaccustomed caution perhaps came from his awareness of how much the pope disliked him. In fact, many at the Vatican court disliked him; Girolamo Soranzo, the Venetian ambassador to Rome, made fun of the Spanish ambassador's arrogance.[39] By the beginning of 1562 Pius had become so hostile toward Vargas that Philip decided his ambassador had to be replaced: he had failed to "stay in His Holiness's good graces," as his initial instructions had ordered.

Unfortunately for Philip, the new ambassador in Rome, Don Luis de Requeséns, would have no more luck remaining friendly with the pope than Figueroa or Vargas had before him. Requeséns, a childhood friend of Philip's, embodied all of the stereotypes of the haughty Spaniard.[40] (Actually, he was half-Catalan, but since the most infamous and hated

37. Philip was so concerned about this question that he sent a special envoy, Juan de Ayala, to Rome just to discuss the problem; nothing came of Ayala's visit. Pastor, *History of the Popes*, Vol. XV, pp. 249–52.

38. Vargas and Ayala to Philip, June 18, 1561; AGSE 889, #96.

39. *Relazione* of Soranzo to the Senate, 1563; *Le relazioni degli ambasciatori veneti al Senato durante il secolo decimosesto*, ed. Eugenio Àlberi, 15 vols.(Florence, 1839–1863), Series II, Vol. IV, pp. 74–76. Soranzo noted that Vargas antagonized Pius because he did not behave with proper modesty; the Venetian also suggested this might be a common characteristic of Spaniards (p. 109).

40. The historian Luciano Serrano writes that (non-Spanish) contemporaries perceived Requeséns as an "insolent imperialist." *Correspondencia diplomática entre España y la Santa Sede durante el pontificado de S. Pio V*, ed. Luciano Serrano, 4 vols. (Madrid, 1914), Vol. II, p. lxvii.

Renaissance pope, Alexander VI, had also been Catalan, this ethnic association would not have helped Requeséns.) In his report of his first meetings with Pius, Requeséns noted that the pope did nothing but complain about Vargas. The new envoy, while he did try to defend his predecessor, also remarked, "an ambassador [from Spain] does not need to satisfy the pope, only Your Majesty."[41] This revealing phrase typifies Requeséns' attitude throughout his tenure in Rome. He displayed an utter disregard for Italian sensibilities, while also expressing puzzlement about Italian resentment towards Spain.[42] In the same letter Requeséns declared that he would never appear in the pope's chambers unless he had been summoned, because he did not want anyone—and particularly the French ambassador—to see him waiting to get in. This fussiness about the dignity of his position as Philip's representative would lead to an open break between the ambassador and the pope.

In February 1564, a dramatic event threatened Spanish influence in Rome. A new French ambassador named Henri D'Oysel arrived in Rome, bringing a demand from King Charles IX that Pius confirm France's ancient right to precedence over the Spanish. D'Oysel warned that if Pius did not comply, France would be forced to withdraw its oath of obedience to the papacy.[43] This threat had power behind it: Calvinist doctrine had taken root in France, and civil war had broken out. The papacy had reason to fear losing France entirely.[44] Pius thus made noises of agreement with the French demand, afraid to refuse.[45] Requeséns, naturally, exploded. He declared that for the pope to entertain French demands for even a moment constituted an insult to Philip II's honor, and he threatened to leave Rome in protest.[46] Philip, who perhaps had little choice, confirmed his ambassador's stance, and the battle for precedence began in earnest.

In response to the French challenge, Requeséns made a series of speeches before the pope and his curia that displayed a newfound sense of Spanish destiny. He declared that Philip, King of a unified Spain and

41. Requeséns to Philip, October 20, 1563; AGSE, 895, #216.

42. During his tenure as governor of Milan (1571–1573), Requeséns' arrogance would get him excommunicated by Archbishop Carlo Borromeo; see José M. March, *Don Luis de Requeséns en el gobierno de Milan, 1571–1573* (Madrid, 1943), pp. 259–84.

43. Pastor, *History of the Popes*, Vol. XVI, pp. 197–98.

44. Mack P. Holt, *The French Wars of Religion, 1562–1629* (Cambridge, 1995), chap. 2.

45. Paolo Prodi notes that in the second half of the sixteenth century, papal diplomacy was weakened because "the religious crisis . . . became a means of permanent blackmail at a political level." *The Papal Prince: One Body and Two Souls*, trans. Susan Haskins (Cambridge, 1987), pp. 167–68.

46. Requeséns to Philip, February 16, 1564; *Pio IV y Felipe Segundo: Primeros diez meses de la embajada de Don Luis de Requeséns en Roma, 1563–1564*, ed. "F. del V." and "S. K." (Madrid, 1891), pp. 236–37.

master of a worldwide empire, should be considered the preeminent monarch of Europe. "These matters of precedence," he claimed, "have always been judged by the greatness of the kingdoms and the kings, and there is no comparing that of Your Majesty with anyone in the world."[47] Vargas had made similar claims, but Requeséns expanded on the idea that Spain, and Philip, held a unique place in the history of the world. Diplomatic ritual and protocol, he argued, should reflect this momentous change.[48] And besides, the ambassador argued, was not Philip the defender of the Catholic faith? And had not the French allied with the infidel Turks, in addition to being spiritually suspect themselves? To grant the French precedence would be a crime against God, as well as an unforgivable insult to Spanish honor. But far more than personal or even national honor was at stake.

Requeséns informed Philip that he had every intention of leaving Rome if the pope ruled against Spain, and encouraged the king to send a personal letter of protest, thus ensuring that "the pope understands that he risks much in not pleasing Your Majesty on this issue, on which depends our reputation in all Italian matters and even in all of Christendom."[49] In Requeséns' opinion, the Spanish cause in Italy, and indeed in all of Europe, would be gravely harmed by defeat in the precedence dispute. Philip evidently agreed, and did what his ambassador suggested.[50] Throughout the early modern period, Spanish Habsburg foreign policy often reflected concern over *reputación*.[51] In this case, Requeséns clearly believed that failure in this contest could have serious repercussions; loss of face could lead to the loss of Italy. The ambassador wrote to his brother, Don Juan de Zúñiga, "I want the King to begin a war [over this conflict] more than I ever wanted anything in my life. . . . if the King does not demonstrate great anger and sorrow in this matter of precedence, no reputation will remain for us to lose."[52] Requeséns may well have been overreacting, but his fear is significant.

47. Ibid.
48. Philip's chronicler, Luis Cabrera de Córdoba, made similar arguments. María José del Río Barredo, "Felipe II y la configuración del sistema ceremonial de la monarquía católica," in *Felipe II (1527–1598): Europa y la Monarquía Católica*, ed. José Martínez Millán, Vol. I, Part II (Madrid, 1998), pp. 678–79. See also Henry Kamen's recent discussion of the meaning of "Spanish empire" in *Empire: How Spain Became a World Power, 1492–1763* (New York, 2003).
49. *Pio IV y Felipe Segundo*, pp. 236–37.
50. On March 26 Requeséns reported delivering Philip's protest letter, but it had no effect. AGSE 896, #46.
51. Geoffrey Parker, *The Grand Strategy of Philip II* (New Haven, 1998), pp. 89–90; and J. H. Elliott, "Foreign Policy and Domestic Crisis: Spain, 1598–1659," in *Spain and Its World, 1500–1700* (New Haven, 1989), pp. 114–36.
52. Letter dated April 30, 1564; *Pio IV y Felipe Segundo*, pp. 343–46.

Pius, caught between Spain and France, delayed making a ruling on precedence. During Holy Week he went so far as to ask the ambassadors not to attend Easter mass, thus avoiding the issue of who would sit where, and they grudgingly agreed. On Easter Day the pope even tricked the ambassadors into waiting in his chambers while he descended a secret staircase to the Sistine Chapel, in order to prevent them from making a scene.[53] Requeséns, of course, was incensed, even more so because he felt isolated. According to him, the cardinals in the Spanish faction gave him only lukewarm support, while the French faction promoted their cause passionately. Meanwhile, the pope himself proved maddeningly stubborn. In April the ambassador reported getting into a shouting match with Pius, who was "insufferable," claiming that the Spaniards had no basis for their protests. The pope also admitted that the French threat of withdrawing obedience to Rome frightened him. Requeséns showed no sympathy, arguing that the French should be punished, not rewarded, for making such threats.[54] But what really drove Requeséns berserk was seeing "how persuaded all Italy is that the French are in the right, it being such great nonsense." From his perspective, Italians sided with France because of their own particular interests, and more importantly, out of "their hatred of [Philip's] greatness."[55] In the eyes of the Spanish ambassador, Italian resentment thwarted a Spanish attempt to assert an imperial agenda.

It is not clear whether Pope Pius was motivated more by the fear of losing France to heresy, as he claimed, or by resentment of Spanish power, as Requeséns believed.[56] The Venetian ambassador in Rome, Giacomo Soranzo, reported that both factors influenced the pope's decision.[57] Pius may well have seen a chance to stick a finger in Philip's eye while claiming to be acting out of conscience. In any case, in May 1564 Pius ruled that France's ancient claims to precedence should not be overturned. Requeséns now had little choice but to carry out his threat. In July he received instructions from Philip: "I charge and command you, that upon receiving this [letter], you go to kiss the foot of His Holiness and take

53. Requeséns to Philip, March 30, 1564; AGSE 895, #52. For details see Michael J. Levin, "A New World Order: The Spanish Campaign for Precedence in Early Modern Europe," *Journal of Early Modern History* 6 (2002), pp. 233–64.
54. Requeséns to Philip, April 6, 1564; AGSE 896, #53.
55. Ibid.
56. Robert J. Knecht writes that French Catholic attempts to form a "league" of Catholic powers at this time were impracticable, because "Pius IV and Philip II of Spain were barely on speaking terms." *The French Civil Wars, 1562–1598* (London, 2000), p. 109.
57. *Relazione* of 1565; *Le relazioni degli ambasciatori veneti al Senato*, Series II, Vol. IV, pp. 147–48.

your leave of him, saying to him how I ordered you to return to these kingdoms."[58] Philip ordered that no one should remain in Rome to negotiate in his name, leaving only the Spanish cardinals to conduct essential business. Despite the gravity of the situation, however, Requeséns did not leave at once, mostly because Pius refused to see him.[59] Eventually, though, he made his dramatic exit, while showing "fitting curtness" to the offending pope.[60] But this dignified display did not hide the fact that Spanish diplomacy had suffered a public relations disaster.[61]

Requeséns went briefly to Florence, and then to Genoa, where he awaited instructions.[62] Philip ordered him to stay put for the time being; he hoped that Pius might have a change of heart, in which case he wanted his ambassador close to Rome.[63] Requeséns ended up stewing in Genoa for over a year, growing increasingly restless and frustrated. He sent Philip and his ministers of state a stream of letters begging for another assignment, as well as a number of diatribes against all Italians.[64] Meanwhile Spanish-papal relations had suffered a serious blow. Giovanni Soranzo, the Venetian ambassador in Madrid, reported that the ill will between Philip and Pius was so strong that he doubted it could be assuaged in this pope's lifetime.[65] And indeed, the situation changed only on the death of Pius IV in December 1565.

The Spaniards now had an opportunity to engineer the election of a pope who might reverse Pius's ruling on precedence. This conclave, however, would be noteworthy for the relative lack of the outside interference that so marred recent elections.[66] Philip wrote to his ambassador that too many cardinals had been alienated in the past by active campaigning, so

58. Philip to Requeséns, July 15, 1564; AGSE 897, #60.

59. Requeséns to Philip, August 11, 1564; *Pio IV y Felipe Segundo*, pp. 409–13.

60. Requeséns to Juan de Zúñiga, August 17, 1564; ibid., pp. 413–19. Requeséns specifies that he kissed the pope's foot. As a royal ambassador, he was entitled to kiss the pope's hands as well; Henry Dietrich Fernández, "The Papal Court at Rome c. 1450–1700," in *The Princely Courts of Europe: Ritual, Politics and Culture under the Ancien Regime 1500–1700*, ed. John Adamson (London, 1999), p. 156. That Requeséns chose not to kiss the pope's hand was perhaps a sign of his displeasure.

61. Both Spanish and French propagandists flooded Europe with tracts arguing their case; see Maria Antonia Visceglia, "Il ceremoniale come linguaggio politico: Su alcuni conflitti di precedenza alla corte di Roma tra Cinquecento e Seicento," in *Cérémonial et rituel à Rome (XVI–XIX siècle)*, ed. Maria Antonia Visceglia and Catherine Brice (Rome, 1997), p. 129.

62. Adro Xavier, *Luis de Requeséns en el Europa del siglo XVI* (Madrid, 1984), p. 169.

63. Philip to Requeséns, September 22, 1564; *Pio IV y Felipe Segundo*, pp. 451–52.

64. For example, the letter quoted in the introduction about preferring Tartars to Italians; see also Requeséns to Gonzalo Pérez, June 12, 1564; AGSE 1394, #165.

65. *Relazione* of Soranzo to the Signoria, 1565; *Relazioni di ambasciatori veneti al Senato*, ed. Luigi Firpo, 13 vols. to date (Turin, 1965–), Vol. VIII, *Spagna*, p. 94.

66. Pastor, *History of the Popes*, Vol. XVII, pp. 8–9.

in this case he would leave the decision in God's hands rather than promoting a particular candidate. Nonetheless he stressed the importance of the election of a pope who would seek to wipe out heresy, and "who also aims to conserve Christendom in peace, unity and conformity, and particularly so in Italy, where there has always been war and which has been so afflicted, which has extremely saddened us."[67] So once again, six years after the Treaty of Cateau-Cambrésis, Philip expressed concern about the peace of Italy.

Requeséns and the Spanish faction did their best to influence the College of Cardinals while avoiding the outrageous behavior Vargas had displayed in the last conclave.[68] The ambassador made several speeches to the cardinals, exhorting them to do their duty, and repeated Philip's words about the peace of Christendom and of Italy specifically.[69] Acting on Philip's instructions, he made no mention of the precedence conflict, and assured the cardinals that Philip wanted them to forget "all passions and particular interests." This of course was both untrue and impossible, and the cardinals knew perfectly well which candidates the Spaniards considered acceptable. One such man was Michele Ghislieri, a Dominican friar and Roman inquisitor. Ghislieri embodied the zeal and austerity of Tridentine Rome, and was thus someone who the Spaniards could pin their hopes on. When he was elected Pope Pius V, Requeséns declared that God had guided the conclave, and that if this man did not become a great pope, there was no hope in anyone.[70]

As it turned out, Requeséns got more than he bargained for. Pius V was indeed a model Counter-Reformation pope, so much so that politics held little interest for him. As one historian writes, "Pius V was an enigma to Philip II and his ministers. Political popes they understood, but a saint confounded them."[71] Requeséns, for one, never seemed to fully understand Pius: he deeply admired the man, but often became exasperated by the pope's indifference to political realities. He also often underestimated Pius's stubbornness, or overestimated his passivity.[72] In particular, he quickly learned that Pius would not be easily swayed on the precedence

67. Philip to Requeséns, December 21, 1565; *Correspondencia diplomática*, Vol. I, pp. 55-59.
68. Setton, *The Papacy and the Levant*, Vol. IV, p. 884.
69. Document entitled "What the Grand Commander of Castile [Requeséns] said on His Majesty's behalf to the Sacred College of Cardinals," dated December 23, 1565, and January 5, 1566; AGSE 900, #82.
70. Requeséns to Philip, January 7, 1566; *Correspondencia diplomática*, Vol. I, pp. 77-78.
71. John Lynch, *Spain under the Habsburgs* 2d ed., Vol. I (New York, 1984), p. 240.
72. He was not the only one. Early in Pius's reign, Antonio Tiepolo, the Venetian ambassador in Madrid, wrote that Pius only ever wanted to promote peace among all princes (*Relazione*, 1567; Firpo, *Relazioni*, Vol. VIII, p. 478). As we will see, Tiepolo was wrong.

issue. A few weeks after his election, Pius wrote directly to Philip, asking that he drop the dispute, since dissension would only push France further into heresy.[73] For his part, Philip ordered his ambassador to praise the pope, and yet make clear that violations of Spanish rights would not be tolerated.[74]

The issue took an unexpected turn when it came time for a Spanish representative to formally swear obedience to the new pope. At first the only question was where the French ambassador would stand during the ceremony; Requeséns wanted the French to be excluded entirely.[75] But then Philip and his ministers began to question whether the king needed to swear obedience at all, since he already done so once before. Did kings make their vows to the institution of the papacy, or to individual popes? Theologians debated this issue in both Rome and Madrid. Requeséns, in consultation with Cardinals Pacheco (the Cardinal Protector of Spain) and Granvelle (a close advisor to Philip on Italian affairs), opined that since Philip was the true Defender of the Faith, he should not have to submit to the same rituals as others.[76] Philip concurred, and stated that his special envoy to Rome, the marquis of Aguilar, should merely congratulate the new pope, and not formally swear obedience in the king's name.[77]

The pope did not respond well to the Spaniards' haughtiness. When Requeséns confirmed to Pius that Philip did not intend to swear obedience, the pope exploded "with greater anger than I have seen from him in my life." The ambassador hastily backpedaled, and suggested that Philip only wanted to avoid ceremonies which would involve the precedence issue. He then sent Philip a surprisingly meek request: "I supplicate Your Majesty to command [me] to resolve this issue as best serves you, and understand that if in this [matter] the pope is not given satisfaction, Your Majesty may lose the goodwill of the best pontiff the Church of God has seen for three hundred years."[78] It would seem that Requeséns realized that he and his fellow Spaniards had misjudged the new pope, and had pushed too hard. Philip also recognized his mistake, and gave

---

73. Pius to Philip, January 24, 1566; *Correspondencia diplomática*, Vol. I, pp. 111–12.
74. Philip to Requeséns, February 1, 1566; ibid., pp. 117–22.
75. Requeséns to Philip, January 24, 1566; AGSE 902, #40.
76. Requeséns to Philip, March 22, 1566; *Correspondencia diplomática*, Vol. I, pp. 168–71.
77. Philip to Requeséns, March 24, 1566; ibid., pp. 172–74. The Spanish Habsburgs spent much time discussing issues of protocol, and the Spanish court was famous for its elaborate ceremonies. See J. H. Elliott, "The Court of the Spanish Habsburgs: A Peculiar Institution?" in *Spain and Its World*, pp. 142–61; and Glyn Redworth and Fernando Checa, "The Courts of the Spanish Habsburgs, 1500–1700," in Adamson, *The Princely Courts of Europe*, pp. 43–65.
78. Requeséns to Philip, April 26, 1566; *Correspondencia diplomática*, Vol. I, pp. 199–203.

permission for his envoy to swear obedience, claiming that the whole thing had been a misunderstanding.[79] Philip did not want to antagonize the new pope either.[80]

When the marquis of Aguilar swore obedience in the king's name, the French ambassador was not present. But the issue of precedence remained unresolved. In December 1566, Requeséns reported a victory of sorts to his king. Pius had agreed to authorize a papal brief that proclaimed Philip the preeminent monarch in Europe. Requeséns warned, however, that "it would be well if Your Majesty commanded that this brief be kept secret . . . because when the French find out about it they may procure another brief which repeals this one, which is one of the things which often happens in Rome."[81] This was truly a limited success, if Philip dare not make use of it! Yet this ambiguous brief represented the climax of the Spanish campaign for precedence. Ten years later, Don Juan de Zúñiga (ambassador to Rome 1568–1579) reported not attending chapel precisely to avoid a conflict over precedence.[82] Still later, in the 1580s and early 1590s, the Spaniards perhaps enjoyed de facto precedence, because of the absence of French ambassadors: due to France's Wars of Religion its diplomatic service collapsed.[83] But no Spanish ambassador in Rome ever enjoyed a public display of preeminence over the French.[84] And even at its zenith the Spanish campaign may have done more harm than good to their *reputación:* Paolo Tiepolo, by now the Venetian ambassador to Rome, described Requeséns as a buffoon, and the precedence dispute as mere noise.[85]

Meanwhile, of course, many other matters pressed for Requeséns' attention. For one thing, Pius was most anxious that Philip should act more decisively to eliminate heresy in the Netherlands. Warning signs of popular and religious discontent had been building in the Low Countries

---

79. Philip to Requeséns, May 13, 1566; ibid., pp. 237–40.

80. Philip and Pius V did, however, have a number of disagreements, particularly over jurisdiction over the Spanish Church; see John Lynch, "Philip II and the Papacy," *Transactions of the Royal Historical Society,* 5th series, 2 (1961), pp. 30–35.

81. Requeséns to Philip, December 27, 1566; *Correspondencia diplomática,* Vol. I, pp. 429–36. A badly damaged copy of this papal brief exists in the Ministerio de Asuntos Exteriores, Archivo General (Madrid), Embajada a la Santa Sede, Legajo 48, #156.

82. Zúñiga to Philip, June 22, 1576; AGSE 926, #138.

83. Garrett Mattingly, *Renaissance Diplomacy* (reprint, New York, 1988), p. 177.

84. William Roosen writes that in the sixteenth and seventeenth centuries Spaniards held ceremonial positions "equal to or above the French." "Early Modern Diplomatic Ceremonial: A Systems Approach," *Journal of Modern History* 52 (1980), p. 463. This might have been true at the Habsburg court in Vienna, but I see no evidence of it in Rome.

85. *Relazione* of 1569; *Le relazioni degli ambasciatori veneti al Senato,* Series II, Vol. IV, pp. 195–96.

for years, but wars in the Mediterranean and France had distracted Philip.[86] From the beginning of his papacy, Pius agitated for Philip to visit the Netherlands and personally address the issue.[87] Requeséns had to fend off the pope's impatient demands for action, insisting that the king had good reasons for everything he did (or did not do).[88] Cardinal Granvelle, recently arrived in Rome after a five-year stint as Spain's governor of the Netherlands, joined with the ambassador in his attempts to appease the pope.[89] But Granvelle also shared the pope's concerns about the consequences of Philip's inaction: as he wrote, "all Italy clearly says that if the disturbance in the Netherlands grows worse, Milan and Naples will follow. . . . matters are in more doubt and danger than could be imagined, and those who know the humors of Italy, and desire the Italians to expel the Spanish, will say the same."[90] So yet another Spanish minister in Italy feared the loss of Italy, in part because of the perceived inconstant nature of Italians.

Philip did his best to reassure Pius as well as his own men. He sent Requeséns a number of letters instructing him on what excuses to make to the pope, including the famous declaration "that rather than suffer the slightest prejudice to religion and the service of God I will lose all my states and a hundred lives if I had them, because I do not wish nor do I intend to be lord over heretics."[91] On the other hand, Philip also ordered his ambassador to remind the pope of the great expense of a Dutch campaign, as well as the fact that the king of Spain had many other responsibilities.[92] Pius, angered by Philip's apparent ambivalence, insisted that financial aid would be forthcoming only if Philip made good on his promises. Requeséns and Granvelle went out on a limb to assure Pius that Philip would indeed journey to the Netherlands, although they could not be sure of this themselves.[93] Finally Philip made what seemed a firm commitment to undertake the venture: the papal nuncio wrote that

---

86. Geoffrey Parker, "Spain, Her Enemies and the Revolt of the Netherlands, 1559–1648," in *Spain and the Netherlands 1559–1659* (London, 1979), pp. 26–27.
87. *Correspondencia diplomática*, Vol. II, pp. xxxi–xxxiv. The papal nuncio in Madrid, Gian Batista Castagna, constantly prodded Philip to act, but got only vague promises. See for example ibid., Vol. I, pp. 204–7.
88. Requeséns to Philip, March 18, 1566; ibid., pp. 152–57.
89. Granvelle shared diplomatic duties in Rome with the resident ambassador from 1566 to 1579.
90. Granvelle to Philip, June 19, 1566; *Correspondance du cardinal de Granvelle, 1565–1586*, ed. Edmond Poullet, vols. I–III (Brussels, 1877–1881), Vol. I, p. 518.
91. Philip to Requeséns, August 12, 1566; *Correspondencia diplomática*, Vol. I, pp. 312–18; quoted in Lynch, *Spain under the Habsburgs*, Vol. I, p. 279.
92. *Correspondencia diplomática*, Vol. I, pp. 308–12.
93. Requeséns, Granvelle, and Pacheco to Philip, September 18, 1566; ibid., pp. 341–48.

the king had publicly declared his intention to go the following spring, and so could no longer back out.[94] Granvelle reported (with relief) that the pope rejoiced at the news.[95] The pope rewarded Philip by authorizing subsidies for the Spanish Crown, one of the powerful leverages the papacy wielded.[96]

But delay followed delay, until August 1567, when Philip announced the suspension of the expedition.[97] Pius reacted with predictable rage, accusing Philip, and his ambassador, of deceiving him in order to get financial concessions. Requeséns argued, feebly, that the king's voyage had merely been delayed due to "impediments and new disturbances," but Pius was not impressed.[98] Philip's mercurial policies had left his ambassador in a bad position, with his credibility undermined; nor would this be the last time such things happened. Loss of face perhaps contributed to Requeséns' decision to request a leave of absence later that year, to return to Spain and settle various family matters. He did not leave in total defeat: the Roman court gave him a solemn farewell celebration, and Pius himself wrote a letter to Philip expressing regret over the ambassador's departure.[99]

Despite this show of approval, however, Requeséns must have regarded his tenure in Rome with mixed feelings at best: he had lost the precedence dispute, and left his post with only tepid relations with the pope (which was, to be sure, an improvement over the previous two Spanish ambassadors to Rome). Nonetheless Philip showed full confidence in Requeséns, appointing him lieutenant general of the Mediterranean fleet, directly under the king's half-brother Don Juan de Austria, in March 1568. Meanwhile, Requeséns' younger brother Don Juan de Zúñiga took over as his "temporary" replacement in Rome—where he would remain for the next twelve years.

94. Castagna to Pius V, November 23, 1566; ibid., p. 397. Philip confirmed his promise to Requeséns, twice: Philip to Requeséns, January 11, 1567 (*Correspondencia diplomática,* Vol. II, p. 43), and Philip to Requeséns, February 16, 1567 (ibid., p. 43).

95. Granvelle to Philip, December 25, 1566; *Correspondance du cardinal de Granvelle,* Vol. II, pp. 167–68.

96. Setton, *The Papacy and the Levant,* Vol. IV, p. 916. For more on Spanish ambassadors and papal subsidies, see below, chapter 5.

97. Castagna to Cardinal Alessandrino [the pope's nephew and close advisor], August 11, 1567; *Correspondencia diplomática,* Vol. II, p. 177. Geoffrey Parker describes this decision as a "fatal error" for Philip and his chances of destroying the Dutch revolt. *The Grand Strategy of Philip II,* p. 122.

98. Requeséns to Philip, September 16, 1567; *Correspondencia diplomática,* Vol. II, pp. 200–201.

99. *Correspondencia diplomática,* Vol. II, p. lxvii. Letter of Pius V to Philip, December 28, 1567; ibid., pp. 281–82.

FIGURE 4. Don Juan de Zúñiga. Anonymous portrait. Courtesy of Geoffrey Parker.

Zúñiga was a very different man from his brother: more reserved and scholarly, although no less the Spanish gentleman. Before coming to Rome, he had served at the royal court in both the Netherlands and Madrid, so he was more experienced than Requeséns had been. As a more seasoned diplomat, Zúñiga showed greater facility at hiding his feelings, and at least appearing more flexible.[100] At first, he expressed doubts about accepting the position; as he wrote to the state minister Don Christobal de Moura after the first month, "I have nothing to say, except I still do not want the office." He also noted that everyone treated him well out of respect for his brother, although they faulted the new ambassador for his taciturnity.[101] Whatever their first impressions, the Roman court welcomed him with the full honors due a royal ambassador, and Pius greeted him with pleasant words.[102]

Zúñiga slowly established himself in Rome. His older brother made periodic appearances as a special envoy, and often took over the current negotiations. This perhaps annoyed Zúñiga (despite his earlier reluctance to take the job), for after a few months he requested that he be given the official title of resident ambassador. He claimed it was the pope's idea, and that Granvelle and Pacheco agreed it would be "convenient" for the king's service, but since he sent this request to several of the king's ministers, he obviously did not object.[103] He also wrote to the papal nuncio in Madrid offering his services and friendship, perhaps in an effort to build his own network of contacts.[104] Philip soon granted Zúñiga the status he wanted (more or less): he informed Pius that Zúñiga should be considered the "ordinary ambassador," equal in status to Requeséns, whenever the elder brother was absent from Rome.[105] Zúñiga was now "the" resident ambassador, at least in the absence of his brother.

Meanwhile, from his first month on the job, Zúñiga was confronted with a number of sensitive issues. Practically the first letter Philip sent him

100. Serrano writes that he was "more dissimulating and less intransigent" than his brother, although also perhaps less forceful. *Correspondencia diplomática*, Vol. II, pp. lxviii–lxxii.

101. Zúñiga to Moura, February 13, 1568; *Colección de documentos inéditos para la historia de España*, Vol. XCVII (Madrid, 1890), pp. 396–97.

102. Zúñiga to Philip, January 20, 1568; *Correspondencia diplomática*, Vol. II, pp. 293–96. According to Zúñiga, Cardinals Granvelle and Pacheco instructed him not to discuss business with the pope during his first visit, since there were currently no urgent issues; perhaps they did not want Zúñiga around long either.

103. Zúñiga to Diego de Espinosa, April 21, 1568 (*Colección de documentos inéditos para la historia de España*, Vol. XCVII, pp. 444–46); and Zúñiga to Ruy Gómez de Silva, April 28, 1568 (ibid., pp. 456–57).

104. Zúñiga to Castagna, October 12, 1568; Vatican Archives, Nunziatura Spagna (Spagna Nuova 3), f. 83r.

105. Philip to Pius, August 2, 1568; *Correspondencia diplomática*, Vol. II, p. 431.

concerned the madness and confinement of the king's eldest son.[106] Over the last year Carlos, heir to the throne, had grown increasingly unstable (including making threats against his father), and finally had to be imprisoned. Philip had to issue a public statement concerning this tragedy. He instructed Zúñiga to explain that Carlos had been confined due to his "condition," not because of any treasonous actions; in other words, the ambassador became involved in a cover-up. Philip also wanted Pius to understand that interference would not be welcome.[107]

Zúñiga did his best to control public opinion, being especially careful to quash any rumors that Carlos had been involved in seditious activity, which the ambassador dismissed as French libels.[108] When the pope asked him directly whether he could confirm a rumor out of France that Carlos had plotted against his father, Zúñiga denied knowing of any such news, and again blamed it on disinformation spread by French heretics.[109] He likewise told other Italian princes, like Duke Cosimo de'Medici of Florence, that Carlos had been imprisoned only for his own safety.[110] Finally, that July Carlos died in jail, and Philip sent his ambassador a "relation" of events which he should use to answer all questions.[111] This episode highlights the ambassador's role as spokesman: as Philip's representative, Zúñiga acted like a modern press secretary, putting "spin" on events which reflected on the Crown.[112]

Zúñiga also quickly became involved with another politically sensitive matter, concerning dynastic marriage alliances. Philip and his Austrian Habsburg relatives had definite ideas about who should marry whom, and brooked little interference.[113] A week after Zúñiga's arrival in Rome, Philip sent him instructions to dissuade the pope from his current attempts to arrange the marriage of King Charles IX of France to Elizabeth, daughter

---

106. See Parker, *Philip II*, pp. 88–91; and Henry Kamen, *Philip of Spain* (New Haven, 1997), pp. 120–23.
107. Philip to Zúñiga, January 22, 1568; *Correspondencia diplomática*, Vol. II, pp. 289–90.
108. Zúñiga to Philip, February 28, 1568; ibid., pp. 311–12.
109. Zúñiga to Philip, March 5, 1568; ibid., pp. 318–20. Zúñiga was at the least being less than completely truthful. Philip had admitted to him that Carlos had been guilty of "some disobedience and disrespect." Zúñiga was also close friends with the Spanish courtier Ruy Gómez de Silva, who had prevented Carlos from carrying out an absurd plot to run off to the Netherlands; James M. Boyden, *The Courtier and the King: Ruy Gómez de Silva, Philip II, and the Court of Spain* (Berkeley, 1995), p. 132. Zúñiga no doubt knew more than he was telling.
110. Zúñiga to Cosimo, March 1, 1568; Archivio di Stato di Firenze, Mediceo 5029, f. 70r.
111. Philip to Zúñiga, July 29, 1568; *Correspondencia diplomática*, Vol. II, p. 427.
112. Philip also wrote a personal letter to Pius, explaining the necessity of his actions; Parker, *Philip II*, p. 91.
113. See Paula Sutter Fichtner, "Dynastic Marriage in Sixteenth-Century Diplomacy and Statecraft: an Interdisciplinary Approach," *American Historical Review* 81 (1976), pp. 243–65.

of Emperor Ferdinand; Philip wanted Elizabeth to marry the king of Portugal instead.[114] Zúñiga accepted the assignment enthusiastically, and sought to frighten Pius with warnings about a tender young Catholic princess abandoned to her fate in heresy-wracked France. As he cautioned the pope, "affairs in France were in such ruinous condition that it would not be well either for religion or for the security of Italy for the emperor to make pledges to the Christian King [of France]."[115] His objection to the marriage on the basis of the peace of Italy is particularly interesting, and of a piece with Spanish strategy overall. Anything that could strengthen French claims or designs on northern Italy had to be stopped. A few months later, Zúñiga talked a senior cardinal out of arranging a marriage between the duke of Urbino and the sister of the duke of Guise, again on religious grounds—but with an obvious political motive as well.[116]

Later that year, Zúñiga became involved in negotiations over his own king's marriage negotiations. Philip's third wife, Elizabeth of Valois, died in October 1568, and speculation about his next wife began immediately.[117] Within a month Zúñiga reported that the French ambassador in Rome had approached Pius, asking for his aid in arranging another French match with Philip. The Frenchman claimed that such a match was the only way to preserve peace between the two nations; Zúñiga suspected the French feared that Philip might marry an Austrian princess, which would strengthen the Habsburg bloc.[118] Requeséns made a point of supporting his brother's position during one of his visits to Rome, underlining the importance of these negotiations. He emphasized how untrustworthy the Valois kings had been in the past, and that the pope should not make any promises to the French without consulting the king first.[119] Both ambassadors used marriage negotiations as opportunities to fill the pope's ears with anti-French propaganda. Their rejection of a French match actually preceded Philip's own decision: he did not rule it out until the following spring.[120]

114. Philip to Zúñiga, January 27, 1568; *Correspondencia diplomática*, Vol. II, pp. 292–93.
115. Zúñiga to Philip, April 7, 1568; ibid., pp. 335–37.
116. Zúñiga to Philip, July 9, 1568; ibid., pp. 500–501.
117. The papal nuncio Castagna wrote to Cardinal Alessandrino on the day of the queen's death, reporting that he was certain the king would remarry, and that common opinion held he would choose an Austrian princess. He also remarked that the French princesses were believed to be sickly and to have bad complexions. ibid., Vol. II, pp. 473–74.
118. Zúñiga to Philip, November 5, 1568; ibid., p. 499. Philip did in fact marry Anne of Austria, the Emperor Maximilian's daughter (and Philip's niece).
119. Requeséns to Philip, November 7, 1568; *Correspondencia diplomática*, Vol. III, pp. 500–501.
120. Kamen, *Philip of Spain*, p. 125.

Zúñiga also quickly learned about the volatility of Italian politics. A conflict between Pope Pius and Duke Alfonso II d'Este of Ferrara, for example, surprised and frightened Zúñiga because of how it escalated. The crisis involved the right to mine and transport salt, and the money generated by it. The papacy controlled mineral rights throughout northern Italy, and raised much capital through their sale or lease.[121] In the 1540s, Pope Julius III had granted the Este family transportation rights, but the license had recently expired, and Pius (who jealously guarded the prerogatives of the papacy) refused to renew it.[122] This was perhaps in retribution for Alfonso's refusal to allow the Roman Inquisition into his territories, or to aid in the pope's military ventures.[123] Hostilities mounted, to the point of actual war, and the duke appealed to Philip for help. Philip agreed to support the duke's cause, and called on the pope to preserve "the peace of Italy, without permitting changes that might threaten its tranquility."[124] His words, however, had the opposite effect. Pius was infuriated, and suspected that Philip had sided against him out of anger over issues of money and jurisdiction.[125] He even feared that Philip might take up arms on Alfonso's behalf. Zúñiga decided not to disabuse Pius of these notions, although he knew that Philip had no intention of going to war; he hoped fear would encourage the pope to be more flexible when negotiating Spanish interests.[126] The stratagem nearly blew up in his face.

In December Zúñiga again reported to Philip that Pius was extremely angry with the Spaniards, but the ambassador's tone remained unconcerned. As he wrote, "I do not think it would do any harm if His Holiness thinks that Your Majesty might break with him."[127] By January, however, Zúñiga began to have doubts. Pius had not softened his position, either toward the duke of Ferrara or Spain, and had become convinced that Alfonso and Philip were plotting against him. Zúñiga, alarmed by the growing tension, suggested that Philip and the Spanish governor general of Milan both write letters to the pope assuring him of their pacific

121. Alum, for example, was a profitable papal monopoly; see Felix Gilbert, *The Pope, His Banker, and Venice* (Cambridge, Mass., 1980); and Jean Delumeau, *L'Alun de Rome XV–XIX siècle* (Paris, 1962).
122. Cardinal Alessandrino to Castagna, July 21, 1568; *Correspondencia diplomática*, Vol. II, p. 419.
123. Pastor, *History of the Popes*, Vol. XVIII, pp. 269–70.
124. Philip to Zúñiga, August 19–20, 1568; *Correspondencia diplomática*, Vol. II., pp. 447–49, quoted in Parker, *The Grand Strategy of Philip II*, p. 83. Parker uses this dispute as an example of the strength of the "pax hispanica," while I see it as another example of the peace's fragility.
125. See chapter 6.
126. Zúñiga to Philip, September 17, 1568; *Correspondencia diplomática*, Vol. II, pp. 459–61.
127. Zúñiga to Philip, December 10, 1568; ibid., pp. 510–14.

intentions.[128] This had no effect. By early summer, Zúñiga faced the real possibility of war in Italy. Duke Alfonso had fielded an army, while Pius and his curia debated the use of force against him. Furthermore, certain cardinals had expressed concern to Zúñiga that Duke Cosimo de'Medici of Florence could use this war as an excuse to seize Ferrara. What had started as an argument over salt mines now threatened to become a general conflagration in Tuscany. Zúñiga told Philip that no one in Italy wanted "to light a fire that would be difficult to extinguish," but this was more of a prayer than a confident pronouncement.[129] Zúñiga urged Philip not to give Alfonso any military aid, because it would only fuel Italian fears of Spanish expansion.

Zúñiga became even more agitated when he learned that Pius intended to grant Cosimo de'Medici the title "Grand Duke of Tuscany," a move with serious political implications. For centuries, popes, emperors, and other princes had contested for ultimate authority over the many feudal territories in northern Italy. Technically, the Holy Roman Emperor held feudal rights over both Florence and Ferrara, although in practical terms this meant little. Cosimo de'Medici, who dreamt of advancing to the front ranks of European powers, sought the title of grand duke from Emperor Maximilian II (his feudal overlord), but was rebuffed.[130] Cosimo then turned to Pope Pius instead. For the last decade Cosimo had cultivated the friendship of the papacy in order to further his ambitions; he successfully petitioned for Pius IV's assistance, for example, in arranging the marriage of his son Francesco to the emperor's sister. Cosimo also strove to impress Rome with his religious zeal, by loaning money and troops to France to help fight Huguenots.[131] As a reward, Pius agreed to grant Cosimo the title he craved, although the pope's legal right to do so was questionable.[132] Pius drew up the papal bull granting the title in August 1569, but he kept it secret until December.[133] Then all hell broke loose.

128. Zúñiga to Philip, January 15, 1569; ibid., Vol. III, pp. 26–28.

129. Zúñiga to Philip, June 13, 1569; ibid., pp. 89–93. The Venetian ambassador in Rome at this time, Paolo Tiepolo, believed that Pius and Alfonso were about to go to war; Pastor, *History of the Popes*, Vol. XVIII, p. 270.

130. Paula Sutter Fichtner, *Emperor Maximilian II* (New Haven, 2001), p. 173.

131. Giorgio Spini, "The Medici Principality and the Organization of the States of Europe in the Sixteenth Century," *Journal of Italian History* 2 (1979), pp. 430–35. In 1561 Cosimo also founded the new military/religious order of St. Stephen, dedicated to the war against the Turks, which impressed Michele Ghislieri; Pio Pecchiai, *Roma nel Cinquecento* (Bologna, 1948), p. 132.

132. Roberto Cantagalli, *Cosimo I de'Medici, granduca di Toscana* (Milan, 1985), pp. 287–88.

133. Pastor, *History of the Popes*, Vol. XVIII, p. 271.

All of Cosimo's rivals in northern Italy immediately objected to his new title, which implied seniority, if not actual power, over them.[134] The duke of Ferrara was particularly incensed, as the papal bull ensured that Cosimo would now have precedence over him.[135] He also suspected that Pius and Cosimo were plotting against him. But of all the envoys in Rome, the imperial ambassador protested most vigorously. Normally the Spanish and imperial envoys cooperated to advance Habsburg interests, but in this case the Austrian ambassador reacted much more strongly, claiming that the pope had infringed on his master's rights. He quickly tried to enlist Zúñiga's help to prevent this affront from happening, by pointing out that Philip's rights had also been trampled: since Philip had invested Cosimo with Siena in 1557, he too was the duke's overlord. Zúñiga temporized, unwilling to commit himself, and urgently requested instructions from Philip.[136] Philip's response indicated his disapproval of the pope's intentions, while also showing his reluctance to antagonize Pius any further. He directed his ambassador to delay the investiture ceremony (without telling him how), while seeking to discover the exact terms of the papal bull. At the same time, he told Zúñiga to act "secretly and with great dissimulation," and not let anyone know that Philip opposed the bull.[137]

These orders left Zúñiga confused and uncertain how to proceed. For the next several months the imperial ambassador constantly pressured him to oppose the granting of the new title.[138] But he was not sure if Philip would approve. At one point he asked for clarification in a diplomatically worded letter, suggesting that it might help matters if he knew what the king was saying to Cosimo and the other Italian princes about this matter.[139] The king did not respond. Meanwhile tensions in Italy, already inflamed, grew worse. The duke of Ferrara wrote to the emperor petitioning military aid against the pope. Lacking any specific instructions from Philip, and sensing a disaster brewing, Zúñiga took it on himself to talk the pope out of provoking a war.

Having "resolved to talk with His Holiness," the ambassador appeared before Pius and said that Philip would approve of the granting of

134. In 1573 Girolamo Lippomano, the Venetian ambassador to Savoy, wrote that Cosimo "has made himself odious to many princes by showing such great desire to acquire new titles, and greater authority . . . he has bought very dearly the hatred of more than one Italian prince." *Le Relazioni degli ambasciatori veneti al Senato*, Series II, Vol. II, p. 217.
135. Pastor, *History of the Popes*, Vol. XVIII, p. 271.
136. Zúñiga to Philip, December 16, 1569; *Correspondencia diplomática*, Vol. III, pp. 196–99.
137. Philip to Zúñiga, December 21, 1569; ibid., p. 206.
138. Maximilian, furious at both Cosimo and Pius, instructed his ambassador to search the Vatican archives for legal arguments against the granting of the title. Fichtner, *Emperor Maximilian*, pp. 173–74.
139. Zúñiga to Philip, January 6, 1570; *Correspondencia diplomática*, Vol. III, pp. 212–14.

Cosimo's new title, but only if it was not "in prejudice of a third party," such as the emperor (which of course it was). He also mentioned that he had heard rumors that the pope plotted war with Florence against Ferrara, but he did not believe them, "because I knew His Holiness's mind, which was to conserve peace in Italy, since it was so beneficial to the service of God and the good of Christendom."[140] Thus he sought to guide Pius into reconsidering his actions, without directly confronting him. His words are noteworthy not only for his skillful handling of a temperamental pope, but also in that Zúñiga chose to emphasize the threat to the peace of Italy, rather than how Philip's feudal rights had been infringed. In any case, Pius responded that he only wanted to thank Cosimo for his services, and that he did not think the granting of the title would result in any *novedades* (as Zúñiga put it). The ambassador complained that Pius might well believe this, but he did not.

Cosimo himself arrived in Rome in mid-February. Zúñiga tried to get Cosimo to reveal his intentions, but the duke cagily asserted that he was only in Rome to give thanks to Pius, and to offer his services to Philip's ministers.[141] His presence in Rome, however, intensified the rumor mill in Italy. According to Zúñiga, the cardinals, the Roman populace, and indeed all of Italy, feared a possible war, and marveled at the pope's apparent political folly.[142] For weeks, Zúñiga shuttled between Cosimo and Pius, begging both of them to preserve the peace of Italy. Both denied plotting war, although they also made clear their hostility toward the duke of Ferrara.[143] Zúñiga grew frustrated, as Pius seemed simply not to understand the possible consequences of his actions.[144] Meanwhile Philip still sent no specific instructions about stopping the proceedings, so Zúñiga ended up watching helplessly as the pope formally invested Cosimo with his new title. Two weeks later, Philip sent Zúñiga a letter commanding him not to use Cosimo's new title in public.[145] Much to Zúñiga's dismay, however, Philip still did not give substantive instructions.[146]

140. Zúñiga to Philip, January 25, 1570; ibid., pp. 227–31.
141. Zúñiga to Philip, February 18, 1570; ibid., pp. 234–38.
142. Zúñiga to Philip, February 28, 1570; ibid., p. 238. The Venetian Senate also greatly feared that the emperor might declare war on the pope, which then might become an opportunity for the Turks to invade Italy; Setton, *The Papacy and the Levant*, Vol. IV, p. 994 n. 74.
143. Zúñiga to Philip, February 28, 1570; *Correspondencia diplomática*, Vol. III, pp. 239–40.
144. Sigismondo Cavalli, the Venetian ambassador in Madrid, reported that Philip also became exasperated with the pope's naiveté. He also suggested that Philip was actually quite patient with Pius, so as not to cause a rupture in their relations. *Relazione* of 1570; Firpo, *Relazioni*, Vol. VIII, pp. 507–8.
145. Philip to Zúñiga, March 25, 1570; *Correspondencia diplomática*, Vol. III, pp. 282–83.
146. Despite the king's silence, the pope was not unaware of Philip's displeasure. In mid-March he dispatched a special envoy, Don Luis de Torres, to Madrid, partly to explain his

Zúñiga's fears about a war in Italy never materialized, but the issue of Cosimo's title continued to be an irritant in Spanish-papal relations for months. A papal envoy in Spain reported that the king and his councilors believed that Pius had acted out of "hatred and malevolence," and might even rupture relations.[147] Philip in fact decided to issue a formal protest, but waited until after Pius had granted papal subsidies.[148] As late as February 1571 Zúñiga was still reporting on heated discussions over the problem at the Roman court, where many believed that Philip and Pius might yet come to blows.[149] Cosimo himself feared Spanish retribution: Zúñiga relayed rumors that the grand duke was raising troops to fend off a possible attack, while people whispered throughout Italy that Don Juan de Austria (commander of the Mediterranean fleet) had secret orders to occupy Florence.[150] When Cosimo confronted Zúñiga directly about these rumors, the Spaniard denied them, although he hinted that Philip had less trust in Cosimo than he used to. Evidently Zúñiga wanted Cosimo to sweat a little.

The pope was harder to intimidate. In a private audience in June 1571, Zúñiga revealed that he held a formal protest letter from Philip. He was clearly nervous about the pope's reaction, and claimed that it was a "modest" protest that would not offend anybody. Nonetheless Pius became angry, declaring that Philip had been "badly advised" on this matter, and that the protest could drive Cosimo into betraying Spain. Zúñiga answered that Cosimo would never be so stupid. He also suggested that if the pope refused to listen to him, he would declaim the protest from the steps of St. Peter's—an uncharacteristically bold threat for Zúñiga, worthy of his brother. It apparently worked: after "marveling" that Philip would risk all of his negotiations with Rome on this matter, Pius agreed to accept the protest letter in private.[151] But this was a hollow victory for the Spaniards, since Cosimo kept his title.[152] Furthermore, Pius remained willfully blind about the hostility his actions had generated among the

actions and intentions in giving Cosimo the new title. Setton, *The Papacy and the Levant*, Vol. IV, p. 956. Some of Torres's correspondence has also been published: *La Lega di Lepanto nel carteggio diplomatico inedito di Don Luys de Torres*, ed. A. Dragonetti de Torres (Turin, 1931).
147. Torres to Cardinal Alessandrino, May 20, 1570; ibid., p. 160.
148. Zúñiga to Philip, December 1, 1570; *Correspondencia diplomática*, Vol. IV, p. 87.
149. Zúñiga to Philip, February 12, 1571; ibid., pp. 198–99.
150. Zúñiga to Philip, February 8 and March 30, 1571; ibid., pp. 195 and 236.
151. Zúñiga to Philip, June 4, 1571; ibid., pp. 328–32.
152. Cosimo died in 1574, and his son Francesco assumed the title of Grand Duke with little to no Spanish opposition. When Francesco swore obedience to the papacy, he demanded that the ceremony reflect his status as grand duke, and Zúñiga did nothing to object. Zúñiga to Philip, May 17, 1576; AGSE 926, #21.

Italian princes, which the ambassador feared might explode.[153] Zúñiga's frustration with the entire situation boiled over in a surprisingly blunt letter to Philip, where he complained about going almost a year without receiving detailed instructions on how to handle this affair. He also suggested that the king had lost face by allowing Cosimo's defiance to go unpunished.[154]

All of these issues—Cosimo's title, Pius's dispute with Ferrara, even the precedence dispute—aggravated Zúñiga all the more because they distracted him from his chief diplomatic task during these years: the negotiation of a new Holy League, among Spain, the papacy, and Venice. The papacy had long cherished the dream of organizing a new military campaign against the Muslims, and the Turkish siege of Malta in 1565 had lent a new sense of urgency to their efforts.[155] Pius V, from the moment of his election, saw it as his mission to unite Christendom against the infidels.[156] Philip's more immediate concern, however, was Spanish Italy, and he instructed his ambassadors to request men and money from the pope to defend these territories.[157] Pius responded positively and quickly, much to the delight of Philip and his ambassador.[158] As for the idea of a Christian military alliance, the Spaniards were skeptical, especially if the pope intended to include the French. During the first two years of Pius's reign Requeséns temporized whenever the pope proposed an alliance, as he had no instructions from the king on the issue; privately, he expressed doubt that the French would ever join such a venture.[159] When the papal nuncio urged Philip directly to join a crusade, the king declined, citing both his various obligations and his doubts about the other Christian princes.[160]

---

153. The ambassador warned the pope that his actions would "cause a fire to be lit [in Italy] which would never be extinguished in all his days." Zúñiga to Philip, June 10, 1571; *Correspondencia diplomática*, Vol. IV, pp. 332–34.

154. Zúñiga to Philip, July 3, 1571; ibid., p. 369.

155. Luciano Serrano, *La Liga de Lepanto entre España, Venecia y la Santa Sede (1570–1573)*, 2 vols. (Madrid, 1918–1920), Vol. I, pp. 28–29.

156. Thus one of his first actions was to ask Philip to drop the precedence dispute, which only served to "drive" the French into friendship with the Turks; Fernand Braudel, *The Mediterranean and the Mediterranean World in the Age of Philip II*, trans. Siân Reynolds, 2 vols. (New York, 1973), Vol. II, p. 1029.

157. John Lynch refers to the period 1569–1570 as "years of crisis" for Spain, when simultaneous wars in the Netherlands and the Mediterranean stretched Spanish resources to the limit; *Spain under the Habsburgs*, Vol. I, p. 239.

158. Setton, *The Papacy and the Levant*, Vol. IV, pp. 882–87.

159. See for example Requeséns to Philip, November 14, 1566; *Correspondencia diplomática*, Vol. I, pp. 385–89.

160. Setton, *The Papacy and the Levant*, Vol. IV, pp. 912–13.

Zúñiga, too, expressed serious doubts about an alliance. In particular he warned the pope about trusting too much in the Venetians, who "would not hesitate to join with the Turks, if it benefits their cause to do so."[161] Clearly, the memory of Venice's abandonment of a Holy League in 1540 still rankled. But circumstances changed. In December 1568 the Muslims living in southern Spain revolted against the Crown, and for the next two years Spanish troops (led by Don Juan) fought a bloody campaign to suppress them.[162] During the "War of Granada" Philip and his councilors greatly feared a Turkish invasion in support of their Iberian brethren.[163] Then in early 1570 came news of a huge Turkish fleet about to set sail, threatening the island of Cyprus, a key Venetian outpost. The Venetian ambassadors in Spain and Rome begged for help. Cardinal Granvelle, viceroy of Naples and Philip's senior minister in Italy, still spoke against an alliance, on the basis of Venetian unreliability.[164] Zúñiga, however, explained that the cardinal's words had an ulterior purpose. Philip's representatives in Italy had agreed to conceal their interest in an alliance, "so that when Your Majesty may wish to enter in [a League] it can be done to your advantage."[165]

This statement illustrates the Spanish position throughout the League negotiations: never agree to anything immediately, and always insist on the best possible terms for Spain. Yet despite their consistent strategy, Zúñiga and his colleagues rarely succeeded in realizing their goals. Recently an historian has suggested that the Holy League "solidified" the close relations between Philip and the papacy, and "demonstrated . . . the central position of Spain in the new world order of the late sixteenth-century Mediterranean world."[166] Actually, it was quite the opposite: the League often acted counter to Spanish interests, the negotiations themselves often degenerated into shouting and insults, and in the end the alliance disintegrated. Spanish imperial power did play a key role in the formation and achievements of the League, but the final results were ambiguous at best.

During the spring of 1570 Philip sent no specific instructions about a League, so his ambassador played for time. Zúñiga continued to pretend disinterest in a League while trying to wheedle financial concessions out of

161. Zúñiga to Philip, August 17, 1568; *Correspondencia diplomática*, Vol. II, p. 443. See chapter 1 on other Spanish opinions of the Venetians.

162. Diego Hurtado de Mendoza, the ex-ambassador, witnessed this campaign and wrote a famous chronicle, *De la Guerra de Granada* (1571–1572), ed. Bernardo Blanco-González (Madrid, 1970).

163. Braudel, *The Mediterranean and the Mediterranean World*, Vol. II, pp. 1063–66.

164. Setton, *The Papacy and the Levant*, Vol. IV, pp. 950–51.

165. Zúñiga to Philip, February 28, 1570; *Correspondencia diplomática*, Vol. III, pp. 242–44.

166. Dandelet, *Spanish Rome*, p. 70.

the pope. He also repeatedly questioned Venice's will to fight, even telling the Venetian ambassador to his face that although Venice was now at war with the Turk, "one could assume that if the Turks ever offered decent terms you would accept."[167] These openly hostile words were perhaps part of an act, or else they reflected Zúñiga's personal attitude; Philip himself treated the Venetian ambassador in Madrid with much greater courtesy.[168] Meanwhile the pope's envoy to Philip, Luis de Torres, argued passionately for a League, or at least for assistance for the Venetians. He flattered Philip, playing on the king's self-image as Defender of the Faith, while warning of the dangers of inaction.[169] Evidently he was persuasive: three days after meeting with Torres Philip informed Zúñiga that he had agreed to muster the Spanish fleet in Sicily, and to provide Venice with wheat.[170]

In mid-May Philip agreed at least to consider entering a League, which launched a whole new barrage of negotiations. On May 16 he dispatched eight lengthy documents to Rome, one of which informed Pius of his decision, while another empowered Zúñiga, Cardinal Granvelle, and Cardinal Pacheco to act as "commissioners" (*comisarios*) to negotiate the terms of the League.[171] The latter document granted the three men (or any two of them) full powers to negotiate in the king's name, and gave them a great deal of independence, although they ultimately had to confirm all decisions with the king and the royal council. The rest of the letters contained detailed instructions on how to conduct negotiations, some addressed to all the commissioners, others specifically to Zúñiga. Philip charged his resident ambassador with sending constant updates on League affairs to Madrid and all Spanish ministers in Italy, as well as to ministers in the Netherlands and Philip's Italian allies.[172] The one mandate repeated in all the letters was that final agreement on a League depended on the pope granting financial subsidies.[173] Philip may have agreed to contribute forces to the League, but he was not going to do it for free.[174]

---

167. Zúñiga to Philip, March 15, 1570; *Correspondencia diplomática*, Vol. III, p. 270.
168. Sigismondo Cavalli, the Venetian ambassador in Madrid (1566–1570), reported that Philip's words and actions reflected "respect and reverence" for the *Signoria*. *Relazione* of 1570; Firpo, *Relazioni*, Vol. VIII, pp. 514–15.
169. Torres to Cardinal Alessandrino, April 24, 1570; *La Lega di Lepanto*, pp. 102–3.
170. Philip to Zúñiga, April 24, 1570; *Correspondencia diplomática*, Vol. III, pp. 295–97.
171. Ibid., pp. 337–39, 330–31. The three men decided amongst themselves that Cardinal Granvelle would be the chief spokesman, due to his status and experience.
172. Ibid., pp. 331–34. Interestingly, Philip named Cosimo de'Medici as one of the Italian dukes Zúñiga was to keep informed, despite the conflict over titles.
173. One of the letters emphasized this requirement and nothing else, underlining its importance; ibid., pp. 336–37.
174. Philip actually ended up spending a great deal on the League; see Geoffrey Parker, "Lepanto (1571): The Costs of Victory," in *Spain and the Netherlands*, pp. 122–33.

Philip also set a number of conditions on his participation in the League, which illustrate his concerns and hopes.[175] Several of his requirements reflected suspicion of Venetian reliability, such as demanding a clause in the terms of the League forbidding any member from signing a separate peace.[176] His most contentious demands, however, concerned the theater of operations: Philip wanted League forces to attack corsair bases in North Africa, which threatened Spain, rather than remain in the eastern Mediterranean, as the Venetians desired. The king also pointed out that since the League would be immediately beneficial for Venice, but not necessarily Spain, costs should be assessed accordingly. Finally, Philip insisted that Don Juan de Austria should be the supreme commander of the League forces, superior to any Venetian or papal officer. Arguments over these demands, which were obviously intended to tailor the League toward Spanish interests, nearly destroyed the League before it even began.

Throughout the League negotiations the Spaniards were ambivalent at best about joining it, none more so than the king.[177] In June 1570, for example, the *comisarios* prodded Philip to order Gian Andrea Doria, the commander of the Genoese fleet, to join up with the Venetians, which he had delayed doing. The Venetians of course had bad memories of Genoese inaction in 1538 (see chapter 1), but the *comisarios* feared that Italians perceived this issue as a test of Philip's commitment: as they wrote, "not only His Holiness and the Venetians but all Italy is watching closely to see if Your Majesty truly wishes to aid the Venetians." Evidently they were worried that Philip could harm his *reputación* in Italy if he did not keep his word. They also suggested that it was to Philip's advantage to help the Venetians, since they would then be in his debt.[178] This letter, in combination with a similar missive from the pope, prompted Philip to order Doria to join the Venetian fleet—although he secretly told Doria to avoid combat for the remainder of the year, and wait for better conditions.[179] This would not be the only time Philip undermined his own representatives.

175. *Correspondencia diplomática,* Vol. III, pp. 339–46.
176. The papal nuncio Castagna warned that distrust between Spain and Venice would be the biggest obstacle to creating a League; Castagna to Cardinal Alessandrino, April 25, 1570; ibid., pp. 304–5.
177. Castagna wrote that Philip joined the League only at the urging of Cardinal Diego de Espinosa, president of the Council of Castile. He suggested that some favor be done for Espinosa, to help keep him friendly. Castagna to Alessandrino, July 13, 1570; ibid., pp. 448–49.
178. *Comisarios* to Philip, June 28, 1570; ibid., pp. 407–11.
179. Setton, *The Papacy and the Levant,* Vol. IV, p. 973.

The negotiations themselves proceeded at an agonizingly slow pace, as the three teams of envoys—Spanish, Venetian, papal—argued terms. The basic distrust between the Spaniards and the Venetians led to quibbles over every word of the League contract. One example will suffice, from a letter describing amendments to the document:

> [On] the annotation labeled "H" in the fifth article concerning *Non timeant* ["Let them not fear"] it seems to us that this chapter should be clarified so as to ask for something reasonable and limited, and to prevent the excuse the Venetians always use, that they fear being invaded by the Turks due to lack of assistance from Your Majesty; and although the Venetian ambassador made a great protest against this, the papal delegates supported us, recognizing the reasonableness of [the clarification], and they saw that the declaration was quite moderate, saying *nisi talis classis turchis exiverit ut verisimile sit eos incursionem a Turchis timere debere* ["unless so great a Turkish fleet embarks that they truly ought to fear a Turkish invasion"].[180]

Thus we see that the Spaniards and the Venetians both feared the other would abandon the League, which made an alliance difficult. Nor were the papal delegates happy: one of them wrote to Castagna in Madrid complaining about the deviousness and selfishness of the *comisarios,* and urged the nuncio to get Philip to rein in his envoys.[181] The Spaniards could report that the pope had granted the subsidies Philip wanted, but even this good news came with a warning that *novedades* in the negotiations could still prevent them from actually seeing the money.[182]

The uninspired military campaign of that summer added to the difficulties at the negotiating table. A Turkish armada landed on Cyprus in July, and by September had captured the capital city of Nicosia. A combined fleet of Spanish, Venetian, and papal forces, long delayed by quarrels among the commanders and general Spanish reluctance, failed to accomplish anything besides taking heavy damage from a storm.[183] In Rome, recriminations flew.[184] Yet the *comisarios* showed remarkably little concern for the Venetian loss, and even expressed suspicion that the Venetians were only pursuing League negotiations in order to bargain for

180. *Comisarios* to Philip, July 21, 1570; *Correspondencia diplomática*, Vol. III, p. 469.
181. Cardinal Rusticucci to Castagna, August 11, 1570; ibid, pp. 503–4.
182. Zúñiga to Philip, July 28, 1570; ibid., p. 479.
183. Kenneth Setton describes the 1570 campaign as "one of the notable failures of the century." *The Papacy and the Levant*, Vol. IV, p. 974.
184. In Madrid, Castagna expressed the pope's "discontent and disgust" with the Spaniards; Castagna to Pius, September 7, 1570; *Correspondencia diplomática*, Vol. IV, p. 1.

better peace terms from the Turks.[185] For their part, the Venetian government's instructions to their delegates emphasized the urgency of their needs and denounced Spanish suspicions.[186] Meanwhile disagreements over various issues, from overall strategy to the price of supplies, still prevented the conclusion of an alliance.[187] The pope himself grew angry with the Spaniards for their refusal to accept anyone but Don Juan as supreme commander of both naval and land forces, and wrote to Philip directly, threatening to pull out of negotiations.[188] From mid-December 1570 to early February 1571, discussions in fact halted completely, which the papal court blamed on the *comisarios*.[189]

Unbeknownst to the Italians, however, the *comisarios* were laboring under a major disadvantage: lack of direction. Philip sent them no instructions at all for months, and when he finally did, in February 1571, they proved remarkably unhelpful as far as solving conflicts were concerned. He repeated that Don Juan should be supreme commander, adding that the appointment of officers was the prerogative of princes, not popes. He also argued that Tunis should be the League's primary target, and that a Levant campaign should be postponed.[190] His orders show disregard for the realities of the negotiating table, as well as for the priorities of the Italians. He did instruct his envoys not to upset Pius when relaying his orders, but he made no suggestions how to accomplish this feat. Evidently Philip felt no urgency to conclude a League.[191]

The *comisarios* did their best to obey Philip and yet keep the negotiations moving forward. They argued with Pius about the inadvisability of having a divided command, and the pope eventually agreed that Don Juan should be in charge. On the other hand, the Spaniards decided not

185. *Comisarios* to Philip, September 8, 1570; ibid., p. 9.
186. Setton, *The Papacy and the Levant*, Vol. IV, p. 992.
187. A lengthy document from the *comisarios* to Philip of December 5, 1570, detailed all of the outstanding issues and the attempts to solve them. The most heated conflict continued to be over the theater of operations: the Spaniards wanted the League contract to include a possible attack on North Africa, but the Venetians (supported by the papal delegates) insisted that the League's objective should be the destruction of the Turkish fleet in the eastern Mediterranean. The Italians were adamant enough on this point that the *comisarios* recommended to Philip that they compromise, by accepting a clause in the contract which stated that an African campaign would be fought at some unspecified time in the future. *Correspondencia diplomática*, Vol. IV, pp. 88–117.
188. Pius to Philip, December 9, 1570; ibid., pp. 118–19.
189. Serrano, *Liga de Lepanto*, Vol. I, pp. 94–95.
190. Philip to *Comisarios*, February 4, 1571; *Correspondencia diplomática*, Vol. IV, pp. 175–82, 185–87.
191. The Venetian ambassador in Madrid warned that Philip was more worried about the Protestants than the Turks at this particular moment; Setton, *The Papacy and the Levant*, Vol. IV, p. 1008.

to mention Tunis for the present, "so as not to upset everything."[192] The *comisarios* appeared surprisingly casual about disregarding Philip's desire to attack Tunis, but they perhaps understood the situation better than their king. The Spanish ambassador in Venice, Diego Guzmán de Silva, warned Zúñiga that while a North African campaign was desirable, if they pressed the issue the Venetians might easily abandon the League.[193] In any case they made progress: the papal delegates expressed satisfaction. The Venetians, however, continued to make objections, most likely because they still hoped to negotiate peace with the Turks.[194] In fact, that January they secretly dispatched an envoy to Constantinople.[195] As late as May 7, 1571, Zúñiga still despaired of getting anything better than a "defensive alliance" out of the Republic.[196] The pope, too, feared that Venice might still back out, and sent a special envoy to the *Signoria* to prompt them into action.[197]

Finally in late May, against all expectations, the various delegates concluded a contract for a League. Zúñiga informed Philip of the good news on May 21, and prayed that the League would produce "great victories over the infidels and enemies of the holy Catholic faith."[198] A few days later the delegates signed the contract in a solemn ceremony in St. Peter's, where all the participants swore oaths to fulfill the contract, and the pope exhorted all to do their utmost for their holy cause. Despite this grand show of solidarity, however, Zúñiga still expressed doubts. Several key details, such as the exact number of ships and men each participant was to provide, remained unresolved.[199] Nor did he or his fellow

---

192. *Comisarios* to Philip, March 9, 1571; *Correspondencia diplomática,* Vol. IV, pp. 213–20.

193. Guzmán de Silva to Zúñiga, March 12, 1571; AGSE 1500, #2. See chapter 1 for more on Guzmán's efforts to promote a League.

194. Braudel, *The Mediterranean and the Mediterranean World,* Vol. II, p. 1091. Zúñiga suspected the Venetians were using the current League negotiations as leverage with the Turks, and wrote to Guzmán about the necessity of foiling such plans. Zúñiga to Guzman, April 7, 1571; AGSE 1501, #18.

195. The envoy even returned to Venice in June with a draft of a peace treaty, but by that time the Venetians had become embittered by their losses in the eastern Mediterranean. Jack Beeching, *The Galleys at Lepanto* (New York, 1982), pp. 169–83.

196. Zúñiga to Philip, May 7, 1571; *Correspondencia diplomática,* Vol. IV, pp. 272–73. Castagna reported that Philip was equally pessimistic, and believed that Venice was making impossible demands as an excuse to sign a separate peace. Castagna to Alessandrino, May 5, 1571; ibid., p. 264.

197. Setton, *The Papacy and the Levant,* Vol. IV, pp. 1012–14.

198. *Correspondencia diplomática,* Vol. IV, pp. 285–89.

199. Zúñiga to Philip, May 26, 1571; ibid., pp. 317–18. Spanish and Venetian officers argued right up to the departure of the League fleet, and beyond. In one particularly ugly incident in early October, several Venetian soldiers were killed in a brawl with Spanish soldiers, who were then in turn executed by a Venetian commander. The incident nearly caused the collapse of the League. Setton, *The Papacy and the Levant,* Vol. IV, pp. 1050–51.

Spaniards instill confidence in their allies: in early June the ambassador delivered Philip's protest letter against Cosimo's new title, which increased tension in Rome.[200] Furthermore Don Juan's departure from Spain was delayed until late July, and he did not arrive at Naples until August 9. The pope became increasingly suspicious that the Spaniards did not really intend to fight, and indeed Zúñiga began to argue that it was too late in the season to attempt anything.[201] It was perhaps to everyone's surprise when the League fleet actually embarked in mid-September. Zúñiga reported with relief that Pius was now content with Spain's efforts, and perhaps could even be induced to grant more subsidies.[202] But the pope's happiness would be increased exponentially by the arrival of news of the victory of Lepanto.

Much as in Venice, Rome erupted with celebration, and pro-Spanish sentiment, when word of Lepanto arrived. Suddenly Spaniards like Don Juan became heroes; Pius, upon hearing the news, quoted Scripture: "There was a man sent from God, whose name was John" (John 1:6).[203] Zúñiga reported the pope's ecstatic reaction, and how he planned to capitalize on it: "certainly his joy is great, and he knows that Christendom could not have enjoyed this [victory] without Your Majesty's help." The ambassador suggested that now was the time to plan for the next year's campaign, and perhaps to stress Spanish priorities.[204] But he was reluctant to do anything without specific orders. In June 1571 Pius and the Venetians had wanted to discuss plans for the following year, but Zúñiga had claimed that he lacked authority to commit Spanish forces so far in advance. Now in October he delayed again, saying he wanted to wait until Don Juan and Requeséns returned before planning strategy. And new conflicts arose with the Venetians over grain supplies and perceived slights to their officers by Spaniards.[205] The League was in danger of collapsing mere weeks after its greatest success.

Although discussions about what the League should do next began almost immediately, they went nowhere fast. The pope and the Venetians wanted to follow up Lepanto with another campaign in the eastern Mediterranean, but Zúñiga again recommended a strike against North

---

200. A few weeks later Pius sent a special envoy to Madrid, with the double mission of appeasing Philip on the "Grand Duke" issue and ensuring that Philip joined the League. See Enrique García Hernán, *La acción diplomática de Francisco de Borja al servicio del pontificado 1571–1572* (Valencia, 2000), pp. 130–32.

201. Zúñiga to Philip, August 17, 1571; *Correspondencia diplomática*, Vol. IV, pp. 410–11.

202. Zúñiga to Philip, September 28, 1571; ibid., pp. 446–47.

203. Pastor, *History of the Popes*, Vol. XVIII, p. 425.

204. Zúñiga to Philip, October 22, 1571; *Correspondencia diplomática*, Vol. IV, pp. 488–89.

205. Zúñiga to Philip, October 29, 1571; ibid., pp. 497–99.

Africa, encouraged by the duke of Alba, one of Spain's leading military strategists.[206] He did this without royal guidance, as once again Philip took his time dispatching instructions to Rome.[207] When the king did send orders, he too stressed the importance of an attack on Africa, although he allowed that such a campaign could be postponed if the other League members demanded it. Even then, however, he insisted that Don Juan should have the last word.[208] But he and his envoys would again have to concede to Italian priorities.[209] The *comisarios* warned Philip that "His Holiness and the Venetians will constrict [the League] to their own concerns," and so they did.[210] The Venetians, once again with papal support, were adamant about sailing to the Levant. In a papal audience in January 1572, the Spaniards announced that while they would prefer an attack on North Africa, for the sake of maintaining the League they would agree to another Levantine campaign. They complained bitterly to Philip that the Venetians seemed to prefer that Algiers and Tunis remained in Turkish hands, rather than in Philip's.[211] Unfortunately, the Spaniards needed Venetian and papal cooperation; they also foresaw that the League would not last long, so they compromised, sacrificing their interests for short-term gains.[212]

When Pius V died in late April 1572, the future of the League became even hazier. Pius had been the driving force behind the Holy League, and his death increased everyone's doubts. As Zúñiga wrote, "his person was of great loss, both for Christendom in general and the particular affairs of Your Majesty."[213] The ambassador was determined, however, to

---

206. Alba wrote to Zúñiga that since the Turkish fleet had been severely damaged at Lepanto, and was thus no longer a threat, the next logical step was to go after their land bases, starting with those close to Spain and Italy. Alba to Zúñiga, November 17, 1571; *Colección de documentos inéditos para la historia de España,* Vol. III, pp. 292–303.

207. On November 25, Philip wrote to the *comisarios* a brief letter suggesting that he lacked the money necessary to maintain the current level of military spending, but he gave no specific instructions about the League. In mid-December, the *comisarios* wrote a plaintive letter back, indicating that they "had greatly hoped to have more precise orders from Your Majesty." *Correspondencia diplomática,* Vol. IV, pp. 540 and 562–70.

208. Philip to the *Comisarios,* December 22, 1571; ibid, pp. 886–91.

209. In January 1572 Philip dispatched a letter empowering the *comisarios* to "negotiate, discuss, document, resolve, and assent to" a League campaign for that year; this time he included Requeséns as one of his delegates. Bibliothèque Publique et Universitaire de Genève, Collection Edouard Favre (hereafter Collection Favre), Vol. LXII, f. 179.

210. *Comisarios* to Philip, December 28, 1571; ibid., pp. 593–600.

211. *Comisarios* to Philip, January 18, 1572; ibid., pp. 615–19.

212. Braudel paraphrases a letter from Granvelle to Zúñiga of March 20, 1572, which acknowledged that Spanish interests were being sacrificed in favor of Venetian concerns. *The Mediterranean and the Mediterranean World,* Vol. II, p. 1114.

213. Zúñiga to Philip, May 1, 1572; *Correspondencia diplomática,* Vol. IV, pp. 731–32.

press forward League negotiations with whomever succeeded Pius, and perhaps even use the next pope's joy at being promoted to improve the terms of the contract.[214] Circumstances seemed favorable: after a quick conclave, Ugo Boncampagni, the Cardinal of San Sisto, was elected Pope Gregory XIII, with support from both the Spanish faction and Cosimo de' Medici.[215] Boncampagni had spent time in Spain as a papal envoy, and was highly regarded by Philip and his ministers; he thus promised to be sympathetic to Spanish interests.[216] Zúñiga immediately took steps to ensure friendly relations with the new pope, and to urge him to follow in Pius's footsteps. Gregory answered positively, promising to proceed with League plans.[217] The ambassador also effused that Gregory "has shown great desire for the conservation of peace between Christian princes, and particularly in Italy . . . and he seems to be a man who will be neutral with everyone."[218]

Unfortunately for Zúñiga, his king's policies would again undermine Spanish-papal relations. News of Pope Pius's illness had prompted Philip to rethink his commitment to a Levantine campaign, which had never been especially strong.[219] He wrote to the *comisarios* that if the pope should die, Don Juan should withdraw from the League and prepare to attack Algiers, a venture that would be more beneficial for "Christendom and my states and vassals" (presumably the latter being a higher priority). The great expense of a campaign, the king suggested, should be put to better use in the western Mediterranean than in the Levant.[220] Philip knew, of course, that Venice and Rome would be angered by such a move, and so instructed his ambassador not to reveal the true reason for the change of plans. The official story was that Don Juan had been ordered to stay in Italy to counter a possible French invasion—a plausible excuse, as France was indeed threatening military action. But Philip specifically ordered his ambassador not to mention North Africa.[221] In other words, Zúñiga had to lie to the new pope, while the Spanish fleet remained idle in Sicily.

214. Zúñiga to Philip, May 1, 1572; ibid., pp. 732–33.
215. Setton, *The Papacy and the Levant*, Vol. IV, p. 1078; and Hubert Jedin, "Catholic Reform and Counter Reformation," in *History of the Church*, Vol. V, ed. Hubert Jedin and John Dolan (New York, 1980), p. 503.
216. Pastor, *History of the Popes*, Vol. XIX, p. 25; and Dandelet, *Spanish Rome*, p. 72.
217. Zúñiga to Philip, May 18, 1572; AGSE 919, #205.
218. Zúñiga to Philip, May 30, 1572; AGSE 918, #225.
219. Braudel, *The Mediterranean and the Mediterranean World*, Vol. II, p. 1117.
220. Serrano, *Liga de Lepanto*, Vol. I, pp. 296–97.
221. Philip to Zúñiga, June 2, 1572; ibid., pp. 305–9; and Braudel, *The Mediterranean and the Mediterranean World*, Vol. II, p. 1117.

Zúñiga, clearly unhappy with his king's decision, tried to warn Philip of the consequences. The pope would take offense, endangering the renewal of papal subsidies, while the Venetians would "scream to the heavens."[222] And his predictions came true. The summer of 1572 was a very uncomfortable time for the Spanish ministers in Rome, as they had to prevaricate every time the pope demanded to know what Philip intended to do.[223] Gregory vacillated between anger and sorrow in his audiences with the ambassador, while the Venetians would barely speak to him. The French ambassador in Rome (whom Zúñiga referred to as a "lunatic") added to the Spaniards' headaches by denouncing the rumors of war circulating in Italy, and claiming it was Philip who threatened the peace.[224] Zúñiga faced a diplomatic catastrophe: the dissolution of the League as a direct result of Philip's policies.

By early July the pressure on Philip had grown so intense that he had to reverse course yet again. Pope Gregory, the Venetians, and his own ministers all objected so vociferously that Philip had to yield.[225] He informed Zúñiga that in order to satisfy the pope and to keep the Venetians in the League, he would order Don Juan to proceed to the Levant with a large part of the Spanish fleet.[226] This concession was all the more remarkable, because by this time, the threat of a French invasion of either Italy or the Netherlands had become more than a mere excuse. King Charles IX of France was deeply involved in plots with Dutch Protestants, and French troops were massing.[227] Requeséns, now the governor of Milan (and thus directly in the French line of fire), complained to Zúñiga that Pope Gregory was completely ignoring French efforts to "disquiet" Italy and disrupt the League.[228] Nonetheless Zúñiga received news of Philip's volte-face with relief. "The other day I had audience with His Holiness," he wrote on August 1, "and I cannot describe how contented I found him, as he had been extremely sorrowful at the prospect of disunity in the

222. Zúñiga to Philip, June 22, 1572; Serrano, *Liga de Lepanto,* Vol. I, pp. 533–36. Zúñiga was not the only unhappy minister in Italy: Granvelle, Requeséns, and Don Juan himself all complained that Philip was driving the Venetians straight into the Turk's arms. Lynch, *Spain under the Habsburgs,* Vol. I, p. 246.

223. In one letter, Zúñiga reported how he and Cardinal Pacheco had met in order to get their stories straight before seeing the pope. Zúñiga to Philip, June 25, 1572; Serrano, *Liga de Lepanto,* Vol. I, pp. 340–44.

224. Zúñiga to Philip, June 26, 1572; ibid., pp. 348–49.

225. Braudel, *The Mediterranean and the Mediterranean World,* Vol. II, p. 1118.

226. Philip to Zúñiga, July 4, 1572; Serrano, *Liga de Lepanto,* Vol. I, pp. 371–73.

227. See N. M. Sutherland, "The Massacre of St. Bartholomew and the Problem of Spain," in *Princes, Politics, and Religion, 1547–1589* (London, 1984), pp. 173–82.

228. Requeséns to Zúñiga, June 21, 1572; Collection Favre, Vol. XXX, ff. 204–6. For Requeséns' tenure in Milan, see March, *Don Luis de Requeséns en el gobierno de Milan.*

[League] fleet at the beginning of his pontificate." Tension had obviously eased, although Zúñiga still complained that the pope and his delegates always gave the Venetians what they wanted, perhaps because they were "all of one nation."[229] Evidently Zúñiga shared some of his brother's anti-Italian prejudices.

On the other hand, the Spaniards had not endeared themselves to the Venetians either. Don Juan, who had been commanded to prepare an attack on North Africa in May, did not receive counterorders until July 12.[230] In his absence the Venetian and papal fleets set sail, and engaged the Turks in an inconclusive battle off Malvasia. Back in Rome, the Republic's envoys expressed suspicion about whether Don Juan really intended to sail to the Levant.[231] They had reason to be mistrustful: the Spaniards were clearly reluctant to let Don Juan leave Italy, because of the French threat.[232] Then came news of the assassination of the French Huguenot leader Admiral Coligny and the St. Bartholomew's Day Massacre of Protestants; suddenly the threat of a French invasion was lifted.[233] Don Juan could now proceed—but when he finally did, it took until early September for him to rejoin the League fleet, and then quarrels among the commanders immediately started up again.[234] A month later, after much indecisiveness, Don Juan declared the campaign over for the year. The League's efforts to capitalize on Lepanto had been a pathetic failure.

The Italian members of the League all blamed the Spaniards for this disaster. Pope Gregory displayed extreme displeasure with Philip and his ministers, while the Venetians openly accused Don Juan of seeking to weaken the Republic.[235] In November the various delegates all met in Rome once again to plan the next year's campaign, but once again Zúñiga refused to make any commitments because he had no instructions from Madrid.[236] Surprisingly, considering his weak position, the ambassador tried once more to argue for a North Africa campaign, which the pope unsurprisingly rejected.[237] Then unexpectedly Philip sent

229. Serrano, *Liga de Lepanto,* Vol. II, pp. 358–61.
230. Braudel, *The Mediterranean and the Mediterranean World,* Vol. II, p. 1118.
231. Zúñiga to Philip, August 21, 1572; AGSE, 919, #69–70.
232. On August 16, Cardinal Granvelle asserted in a letter to Margaret of Parma that Don Juan's presence in Italy had been an effective deterrent against French aggression. *Correspondance du cardinal de Granvelle,* Vol. IV, ed. Charles Piot (Brussels, 1884), pp. 368–69.
233. Sutherland, "The Massacre of St. Bartholomew and the Problem of Spain," pp. 174–75; and J. H. Elliott, *Europe Divided 1559–1598* (reprint, London, 1985), pp. 212–14.
234. Setton, *The Papacy and the Levant,* Vol. IV, pp. 1081–84.
235. Cardinal Como to Castagna, October 28, 1572; Serrano, *Liga de Lepanto,* Vol. II, p. 384; and Setton, *The Papacy and the Levant,* Vol. IV, pp. 1085–86.
236. Zúñiga to Philip, November 11, 1572; Serrano, *Liga de Lepanto,* Vol. II, pp. 389–92.
237. On November 13, 1572, Requeséns wrote to his brother a sympathetic letter about the

Zúñiga orders to prepare for a Levantine campaign, because of the threat of the Turkish fleet.[238] At this point the ambassador must have secretly wanted to strangle his mercurial monarch. Despite private misgivings, however, he proceeded to negotiate another League treaty.[239] The various envoys in fact signed a treaty in February 1573, but it was already too late. The Venetians had secretly begun negotiations with the Turks as early as September 1572, and in March 1573 they signed a separate peace.

A month later, Zúñiga wrote a consoling letter to Philip, assuring him that he had done everything possible for the "peace of Italy" and for the papacy, and that Venice's defection was in no way the king's fault.[240] It is not clear whom he was trying to console, the king or himself. After three years of mind-numbing negotiations, the League had collapsed, for reasons beyond the ambassador's control. The Spanish fleet continued to operate in the Mediterranean for several years more, but the war was essentially a draw; in 1577–1578 Philip and the Turks agreed to a truce, which more or less held for the rest of the century.[241] The Spaniards had tried to dictate every aspect of the League, with ambiguous results, and in the end they could not compel the Venetians to fight. What hurt the ambassador even more, perhaps, was that things might have been better if not for his own king's policies. The monumental task of creating and sustaining an alliance became impossible when support from home suddenly vanished. The League might have dissolved under any circumstances, but without steady royal commitment there had been no chance for it to hold together.

In 1579–1580, Philip seized the Crown of Portugal, and from this point on his attentions turned away from the Mediterranean, and toward the Atlantic. The Protestant Revolt of the Netherlands, and the Protestant Queen of England, became his chief preoccupations.[242] The papacy ceased to be a primary military ally, but it would continue to be a source

unfairness of the Roman court, which blamed Spain for the lackluster 1572 campaign. He suggests that the courtiers were all armchair generals, with no real understanding of military matters. His letter also suggests a total lack of empathy for the Italian point of view. Instituto de Valencia de Don Juan, Envío 81 (3), #1250.

238. Philip to Zúñiga, November 16, 1572; Serrano, *Liga de Lepanto*, Vol. II, pp. 393–95.

239. On December 6, he warned Philip that French agents were trying to facilitate a peace treaty between Venice and the Turks, so somebody needed to pressure the Venetians into signing a League treaty quickly. Ibid., pp. 400–401.

240. Zúñiga to Philip, April 12, 1573; Archivo de Zabálburu (Madrid), Caja 54, #34.

241. Braudel, *The Mediterranean and the Mediterranean World*, Vol. II, pp. 1154–55; and see also Andrew C. Hess, "The Battle of Lepanto and Its Place in Mediterranean History," *Past and Present* 57 (1972), pp. 52–73.

242. Parker, *Philip II*, chap. 9; and Kamen, *Philip of Spain*, chap. 9.

of moral and financial support. Or at least the Spaniards would expect it to be such: as we will see, popes in the later half of Philip's reign often proved as difficult as those in his earlier years. Although Spanish imperial power reached its height in the late sixteenth century, there would be little peace in Italy, any more than in the rest of Europe. More specifically, the papacy remained independent, even when Philip seemed poised to take over the world. While Philip and his ambassadors had grand visions of Spanish hegemony, they never quite converted the papacy into believers.

CHAPTER FOUR

Philip II and the Papacy, 1573–1598

D uring the second half of Philip II's reign, his policies toward the papacy shifted. After the failure of the Holy League, and the near-simultaneous Dutch revolt, Spanish power focused on northern Europe instead of the Mediterranean. Consequently Spanish diplomacy in Rome aimed to win financial and moral support for their grand designs, rather than military involvement. Philip and his ministers also wanted to stop worrying about Italy, so they could concentrate on other problems. The papacy, however, did not acquiesce to the Spanish agenda. On the contrary, as Spanish imperial might reached its zenith in the late sixteenth century, the papacy became more determined to reject Habsburg hegemony, and maintain both its own independence and the balance of power in Europe.[1] In the last half of Philip's reign, various popes had opportunities to support the "Habsburg Bid for Mastery," but they chose not to.[2] Gregory XIII (1572–1585) did not endorse the annexation of Portugal, Sixtus V (1585–1590) refused to pay for the invasion of England, and most painfully, Clement VIII (1592–1605) accepted the ex-Protestant Henry of Navarre as King of France, against Philip's strenuous objections. Moreover, the papacy continued to be active in Italian politics, often threatening the precious peace of Italy that Spaniards held so dear. As we will see, Spanish ambassadors in Rome usually displayed no

1. Paolo Prodi, *The Papal Prince: One Body and Two Souls*, trans. Susan Haskins (Cambridge, 1987), pp. 172–73.
2. The phrase is used by Paul Kennedy, *The Rise and Fall of the Great Powers* (New York, 1987), chap. 2.

more confidence in a "pax hispanica" in this period than they had in the previous twenty years.

Of all of Philip's ambassadors to Rome, Juan de Zúñiga had perhaps the calmest tenure. Zúñiga proved unusual for a Spanish diplomat, in that he seems never to have antagonized the pope to the point of an open break. But that in no way means he had an easy time of it, and the latter part of the decade he spent in Rome was no more carefree than the first half. The pope's policies and interests often diverged from or conflicted with Philip's, which placed the ambassador in difficult circumstances. To begin with, Gregory never ceased agitating for a new campaign against the infidel Muslims, especially after the Turks expelled Spanish forces from Tunis in 1574, which left the pope fearful of an invasion of Italy.[3] He also barraged Philip and his ministers with urgent appeals to invade England and depose the Protestant Queen Elizabeth; at one point he wrote to Philip directly, begging the king to act for the salvation of millions of souls.[4] Philip, however, was fully occupied by the Revolt of the Netherlands, and had no resources to spare. In fact, in September 1575 the king's inability to pay the interest on his many loans forced him to declare bankruptcy.[5] And even if he had had the wherewithal to act, he refused to be rushed, even by the Holy Father. As J. H. Elliott writes, Philip may have been the champion of the faith, "but he would champion it on his own terms, and in his own good time."[6] So Gregory remained frustrated, and Zúñiga often suffered as a result. In a typical letter to Philip written in 1575, the ambassador complained about the pope's balkiness in granting subsidies, and noted darkly that Gregory seemed "little inclined" to help the Spanish cause.[7]

In that same year, Zúñiga's reaction to local political events demonstrated his continued uneasiness about Spanish control of Italy. In 1574, the last French garrisons in Italy had abandoned their positions in Piedmont, so Zúñiga should have felt secure about Spanish hegemony in the peninsula.[8] But he clearly did not. In March 1575 civil unrest broke out

3. Ludwig von Pastor, *The History of the Popes from the Close of the Middle Ages,* trans. Ralph Francis Kerr, 40 vols. (London, 1891–1953), Vol. XIX, p. 343.

4. Angel Fernández Collado, *Gregorio XIII y Felipe II en la nunciatura de Felipe Sega (1577–1581)* (Toledo, 1991), pp. 192–93.

5. Most of the loans came from Genoese bankers, who forced Philip to pay ridiculously high rates, even after he restructured his debts to them; see A. W. Lovett, "The Castilian Bankruptcy of 1575," *Historical Journal* 23 (1980), pp. 899–911.

6. J. H. Elliott, *Europe Divided 1559–1598* (reprint, London, 1985), p. 173.

7. Zúñiga to Philip, March 4, 1575; Archivo General de Simancas, Sección Estado (hereafter AGSE) 925, #40.

8. Geoffrey Parker, *The Grand Strategy of Philip II* (New Haven, 1998), p. 85.

in the Republic of Genoa, one of Spain's key allies in northern Italy. The conflict involved resentment between older and newer aristocratic families in Genoa and control of high political offices.[9] It was thus an entirely local matter, but it threatened to destabilize a strategically important region, as well as disrupt a critical source of finance.[10] Both Zúñiga and Pope Gregory reacted strongly and immediately. The disturbance began on March 15; the following week Gregory dispatched a senior cardinal to Genoa to try to quell the uprising.[11] On March 25 Zúñiga informed Philip about events, and warned that the situation urgently needed attention, or else "major problems" could result.[12] Gregory had already sent a legate to "quiet and pacify" Genoa, "because the pope does not want revolts in Italy." Obviously, neither did the Spaniards. Philip's ministers in Rome, the ambassador stated, were prepared to act without orders if necessary, but in any case something had to be done.

Zúñiga's alarm about the Genoese situation matched the pope's concern about the Spanish response. Cardinal Granvelle, together with the governor of Milan and Gian Andrea Doria, the Genoese admiral in Philip's service, quickly arranged for a show of force, to discourage any thoughts of French intervention.[13] The threat of military action, or even an expansion of Spanish imperialism, frightened Gregory. The pope warned Zúñiga that Philip should not use the current crisis as an excuse to seize more Italian lands.[14] Zúñiga denied that the king had any such intentions, but was unable to allay Gregory's suspicions. Much to the ambassador's dismay, Gregory began making war preparations, evidently as a countermeasure against Spanish aggression. Even worse, Zúñiga suspected that Venice and perhaps other Italian powers had secretly pledged support for this effort, as otherwise Zúñiga could not account for the pope's boldness.[15] So once again a small conflict in one Italian state threatened to explode into a general war, or at least so the ambassador feared. Furthermore, Philip's reticence once again contributed to

9. Eric Cochrane, *Italy 1530–1630*, ed. Julius Kirshner (London, 1988), p. 170; see also Carlo Bitossi, *Il governo dei magnifici: Patriziato e politica a Genova fra Cinque e Seicento* (Genoa, 1990), pp. 46–61.

10. A. W. Lovett writes that Genoese bankers "were the architects of the financial system which made possible and sustained Castile's position as a first-rate power." *Early Habsburg Spain, 1517–1598* (Oxford, 1986), p. 223.

11. Pastor, *History of the Popes*, Vol. XIX, p. 344.

12. Zúñiga to Philip, March 25, 1575; AGSE 925, #23.

13. Manuel Rivero Rodríguez, "La Liga Santa y la paz de Italia (1569–1576)," in *Política, religión, e inquisición en la España moderna*, ed. P. Fernández Albaladejo, J. Martínez Millán, and N. Pinto Crespo (Madrid, 1996), pp. 614–17.

14. Pastor, *History of the Popes*, Vol. XIX, p. 345.

15. Zúñiga to Philip, June 26, 1575; AGSE 925, #89.

Zúñiga's problems, as the ambassador had no idea whether the king really was planning a military intervention.[16] On July 3 Zúñiga wrote to Don Juan directly, warning that many Italians anticipated his imminent attack—if that was what Don Juan actually intended.[17] There is no record of whether Don Juan ever responded.

For a few months, it appeared as if the threat of war had intimidated the pope. Zúñiga reported that Gregory had begun speaking to him with "greater moderation," and had claimed he had acted only in the interest of preserving the peace of Italy, which he knew to be as crucial for Philip as for himself.[18] But then Zúñiga received disturbing intelligence reports that certain Italian powers had approached the King of France, requesting military support in case Philip attempted to conquer Genoa. Supposedly, the king was considering it.[19] This of course represented the sum of all Spanish fears, the return of the Italian Wars. Then later that month Zúñiga heard rumors that the pope, Venice, and several Italian dukes had discussed forming an Italian League, believing that Philip would not dare to fight all of them at once. Interestingly, Zúñiga suggested that the best way to deal with such an alliance might be to join it, since then the Italians would not invite in the French.[20] In any case, as the ambassador wrote, such a development would be exactly the sort of *novedad* that Philip did not want in Italy. Any political change was dangerous, as the French could take advantage of it.

The situation seemed to worsen the following month, with the arrival of a special envoy to Gregory from France. Zúñiga relayed to Philip the warnings of the Spanish ambassador in France, who suspected that the envoy had come to plot with the pope against Genoa. Zúñiga himself, however, doubted that such was the case. As he wrote, "I cannot persuade myself that His Beatitude would ally with the French over Genoa, because he understands that the day [the French] set foot in Italy, this province will be neck-deep in heretics. As I have written to Your Majesty, His Holiness has had discussions with the powers of Italy [about Genoa], but

---

16. Philip may not have known either. At this very time, Philip and his ministers were debating hotly about where to devote their energy and resources, Italy or the Netherlands. Luis de Requeséns, now the governor general of the Netherlands, advocated a reallocation of forces to help him suppress the revolt, while the royal secretary Mateo Vázquez de Leca warned that Italy "will be exposed to complete loss" if the Turks invaded. A. W. Lovett, *Philip II and Mateo Vázquez de Leca: the Government of Spain (1572–1592)* (Geneva, 1977), p. 55.

17. Zúñiga to Don Juan de Austria, July 3, 1575; AGSE 925, #145.

18. Zúñiga to Philip, July 11, 1575; AGSE 925, #147.

19. Zúñiga to Philip, September 2, 1575; AGSE 925, #183. The source of the intelligence was the papal nuncio in France, via Cardinal Como, the papal secretary of state; perhaps the pope was trying to apply pressure indirectly?

20. Zúñiga to Philip, September 30, 1575; AGSE 925, #195.

when it comes to putting things into action they refuse to spend money or to get involved in wars."[21]

This is a very interesting reaction, which seems much calmer than in Zúñiga's previous letters. As it turned out, he was right: the French did not become involved, a general war never materialized, and in March 1576 the Genoese accepted a peace mediated by both Gregory and Philip.[22] Yet Zúñiga's phlegmatic position, which itself seems atypical, ultimately was not based on confidence in Spanish control of Italy, but on the pope's religious zeal and Italian apathy. This hardly seems to qualify as confidence in a "pax hispanica."

Zúñiga also clearly did not believe that Pope Gregory was an unqualified friend of Spain.[23] This became evident when Philip began his campaign to claim the throne of Portugal. In August 1578, when King Sebastian I of Portugal, one of Philip's nephews, was killed in Morocco during a quixotic attempt to revive the Crusades, Philip was the closest male heir. He and his advisors decided that God intended him to claim the throne and thus reunite the Iberian Peninsula for the first time since the Roman Empire.[24] Many of the Portuguese, however, had no particular desire to be ruled by a Castilian king, a fact Philip well knew, so he prepared an army to seize Portugal by force if persuasion did not serve. Pope Gregory strongly objected to the king's actions.

The prospect of Philip gaining control of Portugal and its overseas trading empire terrified the rest of Europe, Pope Gregory included. According to a Venetian ambassador in Rome, Giovanni Cornaro, Gregory desperately wanted peace among all Christian princes, and often complained that Philip was not so moved. The pope believed that the more powerful Philip became, the more jealous of other princes he grew, so that he always sought to become greater.[25] Gregory was thus disgusted by Philip's naked aggression against a Christian neighbor, particularly when at the same time the Catholic King had signed a truce with the Turks. He instructed his nuncio in Madrid to protest against the king's

21. Zúñiga to Philip, November 16, 1575; AGSE 925, #30.
22. Pastor, *History of the Popes*, Vol. XIX, p. 345.
23. The pope had no illusions about the Spaniards either. Gregory and his envoys often expressed anger about Philip's intransigence, especially on matters of Church reform and jurisdiction. See Ricardo de Hinojosa, *Los despachos de la diplomacia pontificia en España*, Vol. I (Madrid, 1896), pp. 229–46.
24. On the messianic significance of the Portuguese campaign, see Geoffrey Parker, "David or Goliath? Philip II and His World in the 1580s," in *Success Is Never Final: Empire, War, and Faith in Early Modern Europe* (New York, 2002), pp. 16–38; and see also Marie Tanner, *The Last Descendant of Aeneas: The Habsburgs and the Mythic Image of the Emperor* (New Haven, 1993).
25. *Relazione* of 1581; *Le relazioni degli ambasciatori veneti al Senato*, ed. Eugenio Alberi, 15 vols.(Florence, 1839–1863), Series II, Vol. X, pp. 283–84.

actions, for which he saw no justification.[26] For the next two years, in fact, Gregory opposed Philip's annexation of Portugal, albeit ineffectually.

Gregory claimed that he had no ulterior political motives, beyond his anguish at seeing Christian princes at war with each other.[27] He might have been telling the truth, but Zúñiga clearly did not believe him. As he wrote, "I have so little confidence that between His Holiness and any Italian there is any desire for Your Majesty to gain another kingdom, that I have been content to ensure that none of the nuncios he sends to Portugal seek to help any of the [other] pretenders to the succession. . . . [I have also tried to convince the pope] that the decent thing would be not to declare support for anyone."[28] The Spanish ambassador, at any rate, had no doubt that the pope opposed the annexation of Portugal for (typically Italian) political reasons. He argued that Philip's possession of Portugal would be to the advantage of all Christendom, but the pope refused to listen (out of jealousy or spite, from Zúñiga's point of view).[29] Zúñiga's perception of an anti-Spanish atmosphere in Italy perhaps explains his ambivalent reaction upon being transferred in April 1579, to the much more lucrative position of viceroy of Naples. In one letter to Philip, Zúñiga expressed gratitude that he was finally leaving Rome, which he had long wanted to do.[30] In another letter written on the same day, Zúñiga stated flatly that he had no wish to die, or for that matter to live, in Italy.[31]

Zúñiga's antipathy toward Italians notwithstanding, he managed not to appear overly arrogant while in Rome. His replacement, however, behaved more like Vargas and Requeséns, and would have an equally difficult time staying friendly with the pope.[32] Enrique de Guzmán, second count of Olivares (and father of the famous count-duke of Olivares), had served at the royal court from an early age, and was wounded at the battle of St. Quentin.[33] He thus enjoyed close personal ties to Philip, and had shed

26. Fernández Collado, *Gregorio XIII y Felipe II en la nunciatura de Felipe Sega* (who seems to take Gregory's word at face value), pp. 52–53.

27. Ibid., pp. 81–82.

28. Zúñiga to Philip, January 31, 1579; AGSE 934, #58.

29. Philip shared Zúñiga's assessment of Gregory's political bias. In 1581, the king complained to one of his ministers that the pope refused to help pay for the suppression of the Dutch revolt, because he did not mind seeing Philip lose some of his states. Parker, *Philip II,* 3d ed. (Chicago, 1995), pp. 57–58.

30. Zúñiga to Philip, April 18, 1579; AGSE 934, #86.

31. Zúñiga to Philip, April 18, 1579; AGSE 934, #87.

32. Philip appointed Olivares as ambassador to Rome in 1580, but due to his various duties he would be unable to take up his post until 1582. During the interim a local Spanish churchman, Abad Briceño, ran the embassy with help from Zúñiga in Naples.

33. *Diccionario de historia de España,* ed. Germán de Bleiberg, 2d ed., 3 vols. (Madrid, 1967–1979), Vol. II, p. 295. For a full description of Olivares' illustrious son, see J. H. Elliott, *The Count-Duke of Olivares: The Statesman in an Age of Decline* (New Haven, 1986).

blood in the king's name. During his tenure in Rome (1582–1591) the Spanish embassy once again became a lightning rod for papal wrath; at one point Pope Sixtus V threatened him with excommunication and expulsion from Rome. Yet, like all Spanish ambassadors, Olivares started with the best of intentions. En route to his new posting he wrote an optimistic letter to Philip, promising to cement firm relations between the king and the pope, and to guard against any *novedades* occurring.[34] In both respects he would be disappointed, and his own haughtiness would often be to blame.

Throughout Olivares' time in Rome, and indeed through the last twenty years of Philip's reign, their main source of conflict with the papacy was its policies toward France. Late sixteenth-century popes, who recognized the decline of papal political power, sought to establish some degree of independence by maintaining a balance between Spain and France.[35] This strategy, of course, exasperated Philip and his ministers, who expected unqualified support against the French, which they rarely received. Philip's instructions to Olivares in May 1582 exemplified the Spanish attitude. The previous year Gregory had sent a new nuncio to France with the specific mission of preventing a French-Spanish war.[36] Philip ordered his new ambassador to disabuse Gregory of his illusions concerning France, which deserved no pity. The French were liars, who abetted rebels and heretics; they had deceived the pope with pious words, while plotting against him; they had deliberately stirred up trouble in various regions, including the Mediterranean, which posed a direct threat to Italy as well as the rest of Christendom. Gregory would thus be fully justified to turn against France, while continued neutrality could not be so rationalized.[37] The overall message was clear: Gregory would be a fool not to side with Spain against France.

Olivares charged into Rome, eager to carry out his assignment. His initial encounters with Pope Gregory were positive, perhaps because they did not talk business.[38] During his first official audience, however, Olivares started in. The first thing he said to the pope was exactly what Philip had told him to say, word for word, about the nefarious French. Unfortunately Gregory did not respond by immediately declaring war on France; instead, he expressed sorrow at the state of world affairs, and claimed he wished for peace above all.[39] The pope and his councilors also seemed to

34. Olivares to Philip, May 19, 1582; AGSE 943, #127.
35. A. D. Wright, *The Early Modern Papacy: From the Council of Trent to the French Revolution, 1564–1789* (London, 2000), pp. 13–15.
36. Pastor, *History of the Popes,* Vol. XIX, pp. 537–38.
37. Philip to Olivares, May 6, 1582; AGSE 942, unnumbered.
38. Olivares to Philip, June 11, 1582; AGSE 942, unnumbered.
39. Olivares to Philip, June 18, 1582; AGSE 943, #40.

be convinced that King Henry III of France genuinely wanted peace as well, whatever the Spaniards might say.[40] This was obviously not the response Olivares had hoped for. In his first few months in Rome, he also noted some disturbing signs. For one thing, the Vatican court seemed to be full of young French nobles, whose intentions were difficult to determine.[41] The ambassador also heard unsettling rumors that the pope might actually be planning a military venture in aid of the French king, or at least French cardinals and their allies were so advising him. Olivares was not sure what to make of this rumor, although anything was possible, given "the mad ideas which the French contemplate."[42] In any case, Olivares realized his task would not be so easy.

In the following years, as Olivares learned more about Italy, his uneasiness would grow. By the early 1580s, the pro-Spanish sentiment Lepanto had inspired among Italians had greatly faded, while resentment of Spanish power increased.[43] Olivares evidently noticed this trend. In 1583, he wrote an unusual number of cautionary letters to Philip, similar to those Vargas and other ambassadors had written over the years. In February, for example, he warned that if war broke out between Spain and France, "those [Italians] who envy Your Majesty's greatness" might fight on the French side; and even if they did not actively aid France, some (like the Venetians) would love to see Spain "occupied" by war, forgetting that Philip was Christendom's "only defender" against heresy.[44] A few months later, Olivares reported a conversation with Pope Gregory, in which the ambassador stated that Italy was dangerously combustible: "it is full of foreigners and unquiet people who desire *novedades* in all of the states of Italy."[45] Soon afterward Olivares alerted Philip that Duke Alfonso d'Este of Ferrara had been acting suspiciously lately, which worried the ambassador, because trouble in Ferrara could easily lead to "a great opportunity for a French invasion and revolts in Italy."[46] And a few months after that, Olivares relayed reports that the Venetian government seemed to have been cozying up to the French recently; in addition, the current Venetian *Signoria* was full of young and restless types, the kind who favored *novedades*.[47]

40. Olivares to Philip, June 25, 1582; AGSE 943, #36.
41. Olivares to Philip, July 23, 1582; AGSE 943, #45.
42. Olivares to Philip, November 8, 1582; AGSE 942, unnumbered.
43. Angelantonio Spagnoletti, "La visione dell'Italia e degli stati italiani nell'età di Filippo II," in *Felipe II (1527–1598): Europa y la Monarquía Católica*, ed. José Martínez Millán, 3 vols. (Madrid, 1998), Vol. I, Part II, pp. 895–96.
44. Olivares to Philip, February 28, 1583; AGSE 944, #48.
45. Olivares to Philip, June 19, 1583; AGSE 944, #88.
46. Olivares to Philip, July 13, 1583; AGSE 944, #95.
47. Olivares to Philip, November 22, 1583; AGSE 944, #119.

Obviously, Olivares had become jumpy. It is not clear if anything other than the generally chaotic situation of Europe made Olivares so apprehensive at this particular time. Civil war wracked France, the Low Countries burned, and the Turks were once again threatening in the eastern Mediterranean; but Olivares specifically worried about Italy. So did Philip. In August 1583, the king wrote to Olivares as follows:

> You know the desire I have that the calm and quiet of Italy should always be conserved, and the orders I have given so that you and all my ministers should procure this, and thus you should not fail to inform me of anything which occurs to disturb it. I have recently come to understand that in certain parts of Italy the ancient names of Guelfs and Ghibellines have started to be revived by fickle types, who may be [just] the first. . . . it is known what harm and damage these bandits have caused that province in the past, [so] report all this to His Holiness most urgently [so that he should oppose them].[48]

Philip concluded by insisting that "those who wish to introduce this *novedad*" must be crushed, and the pope must help. This is an odd letter in several ways. Firstly, in the midst of fighting worldwide campaigns (and three weeks after the death of Philip's three-year-old daughter), the revival of an irrelevant political party in Italy seems like an unimportant detail for the king to be worrying about—and yet he clearly did. Second, the chance of Italy being harmed by a revival of the old medieval conflict of Guelfs versus Ghibellines (those loyal to the pope versus those loyal to the Holy Roman Emperor) should have been nil, particularly under a "pax hispanica." Yet Philip felt threatened enough by the very possibility that he instructed his ambassador to deal with it immediately. Third, if a "Guelf" party really existed in Italy at this late date, why would the pope want to destroy it?[49] The internal illogic of this demand seems to have escaped Philip. All he cared about was to prevent any *novedades* in Italy, and he fully expected the pope to comply.

Novedades, nonetheless, happened constantly, and the next major one to happen was the death of Gregory XIII in April 1585. On hearing the news, Philip expressed sadness, and sent the usual instructions to Olivares about the need for a quick conclave, and for the election of a pope who was not French or one of their supporters.[50] His wish was granted, but he

48. Philip to Olivares, August 29, 1583; AGSE 944, #162.
49. Leopold von Ranke wrote that in this period "the parties of Guelf and Ghibelline still subsisted in fact, though not in name." *The Popes of Rome: Their Ecclesiastical and Political History,* trans. Sarah Austin (London, 1866), p. 172.
50. Philip to Olivares, April 24, 1585; AGSE 946, #168.

did not get an ideal pope either. Felice Peretti, Pope Sixtus V, would become famous for "the power of his mind and the strength of his will."[51] In particular, Sixtus refused to be dictated to by the king of Spain. He shared many of Philip's goals, such as Church reform and the elimination of heresy, but he fiercely defended his independence and often opposed Philip's policies.[52] Their disagreements over European power politics would be especially sharp: the question of how to handle England and France nearly caused a rupture between Rome and Madrid.

Olivares soon detected dangerous signs of willfulness in the new pope. A few months after the election, the ambassador expressed concern that Sixtus had inflated ideas about papal authority over all Christian princes. Worse, the pope seemed determined to prove that he was not overly dependent on Spanish power.[53] This may have been a case of protesting too much, since by the 1580s the Papal States had in fact become greatly dependent on the Spanish empire for military protection, patronage, and even food.[54] But Olivares rarely felt secure about having the pope on a leash (although he clearly would have liked to do so). He did attempt to guide Sixtus onto the right path; in one of his first audiences, he declared that the pope "had to conserve the peace of Italy, and negotiate with the princes of Italy without any *novedades,* in such a way that none of them becomes jealous of another, nor have occasion for dissatisfaction."[55] He thus tried to indoctrinate the pope into the Spanish worldview. But Sixtus did not like being lectured to, and often became angry as a result.

From the beginning, Sixtus and Philip each had definite ideas about how the other should be doing his job. For his part, the pope had the temerity to advise Philip on how to govern Spain.[56] He also urged the king to wield his power in some grand military venture. Olivares had to decline several invitations to launch a new offensive against the Turks, or to besiege the Protestant citadel of Geneva.[57] The pope and the Spaniards agreed, however, that it was finally time to do something decisive about Queen Elizabeth of England. For years Philip had resisted

51. Pastor, *History of the Popes,* Vol. XXI, p. 50.
52. Enrique García Hernán, "La curia romana, Felipe II y Sixto V," *Hispania Sacra* 46 (1994), pp. 644–46.
53. Olivares to Philip, June 24, 1585; AGSE 946, #54.
54. Thomas James Dandelet, *Spanish Rome 1500–1700* (New Haven, 2001), pp. 72–87.
55. Olivares to Philip, June 30, 1585; AGSE 946, #53.
56. José Ignacio Tellechea Idígoras, *El Papado y Felipe II: Colección de breves Pontificios,* 2 Vols. (Madrid, 2000), Vol. II, pp. xii–xiii, 117–19. In a papal brief of August 1586, Sixtus suggested that Philip should steer a middle course between never listening to his ministers and consulting them on everything.
57. Olivares to Philip, July 28, 1585; AGSE 946, #104.

papal pleas to invade England, but in August 1585 Elizabeth signed the Treaty of Nonsuch, which committed her to providing military assistance to the Dutch revolt against Spain. A few months later, Sir Francis Drake landed in northern Spain and wreaked havoc for ten days. Philip could not ignore such blatant acts of aggression, and so the Enterprise of England began in earnest.[58] The problem was, who would pay for it? Philip demanded that Sixtus help defray the enormous cost of an invasion; Sixtus agreed to contribute the extraordinary sum of one million ducats, but insisted that he would not pay until Spanish soldiers actually landed in England. Thus began three very stressful years for the Spanish ambassador in Rome.

What should have been an enthusiastic partnership between Spain and the papacy was marred by a basic distrust: right up to the departure of the Armada, Sixtus did not really believe Philip would go through with the invasion, while the Spaniards suspected that the pope had no intention of honoring his financial pledge. On December 22, 1586, for example, Olivares reported that Sixtus had promised to pay, but asked repeatedly if Philip truly intended to mount an assault.[59] A week later the pope embarrassed Olivares in public, by complaining loudly (within earshot of a French ambassador) that a million ducats was not enough to satisfy the king of Spain.[60] Meanwhile, the Spaniards had their own doubts about the pope's wholehearted support. In February 1587 Philip instructed Olivares to assure Sixtus that he was not planning on becoming king of England, but instead would install his eldest daughter Isabel on the throne, and whomever she married would be king.[61] The implication is that the Spaniards perceived Sixtus to be fearful or jealous at the prospect of Philip gaining another crown. A month later Olivares expressed his concerns explicitly. Barring a miracle, he fumed, Sixtus would never actually pay; furthermore, among the College of Cardinals "There are many who do not favor this business [of England] and close their eyes to Your Majesty's rights, and to the conversion of that kingdom, and to the benefits that would follow from your rule, because of the malice with which they view Your Majesty's greatness. The hostile [cardinals] lose no time in speaking against the campaign, and our enemies seek to impede it."[62]

58. Geoffrey Parker, *The Grand Strategy of Philip II*, pp. 175–77.
59. AGSE 949, #40. Olivares also expressed doubt that the pope could keep the Enterprise secret; he advised Philip to move quickly, because French spies in Rome would quickly learn about the plan. He was right to worry; see Parker, *The Grand Strategy of Philip II*, chap. 7 ("The Worst-kept Secret in Europe?").
60. Olivares to Philip, December 30, 1586; AGSE 949, #6.
61. Philip to Olivares, February 11, 1587; AGSE 949, #15.
62. Olivares to Philip, March 23, 1587; AGSE 949, #28.

Once again the Spanish ambassador in Rome acted like a man in enemy territory, at what should have been a secure moment. Officially, Spain and the Papacy had joined forces in a holy war, but the alliance was hardly firm.

Nevertheless the Enterprise proceeded. The execution of Mary Queen of Scots in February 1587 spurred Philip's efforts.[63] He wrote to Olivares of his sorrow over the death of Mary, who could have been instrumental in restoring Catholicism in England; now, the Enterprise was doubly necessary. The ambassador must hasten to get money out of Sixtus.[64] Olivares acknowledged Philip's orders, but suggested that he should not appear too desperate, as that might warn Spain's enemies of imminent danger. He also encouraged the king to quicken war preparations, which would improve his chances of loosening papal purse strings.[65] Unfortunately for Olivares, the Spanish war machine was sluggish at best. Drake made his famous raid on Cadiz that same month, the treasure ships from America failed to appear, and delay piled on delay. Sixtus raged at the Spaniards; in August 1587, English intelligence reported that the pope had accused Philip of being a liar and a coward.[66] If the English, who did not have any representatives in either Rome or Spain, knew the extent of the pope's displeasure, one can only imagine what Olivares experienced.

If the situation in Rome was tense in 1587, the following year was unbearable. As the months passed, and scraps of information dribbled in about the Armada's progress (or lack of it), Olivares suffered both from the agony of suspense and from the pope's sharp tongue. In February, for example, Olivares complained that the pope constantly criticized the tardiness of Spanish military operations in "outrageous" terms, especially considering that Sixtus had no martial experience whatsoever.[67] Meanwhile the ambassador still sought to wheedle money out of the pope, but Sixtus refused to part with a penny until troops had actually disembarked in England, saying openly that he still doubted whether Philip truly intended to invade.[68] Nor was Sixtus reassured by the fact that Philip neglected to send updates to Rome for months at a time. In June Olivares wrote a delicately worded letter asking when he might expect any news, as

63. Garrett Mattingly, *The Armada* (reprint, Boston, 1987), pp. 50–51.
64. Philip to Olivares, March 31, 1587; AGSE 949, #35.
65. Olivares to Philip, April 23, 1587; AGSE 949, #46. Olivares also warned that many in Rome still worried about the fate of the English throne, and that arguments over this issue could lead to *novedades*.
66. Felipe Fernández-Armesto, *The Spanish Armada* (Oxford, 1988), p. 75.
67. Olivares to Philip, February 6, 1588; AGSE 950, #19. Olivares wrote (in code) that Sixtus talked as if being a military commander was the same as being an abbot in a monastery.
68. Olivares to Philip, March 2, 1588; AGSE 950, #33.

the entire Roman court was most anxious for it, and the pope was "upset" about being ignored; perhaps someone had forgotten to send letters to Rome, or else they had been lost in the mail?[69] Five days later he dispatched a blunter missive to the state secretary Juan de Idiáquez, saying that Sixtus was "terribly offended" that Philip had not written for so long, which made asking for money difficult.[70] When this had no effect, Olivares spoke plainly to the king: "I am extremely worried, it has been thirty-nine days since the Armada [supposedly] embarked and we have had no news. . . . His Holiness is determined not to reimburse us one escudo until word arrives."[71]

What Olivares had no way to know, of course, was that the Armada had been delayed by a combination of ill chance and incompetence. The inevitable time lag between events and notification also complicated matters: letters could take weeks in transit, if they arrived at all.[72] Thus Olivares was not able to inform Sixtus about weather delays experienced by the Armada in late June until the first week of August.[73] Twelve days later, unaware that the Spanish fleet had already been defeated, Olivares wrote Philip thanking him for the great news of the Armada's departure—although he also reported that even at this date Sixtus still suspected the whole thing to be a sham![74] Around the same time (erroneous) reports came in that Francis Drake had been captured, and yet Sixtus remained skeptical.[75] Even so, the pope was obviously just as tense as the Spaniards: on September 5, Olivares informed Philip that Sixtus had recently been suffering stomach pains, and had even vomited in bed.[76] Keeping Madrid updated on the pope's health was a regular part of the ambassador's duties, but this particular letter no doubt had greater significance; everyone was on edge.

Then, slowly, the scale of the disaster became apparent. The first inklings came in mid-September, which caused "the distress which Your Majesty can imagine."[77] Doggedly, Olivares continued to demand that Sixtus pay the

69. Olivares to Philip, June 13, 1588; AGSE 950, #112.
70. Olivares to Idiáquez, June 18, 1588; AGSE 950, #116.
71. Olivares to Philip, July 8, 1588; AGSE 950, #147.
72. Parker, *The Grand Strategy of Philip II*, chap. 2.
73. Document entitled "What the Count of Olivares said to His Holiness on His Majesty's behalf," August 7, 1588; AGSE 950, #154.
74. Olivares to Philip, August 19, 1588; AGSE 950, #172. The same day Olivares wrote to Idiáquez a bitter letter, complaining of the pope's cruelty, as he continually abused the ambassador verbally (AGSE 950, #174).
75. Mattingly, *The Armada*, pp. 358–60.
76. Olivares to Philip, September 5, 1588; AGSE 950, #164.
77. Olivares to Philip, September 16, 1588; ASE 950, #185.

million ducats he had promised.[78] But by October the truth could not be denied: the English Enterprise had failed. All that remained was to apportion blame. Olivares reported that evil tongues were wagging in Rome, some castigating the duke of Medina Sidonia for not following orders, others insinuating that the duke of Parma had never intended to leave the Netherlands with his army. All of them, Olivares angrily declared, were ingrates.[79] And what of the pope? He expressed his disappointment by being coldly angry.[80] As the ambassador wrote in November, "for many days the pope had not said a word about England, and takes care not to mention to me the return of the Armada [to Spain] . . . instead he talks of lesser matters."[81] The pope also definitively refused to produce the money he had promised. To add insult to injury, Italian politics suddenly flared up again: the duke of Savoy invaded the Marquisate of Saluzzo, on the French border, with papal connivance.[82] A senior cardinal warned the ambassador that either the French or the Protestants of Geneva might well get involved in this conflict. Simultaneously, the dukes of Ferrara and Mantua began squabbling, and rumors surfaced that the latter had offered his services to France. "Your Majesty cannot imagine the turbulence of all these princes," Olivares wrote, obviously frustrated with the whole situation.[83]

Unfortunately for Olivares, yet another crisis was brewing, this time in France. For years, the fate of France obsessed both Philip and the papacy. In 1584, the duke of Anjou, next in line for the Crown of France, died, leaving Henry of Navarre as the heir presumptive. But Henry was a Protestant, and the prospect of a heretic becoming king of France galvanized French Catholics and Philip alike. The leaders of the French Catholic nobility formed the Catholic League, dedicated to preventing Henry's ascendancy, and received support from Spain.[84] Naturally, Philip

78. Olivares to Philip, September 26, 1588; AGSE 950, #274.
79. Olivares to Philip, October 29, 1588; AGSE 950, #226. Olivares took particular care to defend the duke of Medina Sidonia, who was his cousin. Peter Pierson, *Commander of the Armada: The Seventh Duke of Medina Sidonia* (New Haven, 1989), p. 175.
80. Pastor writes that the haughty behavior Olivares displayed toward the pope at this time indicated "how little suited Olivares was to deal with a man like Sixtus V." *History of the Popes*, Vol. XXI, p. 272.
81. Olivares to Philip, November 29, 1588; AGSE 950, #257.
82. Pastor, *History of the Popes*, Vol. XXI, p. 303 n. 1.
83. Olivares to Philip, November 6, 1588; AGSE 950, #242. Philip's distress was also evident. He wrote to Olivares about the importance of convincing the pope and the other Italian princes that he had nothing to do with the duke of Savoy's actions, for "the movement of arms in Italy could not be worse for anyone than for me, especially at this time." Philip to Olivares, November 1, 1588; Ministerio de Asuntos Exteriores, Archivo General, Embajada a la Santa Sede, Legajo 38, #334.
84. See De Lamar Jensen, *Diplomacy and Dogmatism: Bernardino de Mendoza and the French Catholic League* (Cambridge, Mass., 1964).

expected the unqualified backing of the papacy in this effort, but he did not always get it. Sixtus distrusted Philip's motives in meddling with French internal affairs, and was more willing to compromise in order to bring peace to France. This philosophical difference would lead to the worst conflict yet between Sixtus and the Spanish ambassador.

Early on, Sixtus and Philip seemed to be in agreement about France, and more specifically, about Henry of Navarre. In September 1585 Sixtus excommunicated Henry and declared him ineligible for the throne. This pleased Philip, but he and the pope disagreed about whom to support among the various factions that rived France. The king backed the Guises, the ambitious noble family that led the Catholic League, but Sixtus disliked them, fearing that they might be too independent.[85] As constant warfare ripped France apart, the Spaniards and the pope argued over what to do. In 1587, for instance, Olivares and Sixtus had a number of heated discussions. In the spring of that year the "War of the Three Henrys" broke out among the main contestants for power in France; essentially, anarchy ruled.[86] On June 30, Olivares reported that the pope had recently thrown a temper tantrum, abusing his servants and smashing plates—not a unique occurrence, he added, but on this occasion it was more violent than usual.[87] Olivares noted that a meeting between the pope and the French ambassador seemed to have triggered this scene. The next day in an audience with Sixtus, the pope revealed the source of his anger: the Guises. King Henry III, the pope declared, was jealous of the Guises, and the hostility between them threatened the Catholic cause in France. Olivares answered that he understood the antagonism between Henry III and the Guises to be a deception. Whether he really believed this is not clear, but he evidently sought to deflect the pope's anger away from Philip's chosen allies in France. A few months later Olivares wrote that Sixtus displayed desperation and confusion about France, emotions which he shared.[88]

In the following few years, the French situation deteriorated even further. In December 1588, King Henry III had the duke of Guise assassinated, and then was himself fatally stabbed in August 1589. On his deathbed, the king named Henry of Navarre as his heir. Henry began to win supporters among French Catholics, and also won a number of battles against his enemies. Henry was an extraordinary leader, and many perceived him to be France's greatest hope, both as a healer and as a man

85. Ibid., pp. 71–72.
86. R. J. Knecht, *The French Civil Wars, 1562–1598* (London, 2000), pp. 227–31.
87. Olivares to Philip, June 30, 1587; AGSE 949, #69.
88. Olivares to Philip, October 30, 1587; AGSE 949, #101.

who maintained his independence from the king of Spain. This perception extended to Italy as well as to France: in October 1589, the Republic
of Venice recognized Henry as the legitimate king of France. Both Sixtus
and the Spaniards knew perfectly well that the Venetians had been motivated by resentment of Spanish power.[89] The pope and his curia
denounced Venice, but the Spaniards suspected that Rome secretly
applauded. Philip, on being informed that several French cardinals had
recognized Henry as heir, blamed the pope.[90] Then in January 1590 an
emissary from Henry, Duke Francis of Luxemburg, arrived in Rome to
negotiate papal support for his master. To Olivares' horror, Sixtus agreed
to listen to him. The clash that followed nearly caused a total rupture in
Spanish-papal relations.

Olivares, leading a war party of pro-Spanish cardinals, confronted Sixtus with a demand for Luxemburg's expulsion.[91] Sixtus refused, at which
point the fireworks really began. In late February, during a papal audience, Olivares claimed that Philip did not want to tell the pope what to
do, but then he proceeded to do just that. He more than suggested that
Sixtus was being stupid, as well as forgetful of his religious duty to oppose
Henry.[92] Olivares dared to threaten the pope, implying that Philip might
resort to violence if Sixtus did not come to his senses.[93] The pope
responded with rage, and the entire Vatican court trembled. A Venetian
ambassador reported that Sixtus and the Spanish ambassador passed an
"extremely distressing morning," full of vituperation. The pope thundered at Olivares that Philip, who had signed a peace treaty with the
Turks, had no right to criticize him on religious grounds.[94]

But Olivares did not flinch. In another face-to-face meeting with Sixtus,
he threatened to make a public protest if the pope did not immediately
expel Luxemburg, condemn Henry of Navarre, and excommunicate any
French Catholics who supported the heretic prince. In the face of these
demands Sixtus snapped completely, accusing Philip of trying to make
himself pope, and threatening Olivares with excommunication, expulsion from Rome, and even execution.[95] (So much for a "pax hispanica.")
But if this frightened Olivares, he did not show it. Later that week,
"sources" told him that the pope rebuffed everyone who tried to talk with

89. Pastor, *History of the Popes*, Vol. XXI, pp. 332–39.
90. Henry Kamen, *Philip of Spain* (New Haven, 1997), p. 296.
91. Pastor, *History of the Popes*, Vol. XXI, p. 344.
92. Olivares to Philip, February 28, 1590; printed in *Sixte-Quint*, ed. Baron de Hübner, Vol. III (Paris, 1870), pp. 372–76.
93. Pastor, *History of the Popes*, Vol. XXI, p. 346.
94. Alberto Badoer to the Doge, March 3, 1590; Hübner, *Sixte-Quint*, Vol. III, pp. 376–78.
95. Pastor, *History of the Popes*, Vol. XXI, p. 350.

him, and that when eating meals he spoke not a word to anyone; according to Olivares, "these are two very good signs."[96] Convinced he could still batter the pope into submission, he made his most serious threat yet: if Sixtus did not relent, Spain would withdraw its obedience to the papacy.[97] It is not clear if he was authorized to make such a declaration, but it seems unlikely; other Spanish ambassadors, as well as Philip, had always made a point of not making this particular threat. Olivares may have blurted it out in the heat of the moment. In any case Sixtus remained obdurate.

Whether or not his ambassador had overstepped his bounds, Philip decided Olivares had to go.[98] Although he supported his ambassador's positions, Olivares' harsh negotiating tactics had become destructive. Anti-Spanish sentiment in Rome had risen to fever pitch: people were unfavorably comparing Philip to the Emperor Nero for his arrogance.[99] So, for the third time in his reign, the king replaced his ambassador in Rome in hopes of improving relations. This time he chose Don Antonio Folch y Cardona, the fourth duke of Sessa, who had a reputation for composure and flexibility.[100] Philip sent the young and gifted Sessa to Rome with the explicit mission of winning over the pope with persuasion rather than force. He instructed the new ambassador to be gentle yet firm. Sixtus was wrong to reject the king's advice on policy; popes had always sought council from secular princes, especially in matters as grave as these. The loss of France to heresy was too terrible an outcome to contemplate, and so must be prevented not with words and weeping, but with action.[101] But most important of all, the pope must never do anything to help Henry of Navarre become King of France.

Sessa arrived in Rome on June 21, 1590. He had the customary first audience with Sixtus to introduce himself, and then two days later he got down to business. Olivares accompanied him to the pope's chambers, but Sessa did all the talking, doing his best to obey Philip's orders and "attempt the road of gentle methods [*el camino de medios suaves*] with His Holiness."[102] If Henry and his heretic followers prevailed, he emphasized, not only would France be irreparably harmed, but so too all of Christendom, and particularly Italy and the Holy See. On the other hand, should

96. Olivares to Philip, March 5, 1590; Hübner, *Sixte-Quint,* Vol. III., pp. 378–82.
97. Pastor, *History of the Popes,* Vol. XXI, p. 353.
98. Olivares would actually stay in Rome until November 1591, acting as advisor to the new ambassador, before leaving for his new post as viceroy of Sicily.
99. Dandelet, Spanish Rome, pp. 86–87.
100. *Diccionario de historia de España,* Vol. III, p. 656.
101. Philip to Sessa, July 15, 1590; Hübner, *Sixte-Quint,* Vol. III, pp. 448–49.
102. Sessa to Philip, June 30, 1590; ibid., p. 459.

Sixtus save France from Henry, he would thereby gain eternal glory. Philip, Sessa declared, was ready, willing and able to assist the pope in such a noble and holy cause. Obviously the new ambassador attempted a different approach, and it was successful in that Sixtus did not shout at him—but the pope did not change his mind either. He still refused to condemn Henry's Catholic adherents, or proclaim Henry ineligible for the throne. In other words, Sessa's first shot missed.

The next few months continued to be fruitless for the Spaniards. "It is a great pity," Sessa wrote, "that His Holiness is so blind."[103] Philip used even stronger terms, warning that the pope was introducing extremely danger-ous *novedades* into an already precarious situation.[104] But Sixtus absolutely refused to let the Spaniards dictate policy. "We are not the slave of your king," he declared, "we do not owe him obedience, nor are we account-able to him for our actions. We are his father, and it is not the place of sons to give him their advice without being asked for it."[105] The Spanish diplomatic corps had met its match in imperiousness. Yet it cost the pope a great deal to be so immoveable: two weeks after making that statement he fell seriously ill, and a week after that he was dead.[106] Philip and his ambassadors sighed in relief, as many Italians noted.[107]

What they did not know, however, was that they were about to enter into a very strange two-year period in Spanish-papal relations. Spanish diplomacy was quite successful in replacing Sixtus with more malleable candidates, but this had to be done over and over. Between August 1590 and December 1592, there were no less than four papal elections: Urban VII (September 14–24, 1590), Gregory XIV (1590–1591), Inno-cent IX (October 29–December 30, 1591), and finally Clement VIII (1592–1605). This rapid turnover, of course, left Roman politics extremely unsettled, at a time when the Church needed a firm hand. The fate of France still hung in the balance, while Italy itself experi-enced a series of economic and social upheavals.[108] During this period the Spanish embassy oscillated between glee and despair, as one pope

103. Sessa to Philip, July 8, 1590; ibid., pp. 470–71.
104. Philip to Sessa, July 26, 1590; ibid., p. 494.
105. Sessa to Philip, August 7, 1590; quoted in Pastor, *History of the Popes*, Vol. XXI, p. 369.
106. Pastor writes that Sixtus's quarrels with the Spaniards hastened his death, and that the pope "fought like a hero for his convictions" (ibid., p. 373). Pastor, as I have mentioned before, seems to have had a certain anti-Spanish bias.
107. Tommaso Contarini, a Venetian ambassador in Madrid, stated that the Spaniards were "grateful" for the death of Sixtus. *Relazione* of 1593; *Relazioni di ambasciatori veneti al Senato*, ed. Luigi Firpo, 13 vols. (Turin, 1965–), Vol. VIII, pp. 881–82.
108. See *The European Crisis of the 1590s: Essays in Comparative History*, ed. Peter Clark (Lon-don, 1985), chaps. 8–9.

after another ascended the throne and died. For a while, the Spaniards had it all their way: the first three elections after Sixtus were practically stage-managed by the ambassadors.[109] The election of Pope Gregory XIV particularly pleased Philip and his ministers, as he was devoted to the Spanish cause.[110] More to the point, Gregory vehemently opposed Henry of Navarre, and had no interest in trying to reconvert Henry to Catholicism.[111]

During Gregory's one-year papacy, the Spanish ambassadors strutted confidently around Rome. Olivares boasted that Philip was the "absolute lord" of the Vatican court, where his every wish quickly came true.[112] He and Sessa double-teamed the pope, demanding money in support of the Catholic League. At first Gregory hesitated, seeing manifest danger to France, Italy, and all of Christendom on one side, but a strained bank account on the other.[113] He soon relented, however, and authorized a loan of 400,000 escudos for use in France.[114] Philip and his ambassadors exulted. But even so, not everything ran smoothly. As always, Philip warned that no *novedades* should be allowed in Italian politics.[115] But the seeds of a crisis appeared. Duke Alfonso II of Ferrara, old and childless, began to make noise about his successor. His nephew Cesare d'Este was next in line, but Alfonso did not like him, and neither did the Spaniards, and so they tried to win Gregory's permission to name an alternate successor.[116] Olivares worried that Philip might lose *reputación* if the proposal failed.[117] And in fact, a group of anti-Spanish cardinals blocked the proposition.[118] Gregory died before the matter could be settled, and the question of Ferrara would fester for the remainder of the decade.

Still, Spanish diplomacy enjoyed great success under Gregory; one modern historian describes Rome in this period as a "Spanish Avignon," so great was their influence over the papacy.[119] Unfortunately, Gregory did not last long. He died in October 1591, and considering the urgent need to get another amenable pope elected, Philip ordered Olivares to

109. The historian Tellechea Idígoras writes that Sessa and Olivares acted "impudently and provocatively and success smiled on them" when Pope Gregory XIV was elected. *El Papado y Felipe II,* Vol. II, p. xiv.
110. Pastor, *History of the Popes,* Vol. XXII, pp. 354–55.
111. Michael Wolfe, *The Conversion of Henry IV* (Cambridge, Mass, 1993), p. 95.
112. D. Luigi Càstano, *Gregorio XIV (Niccolò Sfondrato) 1535–1591* (Milan, 1993), p. 375.
113. Sessa to Philip, March 2, 1591; AGSE 958, unnumbered.
114. Càstano, *Gregorio XIV,* pp. 402–3.
115. Philip to Olivares, January 22, 1591; AGSE 958, unnumbered.
116. Pastor, *History of the Popes,* Vol. XXII, pp. 379–80.
117. Olivares to Philip, July 5, 1591; AGSE 957, unnumbered.
118. Pastor, *History of the Popes,* Vol. XXII, p. 381.
119. Dandelet, *Spanish Rome,* pp. 87–89.

postpone his departure from Rome yet again. Gregory had pledged money and soldiers for the Catholic cause in France, and Philip instructed his ambassadors to head off any changes in papal policy. "I am certain," the king wrote to Sessa, "that while the Holy See is vacant you will prevent any *novedades* in the matter of the aid promised to [the Catholic League in] France."[120] Luck seemed to be with the Spaniards once again with the election of Innocent IX. In an audience with Sessa, Innocent declared his love and esteem of Philip, and praised the king's greatness, which protected the peace of Italy as well as all of Christendom.[121] How could things be any better? In November 1591 Olivares wrote a self-satisfied letter to Philip, saying that he no longer needed to delay his exit. He would leave content, he said, that Philip's *reputación* in Rome was greater than ever, and that all of the king's wishes would quickly be granted.[122] But he spoke too soon: a month later Innocent, too, was dead. Sessa lamented, "of all the universal misfortunes in Christendom, in my opinion the worst is having to advise Your Majesty so often of the deaths of popes."[123]

So in January 1592 Sessa and the Spanish faction once again campaigned to get a pope elected who shared their point of view about Henry of Navarre. This time the outcome proved an ambiguous victory for the Spaniards: the new pope, Clement VIII (Ippolito Aldobrandini), had been last on the king's list of acceptable candidates.[124] Philip and his ministers worried that Aldobrandini seemed too neutral on the question of the French throne. And over time, it would become apparent that they had badly underestimated how much Clement differed from Spanish opinions. Above all, Clement wanted to bring peace to France, but he also wanted to restore the balance of power in Europe.[125] Moreover, Clement (like Sixtus V) had strong opinions about the pope's prerogatives both as reform leader and as an Italian prince.[126] Arguments over jurisdiction and Church reform, which had always been a problem in Spanish-papal relations, increased in frequency and intensity under Clement. But the worst blow came in 1595, when the pope defied Spanish wishes and welcomed Henry of Navarre back into the Church.

120. Philip to Sessa, November 8, 1591; AGSE 958, unnumbered.
121. Sessa to Philip, December 22, 1591; AGSE 958, unnumbered.
122. Olivares to Philip, November 11, 1591; AGSE 957, unnumbered.
123. Sessa to Philip, December 30, 1591; AGSE 958, unnumbered.
124. See Agostino Borromeo, "España y el problema de la elección papal de 1592," *Cuadernos de investigación histórica* 2 (1978), pp. 175–200.
125. Hinajosa, *Los despachos de la diplomacia pontificia en España*, pp. 348–52.
126. Eric Cochrane describes Clement as a "psalm-chanting defender of the papacy's just territorial rights." *Italy 1530–1630*, p. 194.

From the beginning of his papacy, Clement had been courted by Henry's moderate French Catholic supporters.[127] The new pope also demonstrated a disturbing willingness to listen to these overtures, as well as political shrewdness. A few months after his election, Clement argued with Sessa that it would be to Philip's advantage to allow a reconverted Henry to become king of France, because he would thus lay to rest Italian fears that Philip had "other plans" for France. He also suggested that it would cost much less to support Henry than to oppose him.[128] These were very shrewd arguments: Clement was playing on Spanish fears about Italian resentments, as well as on Spain's perennial money problems. He neatly turned the tables on Philip and Sessa by suggesting that the king's opposition to Henry was actually hurting Spanish interests in Italy, thereby increasing fears and suspicions of Spanish power. Later that year Clement urged the Spaniards to join with him and other Italian princes in a defensive Italian League, "it seeming to him that it could not be bad for Your Majesty, who has always procured the peace and quiet of this province." The pope pointed out that if Spain joined this alliance, other powers (such as Venice) would be more likely to side with them and against France.[129] What Clement really wanted was a renewed war against the Turks.[130] He knew, however, that Philip's attentions were focused elsewhere, so again he jabbed at the Spanish sore spot, their paranoia about control of Italy. His suggestion that Philip might win back Venice was particularly crafty, since he knew how Venetian support for Henry must gall the Spaniards, in addition to which the pope was leaning toward Henry himself.

In July 1593 Henry raised the stakes by converting to Catholicism (for the second time), supposedly declaring, "Paris is worth a Mass!"[131] He still remained under a papal bull of excommunication, however, which had to be lifted if he was ever to be accepted as the legitimate king of France. For the next two years, Henry negotiated with Clement for absolution, battling both French and Roman politics.[132] In August 1593 Henry sent the duke of Nevers, one of his French Catholic supporters, to Rome for this purpose. Spanish diplomacy was slow to respond to this turn of events. For the last several years, Philip had been advocating what seemed to him

127. Wolfe, *Conversion of Henry IV*, pp. 110–11.
128. Sessa to Philip, April 23, 1592; AGSE 959, unnumbered.
129. Sessa to Philip, December 22, 1592; AGSE 959, unnumbered.
130. Hinajosa, *Los despachos de la diplomacia pontificia en España*, p. 352.
131. Most historians believe this to be an apocryphal story, perhaps invented by Henry's Catholic League opponents. Frederic J. Baumgartner, *France in the Sixteenth Century* (New York, 1995), p. 228.
132. Wolfe, *Conversion of Henry IV*, pp. 172–73.

the perfect solution to the French succession problem: to place his eldest daughter Isabel on the throne. As the granddaughter of King Henry II of Valois, Isabel did indeed have a claim, but French law and French anti-Spanish sentiment blocked Philip's plan.[133] Philip was still hopeful, but Henry's conversion, moving him one step closer to the throne, apparently came as a shock. Two months after the event, Sessa wrote to Philip to express the pope's (and his own) amazement that the king had not yet sent word of his reaction. Sessa had been making excuses on Philip's behalf, but the ambassador desperately needed instructions. Nevers was in Rome, and Sessa did not know what to do about it. As he wrote,

> Your Majesty should not marvel at what I write about the *reputación* we lose here due to our delays. I would not be fulfilling my duty as servant and loyal vassal if I were silent or spoke with gilded words. It is certain that on this business depends whether Your Majesty's greatness will be esteemed or disrespected in Italy and beyond, and although I suspect [our image] seems great Your Majesty may believe in this case it is not. . . . in short the pope and everybody else are watching for what we will do, and they clearly say they will believe only what they see.[134]

Once again the Spanish ambassador in Rome complained that lack of direction from Madrid was damaging the king's interests; Sessa feared that Italians would interpret Spanish indecision as weakness. Sessa's suggestion that the view from Madrid was too rosy is especially revealing: as the man on the spot, he knew better than his masters.

Nonetheless no instructions were forthcoming. Sessa's only comfort came from the fact that the duke of Nevers suffered from a similar lack of direction.[135] At the end of November 1593 Sessa reported that the Frenchman's negotiations had stalled, but Spanish diplomacy had nothing to do with it. Sessa seemed lost: the pope asked him constantly whether Philip had sent any word, "and I don't know what to tell him." Even worse, the Venetian ambassador in Rome had been urging Clement to absolve Henry, "warning that otherwise it could lead to schism not just in France but also in Italy, because the majority of Italian princes and cardinals are of the same opinion."[136] From Sessa's perspective, Spanish diplomacy was losing the battle for the hearts and minds of the Italian powers on the French question. The Venetian ambassador, Giovanni Gritti, agreed with

133. Kamen, *Philip of Spain,* pp. 296–99.
134. Sessa to Philip, September 27, 1593; AGSE 961, unnumbered.
135. Sessa to Philip, November 4, 1593; AGSE 961, unnumbered.
136. Sessa to Philip, November 29, 1593; AGSE 961, unnumbered.

him. According to Gritti, the Vatican court was increasingly resentful of Spanish arrogance, resulting in a resurgence of the French faction; in addition, the pope, who normally "esteemed" the Spanish nation, was now angry at Philip's "oppressive" policies in France.[137]

The situation continued to slip further out of Spanish hands. In July 1593 Henry solemnly forswore Protestantism, paving the way for his coronation in February 1594. Meanwhile another delegation from Henry came to Rome, and enjoyed much greater success.[138] Henry then declared war on Spain, in part to demonstrate that his conversion to Catholicism had not made him a Spanish tool.[139] By 1595 the momentum behind his negotiations in Rome had become unstoppable. Sessa made several last-ditch efforts, including attempting to bribe cardinals and lying about the Catholic League's strength, but to no avail.[140] In a short and stark letter to the count of Fuentes, governor of the Netherlands, Sessa warned that it would be a terrible blow to Spanish *reputación* if the pope absolved Henry.[141] That same week, it was done. Sessa issued a protest, which the pope ignored.[142] Philip and his ministers had been totally defeated.

The ties between Clement VIII and Henry IV of France (as he now was known) would grow stronger, even as Philip II succumbed to old age and sickness.[143] From 1594 on, the king of Spain weakened visibly.[144] The entire Spanish empire seemed enervated as well. In the Netherlands and France, Philip's ministers tried to disentangle themselves from war. Italy, meanwhile, rippled with unsettling events.[145] In October 1597 Sessa dis-

137. *Relazione* of 1595; *Le relazioni degli ambasciatori veneti al Senato*, Series II, Vol. IV, pp. 380–81 and 425–26.
138. Wolfe, *Conversion of Henry IV*, p. 173.
139. Knecht, *The French Civil Wars*, p. 272.
140. Pastor once more exhibits his anti-Spanish tendencies, writing that "all the effrontery and threats of the Spaniards had no other effect than to increase [Clement's] desire to put an end to their tyrannical influence in Rome" (*History of the Popes*, Vol. XXIII, p. 119).
141. Sessa to Fuentes, September 19, 1595; Instituto de Valencia de Don Juan, Envío 9, Caja 15, #367.
142. Pastor, *History of the Popes*, Vol. XXIII, pp. 134–35.
143. Dandelet describes this period as one of "transition," when Spanish influence in Rome waned, albeit "temporarily" (*Spanish Rome*, pp. 94–95).
144. See the recent description of Philip's deterioration, as seen by papal ambassadors in Madrid: J. Ignacio Tellechea Idígoras, *El ocaso de un rey: Felipe II visto desde la nunciatura de Madrid 1594–1598* (Madrid, 2001).
145. In 1595, a Spanish doctor of law residing in Rome sent the duke of Sessa an apocalyptic treatise, which pointed to the combined threat of Henry IV and the Turks as signs of the End Times. This work reflects the general unease of the time, as well as a dialogue amongst intellectuals about the crisis and nature of the Spanish empire. John A. Marino, "An Anti-Campanellan Vision on the Spanish Monarchy and the Crisis of 1595," in *A Renaissance of Conflicts: Visions and Revisions of Law and Society in Italy and Spain*, ed. John A. Marino and Thomas Kuehn (Toronto, 2004), pp. 367–93.

patched an odd letter describing the actions of Virginio Orsini, duke of Bracchiano and scion of an ancient Roman noble family. Orsini, according to Sessa, had been raising troops in Tuscany, with the intention of "molesting" the Papal States, perhaps with clandestine aid from other Italian princes. Fortunately Orsini was killed before he could cause any real damage. This minor tussle might have gone unnoticed, but the story takes an unexpected twist: the pope shared intelligence with Sessa which suggested that Henry IV of France had abetted Orsini's adventure, and the real aim had been "to do damage to Your Majesty's states in Italy."[146] The truth of this claim is not clear, nor is it evident what Clement's motives might have been in sharing this information. Nonetheless it illustrates why Sessa acted as if he were under siege. Nor was he the only Spanish minister in Italy who felt threatened. In November 1597 Juan Fernández de Velasco, the governor of Milan, warned Philip, "there is a general desire in Italy to expel the Spaniards. Our salvation can only lie in more troops, money, and above all dispatch."[147] These words echo those of Francisco de Vargas in 1560, and every Spanish ambassador in Rome since. But there were no troops or money to spare. Then at this very moment, a new crisis in Ferrara erupted.

Much like Iñigo de Mendoza in Venice (see chapter 1), Sessa was surprised and alarmed by the Ferrara affair. He alerted Philip to the new problem on November 7, 1597, a day before Mendoza. News of Cesare d'Este's seizure of Ferrara had arrived on November 1, and although the pope was sick in bed at the time he leapt up, summoned the College, and began war preparations. Meanwhile the Venetian ambassador in Rome, Giovanni Dolfin, sought out Sessa to warn of the possible consequences if Philip did not do something "to preserve the peace and quiet of Italy." Sessa asked who the Venetians preferred in control of Ferrara, but Dolfin gave an ambiguous response. "I deduced from his talk," Sessa wrote, "that although Venetians often dissimulate, they have little desire to see the Papal States grow any larger, besides which they possess a large part of the territory which has long been said to belong to the Ferrarese."[148] He guessed that Venice was inclined to support Cesare d'Este, evidently

146. Sessa to Philip, October 12, 1597; AGSE 969, unnumbered. The pope's source was an intercepted letter from Henry to the Turkish Sultan Mehmet III, which proposed an alliance against the "common enemy," Spain.
147. Quoted in Fernand Braudel, *The Mediterranean and the Mediterranean World in the Age of Philip II*, trans. Siân Reynolds, 2 vols. (New York, 1973), Vol. II, p. 1219. Velasco also warned that Clement "loves [Henry IV] as a son and a protégé" while "he has made clear in many conversations and circumstances the lack of goodwill he bears Your Majesty's affairs and his dissatisfaction at the greatness of your states."
148. Sessa to Philip, November 7, 1597; AGSE 969, unnumbered.

unaware of Mendoza's reports to the opposite effect. In any case Sessa made sure to argue against making things worse: he told Dolfin that he "believed his Republic would not want foreigners, and much less heretics, to enter Italy," an obvious reference to inviting French intervention. Dolfin cagily answered that preventing foreign troops from entering Italy would require raising an army, "which would be very costly for those who are not at war with anyone." The Venetians thus declared neutrality, while clearly rejecting aiding Spain. Not a promising start for Sessa.

Over the next few weeks, even the phlegmatic Sessa began to exhibit the same signs of panic as Iñigo de Mendoza in Venice. On November 10, he reported an alarming conversation with Clement, in which the pope threatened that if Philip remained "neutral" in the Ferrara conflict, other Italian powers might be tempted to aid Cesare; and if that happened, it would force Clement to seek military assistance from France. Moreover, Sessa knew that the French ambassador had indeed offered the pope troops.[149] In other words, the pope was blackmailing Philip, and he was not bluffing. This turn of events represented exactly the sort of nightmare all Spanish ambassadors feared. Even apparently encouraging news failed to lift Sessa's mood. On November 19, he reported that Ferdinand de'Medici, grand duke of Tuscany, had offered his services to the Spaniards in defense of the peace of Italy. A Florentine ambassador told Sessa that Ferdinand feared that "the blaze that erupts in Ferrara, if it is not extinguished quickly, could jump to other parts of Italy." Ferdinand hoped that Philip could settle the Ferrara dispute, and promised to help.[150] This was a surprising offer, considering that up to now Ferdinand's policies had been based on counterbalancing Spanish power (for example, he had supported Clement's decision to absolve Henry IV).[151] He also happened to be married to the French princess Christine of Lorraine.[152] If Ferdinand really had reversed his policies and adopted Spanish concerns about war in Italy, it would have been quite a coup, but Sessa, who perhaps wondered at Ferdinand's motives, gave a lukewarm response. He "praised the grand duke's good will" and promised to pass the offer on to Philip. No doubt the Spaniards would have appreciated some help,

149. Sessa to Philip, November 10, 1597; AGSE 969, unnumbered.
150. Sessa to Philip, November 19, 1597; AGSE 969, unnumbered.
151. Elana Fasano Guarini, "'Rome, Workshop of All the Practices of the World': From the Letters of Cardinal Ferdinando de'Medici to Cosimo I and Francesco I," in *Court and Politics in Papal Rome, 1492–1700,* ed. Gianvittorio Signorotto and Maria Antonietta Visceglia (Cambridge, 2002), p. 77.
152. The marriage took place in 1589, occasioning a month-long pageant; see James M. Saslow, *The Medici Wedding of 1589* (New Haven, 1996).

for Clement obviously meant business. The pope all but strapped on a sword, while again informing Sessa that he "trusted in Philip's Christianity and piety not to support Cesare, or remain neutral."[153] Thus Clement practically dared Philip to oppose him.

Philip, however, did nothing. He was deathly ill, grief-stricken (his younger daughter Catalina had died the previous month), and losing a war to France. Paralysis had gripped Madrid. Sessa waited for instructions, but the only communication he received from the king was a short note expressing regret for the trouble in Italy, "which is not helpful with everything else we have on our hands." He hoped the pope would act with his "accustomed prudence," and recommended that a peaceful end to the conflict be sought.[154] Sessa must have been frustrated to receive such a disconnected and useless letter. Meanwhile the possibility of French intervention in Italy loomed ever larger. On December 18 Sessa passed on an intelligence report that Henry IV had offered Clement twenty thousand infantry and three thousand cavalry in support of a war against Cesare, and had even pledged to come in person if the pope so desired.[155] This was a truly terrifying prospect, suggesting a return to the Italian Wars, when Charles V and Francis I had dueled for mastery—only the present king of Spain was in no condition to fight anybody. The Treaty of Cateau-Cambrésis, and whatever hegemony Spain had in Italy, appeared to be in serious jeopardy.

In the end, of course, the affair ended with the whimpering of Cesare rather than the bang of French guns. The mere threat of French intervention had been enough to deprive Cesare of any Italian allies.[156] Spanish power, on the other hand, seems to have been irrelevant. Perhaps most revealing of Spanish impotence is Philip's evident crumbling in the face of Clement's threats. On January 22, 1598, ten days after Cesare formally sued for peace, Philip wrote to Sessa that he had decided to support Clement's just war. He rejected Cesare's plea for aid, the king explained, because it could lead to "the infliction of foreigners on Italy."[157] So the pope's blackmail had been effective, even if it turned out to be unnecessary. Nothing could underline more clearly Spain's lack of control. A few months later, Sessa reported that the Roman court was grumbling about the expense of traveling to Ferrara, where Clement celebrated his victory. In the same letter, Sessa described telling Clement about the peace nego-

---

153. Sessa to Philip, November 19, 1597; AGSE 969, unnumbered.
154. Philip to Sessa, December 1597 (exact date unknown); AGSE 969, unnumbered.
155. Sessa to Philip, December 18, 1597; AGSE 969, unnumbered.
156. Pastor, *History of the Popes*, Vol. XXIV, pp. 390–91.
157. Philip to Sessa, January 22, 1598; AGSE 970, unnumbered.

tiations in Vervins, where Spain was admitting defeat. The pope demonstrated "great satisfaction."[158] Sessa does not say what he felt.

Sessa's reactions to the Ferrara crisis parallel those of Juan de Zúñiga during the 1575 revolt in Genoa. In neither case did their fears of a general war materialize, but the very fact that they feared so greatly tells us much about the situation in Italy. The "pax hispanica" was no more absolute in the second half of Philip's reign than in the first half. Spanish diplomats, with the exception of a brief period in the early 1590s, proved singularly unable to bend the papacy to their will. Popes sometimes aided Spain, but they were never its puppets. And they often defied Spanish wishes on crucial issues: the annexation of Portugal, the invasion of England, the absolution of Henry IV. When Philip II died in September 1598, his desire for mastery of Italy had still only been partially fulfilled. Clement VIII had not declared war on him, as Paul IV had done, but he had moved decisively toward France. There had been a buildup of Spanish military power in Italy, and the Crown had paid many princes and prelates to be friendly, but Philip's ministers in Italy felt little safer in 1598 than they had in 1559, or in 1529 for that matter. Rome, in particular, was rarely a peaceful haven for Spanish diplomats; as we will see in the next chapter, even on good days they had too much to worry about.

158. Sessa to Philip, April 26, 1598; AGSE 970, unnumbered.

CHAPTER FIVE

Special Problems and Ordinary Duties in Rome

In addition to the endless political crises that cropped up, every Spanish ambassador in Rome faced a long list of everyday concerns that made life difficult. These ordinary responsibilities could cause just as much stress as unforeseen events, and sometimes even more, because of their importance and their potential for frustration. The basic problem was that the Spanish Crown needed many things from the papacy, a fact that popes could use to their advantage. Obviously this dependency worked both ways, yet ambassadors often found themselves begging for something, usually successfully, but always at a cost. Money, of course, figured heavily in this struggle, but on a deeper level Spanish ambassadors and the papacy were fighting for control. Who really controlled the Spanish Church, and its finances? Who really directed the Catholic Reformation mandated by the Council of Trent? Every time Spanish diplomats asked for loans, or an appointment to a vacant ecclesiastic post, the underlying struggle for supremacy became clear. The "pax hispanica" was as problematic at this level as in the arena of geopolitics. True, the Spaniards often got what they asked for, but there were some spectacular exceptions. And even when they did succeed, it was never easy. Once again the Spanish Habsburg sense of entitlement clashed with the realities of Italian politics. As we have seen, Spanish ambassadors did not excel at asking nicely.

To begin with, the Spanish Crown needed papal permission to raise funds from religious institutions. During the reign of Philip II, the Crown had three major sources of revenue tied to the Church: the *subsidio* (a third of all tithes collected in Spain), the *cruzada* (an indulgence intended to finance wars against Muslims and heretics), and the *excusado* (the tithe paid by the richest property in each Spanish parish). These financial concessions, known as the *tres gracias* or "Three Graces," were extremely lucrative: in 1565, a Roman official calculated that they generated two million ducats for Spain annually.[1] Obviously Philip valued these privileges highly; the catch was that each of them needed to be renewed periodically by the papacy. If a particular pope did not approve of how Spain was spending the money, or simply did not like Philip, he could cut off the flow, or hold the concessions hostage to advance his own agenda. Thus Philip's ambassadors often had to plead for the money they felt entitled to for doing God's work.

In March 1561, for example, Francisco de Vargas spent a trying day arguing with Pope Pius IV about the *tres gracias*. Vargas pointed out that Philip was the defender of Christendom, a heavy burden indeed. It was the pope's duty to do his part. Pius answered that he had every wish to please Philip (an outright lie), but he had some scruples about granting the concessions. So Vargas sought out Cardinal Morone, a close advisor to the pope whom Vargas suspected as the source of the problem. Morone had raised objections to the concessions in consistory, and had proposed a disputation on the subject, "which is the way they are accustomed to not do something here [in Rome]." Morone was a member of the Spanish faction, so Vargas displayed understandable vexation. He "begged [Morone] as a good servant of Your Majesty . . . to take action on this matter, and do it without delay, and without consultation, or consistories, or deputations." The cardinal replied that he had already done what he could. Now boiling, Vargas went back to Pius, who insisted on discussing the matter further with the consistory. The pope also suggested that Philip's ministers of state were advising the king badly by insisting on getting papal concessions.[2] Vargas experienced many such maddening days in Rome.

Luis de Requeséns had an even harder time getting concessions out of Pope Pius V. In 1566, in the midst of arguments over precedence, politics, and other matters, Pius refused to renew the *cruzada*. In addition to being extremely jealous of the Church's rights, Pius thought Philip had not earned the *cruzada,* because the king was not doing enough to suppress the Dutch revolt (see chapter 3). The pope's rebuff scandalized

---

1. Peter Pierson, *Philip II of Spain* (London, 1975), p. 113.
2. Vargas to Philip, March 14, 1561; Archivo General de Simancas, Sección Estado (hereafter AGSE) 889, #86.

Philip. In a letter to Requeséns, the king expressed outrage that the pope had introduced such a *novedad* into his relations with Spain, especially one that caused such harm. Philip even speculated that Pius intentionally sought to weaken Spain, or else planned to force Philip to do what he wanted.[3] And in fact Pius did extract a promise from Philip to visit the Netherlands. In return, Pius granted Philip the *excusado*, for the express purpose of financing the king's journey, which of course never occurred. After it became clear Philip would not in fact be going to the Netherlands, Pius abused Requeséns repeatedly, prompting the following plaintive letter:

> After the pope's election, I have sought [the granting of the *cruzada*] with as many petitions as possible, and God knows the pain this has caused and still causes me, as I have so little hope that the pope will forgo the scruples he has in this matter, and much more so now. He is extremely angry after receiving word from the nuncio [in Madrid] . . . that Your Majesty's journey to the Netherlands will not take place this year. . . . He is ashamed to think he was deceived, and that [the promise of the journey] was publicized only in order to get the *cruzada*.[4]

When Requeséns left Rome in 1568, the issue remained unresolved, and so his brother Juan de Zúñiga took up the fight. Two years later he was still fighting. He attacked the pope's religious scruples, claiming "there was no theologian in Spain or Italy who did not say that His Holiness could grant [the *cruzada*] in good conscience." Pius answered that all the world could not make him change his mind.[5] Zúñiga did eventually persuade Pius to renew the *cruzada* in 1571, but it took an extraordinary effort—and this from a relatively friendly pope.

In spite of such events, the difficulties Spanish ambassadors had getting financial concessions should not be overemphasized. The papacy did regularly grant the *gracias,* even if they sometimes made the Spaniards sweat over it. Sixtus V, for example, renewed the *subsidio* for five years, and the other two *gracias* for six years each, despite refusing to help pay for the invasion of England.[6] Nonetheless renewal was never automatic; all Span-

3. Philip to Requeséns, February 11, 1567; British Library, Additional Manuscripts 28.404, ff. 83–84.
4. Requeséns to Philip, September 16, 1567; *Correspondencia diplomática entre España y la Santa Sede durante el pontificado de S. Pío V,* ed. Luciano Serrano, 4 vols. (Madrid, 1914), Vol. II, pp. 200–201.
5. Zúñiga to Philip, February 25, 1570; British Library, Additional Manuscripts 28.405, ff. 103–6.
6. Thomas James Dandelet, *Spanish Rome 1500–1700* (New Haven, 2001), p. 84.

ish ambassadors in Rome worried about the issue, and spent considerable time and effort on what they felt should have been a given (literally). Keeping the money flowing was one of their prime responsibilities, as well as a constant headache.

Another, and sometimes even greater, source of conflict concerned the Crown's jurisdictional rights over the Church in Spanish-controlled territories. According to a popular saying in the sixteenth century, "there is no pope in Spain." This aphorism reflected the extent of the Crown's control—or its ambitions of control—over religion and religious institutions within the Iberian Peninsula, as well as the rest of the Habsburg empire. During the early modern period the papacy granted the king of Spain the right to appoint his own men to many high ecclesiastical positions, as well as permission to publish or withhold papal bulls in Habsburg territories (particularly Spain, Naples, and Sicily).[7] But throughout Philip's reign conflicts over jurisdiction often arose, especially after the Council of Trent. Both the papacy and Philip promoted Church reform, but the king, encouraged by his councilors and leading Spanish theologians, demanded control over the process in his own lands.[8] The post-Tridentine papacy was equally determined to protect its prerogatives, and the Spanish ambassadors often found themselves caught in the middle.

Requeséns in particular engaged in many skirmishes over this issue, not surprisingly given his imperious nature. Early in his tenure at Rome, for example, he reported that Pope Pius IV was threatening to revoke the *cruzada* because of perceived Spanish interference in Church affairs. This subject, in fact, often caused the pope to become angry, and to say "many things detrimental to his person and dignity . . . which I would pardon if he said them behind closed doors, but he says them in public."[9] Given the pope's attitude, when Philip wanted to get papal permission to institute reforms within Spanish monasteries, he thought it wise to try to smooth the way. The king ordered Requeséns to enlist the aid of the Milanese Cardinal Carlo Borromeo, the pope's nephew and secretary of state, to facilitate the request.[10] Since Borromeo was Philip's royal subject, the Spaniards expected compliance, but the cardinal chose Church over Crown. (The Church would later declare Borromeo a saint.) When

---

7. Pierson, *Philip II*, pp. 113–14.
8. See José Martínez Millán, "En busca de la ortodoxia: El inquisidor general Diego de Espinosa," in *La corte de Felipe II*, ed. José Martínez Millán (Madrid, 1994), pp. 189–228.
9. Requeséns to Philip, October 29, 1563; AGSE 895, #211.
10. Philip to Requeséns, November 15, 1563; *Pio IV y Felipe Segundo: Primeros diez meses de la embajada de Don Luis de Requeséns en Roma, 1563–1564*, ed. "F. del V." and "S. K." (Madrid, 1891), pp. 70–84.

Requeséns approached him, Borromeo refused to help, on the grounds that religious reform was solely within the Church's domain. This reaction baffled the ambassador; he wrote of Borromeo that he was a very good man, but he had some very strange opinions.[11] This would not be the only encounter between these two men. Ten years later, when Requeséns was governor of Milan and Borromeo its archbishop, they would again clash over jurisdiction, and the latter ended up excommunicating the Spaniard.[12] In any case, the ambassador had serious problems on this issue from the beginning.

Once again, the situation became worse under Pope Pius V, the zealous crusader with no regard for political or practical considerations. The conflict between him and the Spaniards over jurisdiction would become especially sharp over the Carranza case.[13] Bartolomé Carranza, archbishop of Toledo, had been imprisoned in 1559 by the Spanish Inquisition, under suspicion of heresy. Pope Pius IV had claimed jurisdiction over the case, given the high rank of the accused, but Philip, backed by many Spanish theologians and church officials, had refused to surrender the prisoner. When Pius V took the throne, he made even stronger demands. Philip again resisted, and the conflict became a general war over control of the Church in Spain. In May 1566, five months after Pius's election, Requeséns reported a typically fruitless argument with the pope on the issue. The ambassador carefully explained the reasons why Carranza should remain in Spain. "[Pius] listened to me very patiently," Requeséns wrote, "without getting excited as he usually does when discussing this matter, so that I thought I had persuaded him, but then he told me all the reasons I had not done so." Among other things, the pope accused Philip of deliberately delaying the archbishop's trial, so that he could continue to collect revenues from Carranza's see.[14] Requeséns tried to make a joke out of this accusation, although it was probably true. In any case, he continued to argue to the pope's deaf ears for months, but as the ambassador noted, Pius cared nothing for reasons of state.[15]

---

11. Requeséns to Philip, December 16, 1563; ibid., pp. 121–29.

12. See José M. March, *Don Luis de Requeséns en el gobierno de Milan, 1571–1573* (Madrid, 1943), pp. 259–84. During this power struggle, Requeséns wrote to Philip that "in matters of jurisdiction, I not only judge that [Borromeo] is deceived, but I believe him to be the most obstinate man I have ever seen in my life." August 16, 1573; AGSE 1236, #166.

13. John Lynch, *Spain Under the Habsburgs*, Vol. I, 2d ed. (New York: 1984), 276–77. See also J. I. Tellechea Idígoras, *Bartolomé Carranza y su tiempo* (Madrid, 1968).

14. Requeséns to Philip, May 3, 1566; *Correspondencia diplomática*, Vol. I, pp. 223–27.

15. Requeséns to Philip, September 18, 1566; ibid., pp. 348–51.

Eventually, Philip submitted. In December 1566, after seven years of imprisonment, Carranza was transported to Rome for trial. Were the Spaniards convinced by the pope's arguments? The ambassador's correspondence suggests not. If the king agreed to let Pius have Carranza, Requeséns wrote, the pope might be more willing to grant the *cruzada*.[16] He was wrong, but it is important to note his conclusion, which evidently agreed with Philip's: financial need trumped national pride, as well as the Crown's pretensions to control over the Spanish Church. The papacy again displayed its independence from Spanish control.

But the fight was not over. Carranza's trial would be delayed and prolonged for years, in large part due to Spanish uncooperativeness. When Juan de Zúñiga arrived in Rome in 1568, Spanish and Italian theologians were still arguing over what Carranza should be accused of. In one of his first papal audiences, Zúñiga had to defend the Spanish Inquisition against charges of carelessness. According to the new ambassador, Pius had "calumniated the Holy Office of Spain's methods of procedure," and "most of the Italian [cardinals] did not object."[17] So from the very start Zúñiga perceived Rome to be hostile territory. Nor would matters improve. A year later, Zúñiga wrote that "It greatly pains me to see that His Holiness does not favor us in matters of the Spanish Inquisition, as would be just. He has it in his head that the inquisitors do not want to obey him and that Your Majesty is to blame. I have constantly pointed out to him the damage he will do to all Christendom and particularly to this Holy See by disparaging the Inquisition, [because] Your Majesty uses it to sustain religion in your kingdoms."[18]

Once again we see the Spanish assumption that the papacy should naturally acquiesce to their needs, and their consequent inability to understand the Italian point of view. In the end, Zúñiga never was able to get this pope, or any pope, to let the Spanish Inquisition have its way with Carranza. The best the Spaniards could do was to prolong the trial, in effect condemning Carranza to perpetual imprisonment. Finally, in 1575, he was found not guilty, although he had to renounce certain passages from his writings and was suspended from office. Two months after sentencing, he died.[19]

The Carranza trial was a unique case, but other conflicts over jurisdiction arose periodically throughout the sixteenth century. Control over the Church and religion in Spanish Italy, for example, represented a constant

16. Requeséns to Philip, December 27, 1566; ibid., pp. 429–36.
17. Zúñiga to Philip, August 17, 1568; ibid., Vol. II, pp. 439–42.
18. Zúñiga to Philip, September 7, 1569; ibid., Vol. III, pp. 140–42.
19. Lynch, Vol. II, p. 277.

problem. The Spanish monarchy possessed exclusive rights of patronage (called the *Patronato Real*) in the Kingdoms of Naples and Sicily, but technically the papacy also held feudal rights over those territories, in addition to its ecclesiastic claims.[20] The Spanish and Roman branches of the Inquisition likewise tangled often, especially in Naples (where popular opposition to the Spanish Inquisition was so great that a local diocesan inquisition had to be installed).[21] Both Charles V and Philip II wrestled with the papacy over everything from publishing papal decrees to filling vacant Church offices. In April 1550, for instance, Charles wrote to Diego Hurtado de Mendoza about getting Pope Julius III's approval for a new archbishop of Messina. "We would not want to lose this church to His Holiness's deliberations," he informed his ambassador.[22] Since Mendoza had intentionally insulted Julius the previous year—the "gift" of a broken-down nag from Naples (see chapter 2)—the emperor might also have been reminding his ambassador to be more diplomatic.

Almost twenty years later, Requeséns and Zúñiga became entangled in a series of fights over jurisdiction with Pope Pius V. One of the triggers was the proclamation of a papal bull called *In Coena Domini,* an annual declaration of censures against abuses within the Church. In 1568, Pius issued a particularly scathing list of perceived abuses in Spanish Italy, as well as other Habsburg territories. Earlier that year, the papal nuncio in Spain had reported that Spanish government officials, from local tribunals all the way up to royal councilors, repeatedly interfered with Church functions, and usurped Church authority. Pius aimed his bull directly at such abuses.[23] As Zúñiga wrote to the archbishop of Santiago de Compostela, the pope was "very annoyed that in all the King's realms His Majesty's ministers meddle too much with ecclesiastical jurisdiction, and on this subject we have a hundred thousand debates every day."[24] Philip, angered by what he saw as a pope overstepping his bounds, refused to let the bull be published in his realms. The real issue, of course, was power, a classic confrontation of

20. See W. Eugene Shiels, *King and Church: The Rise and Fall of the Patronato Real* (Chicago, 1961); and H. G. Koenigsberger, *The Practice of Empire: The Government of Sicily under Philip II of Spain,* emended 2nd. edition (Ithaca, 1969).

21. See William Monter, *Frontiers of Heresy: The Spanish Inquisition from the Basque Lands to Sicily* (New York, 1990); and on Naples, Henry Charles Lea, *The Inquisition in the Spanish Dependencies* (New York, 1922), chap. 2.

22. Charles to Mendoza, April 26, 1550; AGSE 876, #15.

23. Ludwig von Pastor, *The History of the Popes from the Close of the Middle Ages,* trans. Ralph Francis Kerr, 40 vols. (London, 1891–1953), Vol. XVIII, pp. 32–35.

24. Zúñiga to the archbishop, April 4, 1568; *Colección de documentos inéditos para la historia de España,* Vol. XCVII (Madrid, 1895), pp. 417–18.

prince versus pope.[25] The king felt strongly enough that he sent Requeséns, only just released from duty as the resident ambassador, back to Rome to argue his case. As Philip wrote to Requeséns, "you will see the cause which has forced us to send you to Rome, and the gravity and importance of this business, which is greater than any other."[26] Philip did not give precise instructions, instead trusting in Requeséns' "prudence and skill" to smooth over the conflict. Both king and ambassador would be disappointed.

In Rome, Zúñiga, who had been on the job only six months, anxiously awaited his brother, "for the good of the pending negotiations, because I would not wish to pursue [discussions] concerning the *cruzada* and the bull *In Coena Domini* alone."[27] (Note that once again jurisdiction conflicts were linked to financial negotiations.) When Requeséns arrived, he did his best. In December 1568, he described broaching the topic of jurisdiction on a day when Pius was in a good mood. Speaking to the pope as "a Christian and a servant,"

> I told him that I had often considered the state Christendom is in, bring-
> ing to his attention affairs in the Netherlands, France, Germany and Eng-
> land, and even Italy, where heretics are discovered every day; and that I
> would be much less concerned about all of this except for fear of the dis-
> unity which has existed between Your Majesty and His Holiness, which I
> am certain has been caused by the devil. . . . This is a great shame, as Your
> Majesty's interests and goals are the same as His Holiness's, but the devil
> has placed between you these issues of jurisdiction, which is all that could
> keep you apart.[28]

This plea, while dramatic, also drastically simplified the problem. Requeséns dismissed the conflict over jurisdiction as mere illusion, a distraction concocted by the Evil One. He implied that Pius should be concentrating on more important issues. Even more interesting, Requeséns then claimed that stories of church abuses in Spanish Italy were lies, invented by those prejudiced against Spain. These people

---

25. See Massimo Carlo Giannini, "'El martillo sobre el anima': Filippo II e la bolla In Coena Domini nell'Italia spagnola tra religione e sovranità (1568–1570)," in *Felipe II (1527–1598): Europa y la Monarquía Católica*, ed. José Martínez Millán, Vol. III (Madrid, 1998), pp. 251–70.
26. Philip to Requeséns, July 31, 1568; *Correspondencia diplomática*, Vol. II, pp. 428–29.
27. Zúñiga to Philip, June 10, 1568; *Colección de documentos inéditos para la historia de España*, Vol. 97, pp. 500–502.
28. Requeséns to Philip, December 10, 1568; *Correspondencia diplomática*, Vol. II, pp. 512–18.

(never identified) hated and feared Philip's greatness, as well as "generally disliking our nation." Some of these same people, the ambassador
continued, hated the pope because of his religious zeal and rigor. Thus
Requeséns projected his own defensiveness and grandiosity onto the
pope, or at least pretended to do so.

And how did Pius react? He listened quietly, thanked Requeséns for his
affection and zeal, and admitted that the devil might well be behind the
jurisdiction conflict; but he "did not want to confess that his concerns
were not justified."[29] So much for Requeséns' "prudence and skill." The
ambassador's tactics proved ineffective, primarily because he did not
admit that the pope had legitimate complaints. Many Spanish officials
did in fact interfere with papal authority, taking their cue from the king
himself, who made no secret of his proprietary attitude toward the Iberian Church.[30] For Requeséns to deny that a problem existed seems either
disingenuous or arrogant, or perhaps both. In any case, Pius did not like
being patronized, and the conflicts continued throughout his reign.

Nor did the problem of jurisdiction improve under Pius V's successors.
If anything, it worsened. In April 1580, for example, Philip felt it necessary to send a special envoy to Rome, the marquis of Alcañices, to discuss
the issue of religious reform in Habsburg territories with Pope Gregory
XIII. Gregory, however, rebuffed Alcañices' attempts to mollify him, complaining of Spanish intransigence instead. The pope even accused
Philip's Council of Castile (the highest royal council) of deliberate and
criminal defiance of papal commands.[31] The papal nuncio in Madrid at
the time, Felipe Sega, echoed his master's words in a letter to his replacement in July 1581. According to Sega, throughout Spain and Spanish
Italy Habsburg officials usurped the authority and jurisdiction of the
Church, while the king stood idly by.[32]

Church officials repeated such sentiments through the reign of Sixtus
V, and even more so under Clement VIII, often in response to perceived
Spanish arrogance. In 1592, just after Clement came to the papal throne,
a theologian at Philip's court named Juan Rosa Davila published an *Apology for the Rights of Princes*, which argued for the Crown's prerogatives over
the Church. Clement quickly placed this work on the Index of Forbidden
Books.[33] Meanwhile the pope's representatives in Spain were equally

29. Ibid.
30. A. W. Lovett, *Early Habsburg Spain, 1517–1598* (Oxford, 1986), pp. 280–81.
31. Ricardo de Hinajosa, *Los despachos de la diplomacia pontificia en España*, Vol. I (Madrid,
1896), p. 229.
32. Ibid., pp. 242–45.
33. Pastor, *History of the Popes*, Vol. XXIII, p. 197.

upset. In 1596, the nuncio Camilo Caetani wrote a series of letters bewailing the state of religious affairs in Spain. For thirty years and more, he claimed, Spanish ministers of state and theologians had encouraged Philip to defy the papacy and usurp the Church's authority in religious matters. Caetani reported that the Spanish Church was in woeful condition, and that the Habsburg government's interference seriously threatened the Church's well-being.[34]

Pope Clement took his nuncio's warnings seriously. He made numerous attempts to force the Spanish Church to abide by the Council of Trent's mandates; for example, he ordered the Spanish bishops to reside in their sees, something many of them had refused to do. Philip, however, perceived the pope's efforts as an infringement on his rights within his own realm, and refused to publish Clement's edicts.[35] One of Clement's personal advisers responded thus: "The oppression of the clergy by the civil power, such as prevails in the Spanish dominions, is equivalent to crypto-heresy."[36] So, to the end of Philip's reign, conflicts over jurisdiction often poisoned the atmosphere between Rome and Madrid.

Despite all of these conflicts, however, the Spanish ambassadors in Rome got a remarkable amount of routine work done. In addition to the ambassadors' many large concerns, like money and jurisdiction, they also had to ask the pope for many smaller—yet still important— favors. For example, we have already seen how ambassadors relayed royal recommendations for vacant ecclesiastic offices. The archives are full of such letters. Sometimes the king simply passed on names he had been given by his staff. In May 1560, for instance, Philip wrote to Francisco de Vargas that a certain Dominican friar named Bernardo de Albuquerque had been recommended to him for the bishopric of Antequera, in Oaxaca, Mexico. The king noted that Fray Bernardo came with excellent references, and that the annual rents of the see amounted to two hundred ducats a year. Philip asked the ambassador to ask Pope Pius IV to expedite the appointment, for the good of the citizens of Antequera.[37] This is a typical request; in 1561, Philip sent at least forty such letters to Vargas, for church positions throughout the

---

34. J. Ignacio Tellechea Idígoras, *El ocaso de un rey: Felipe II visto desde la nunciatura de Madrid 1594–1598* (Madrid, 2001), pp. 50–51.
35. See Ignasi Fernández Terricabras, "El episcopado hispano y el patronato real: Reflexión sobre algunas discrepancias entre Clemente VIII y Felipe II," in Millán, *Felipe II (1527–1598)*, Vol. III, pp. 209–23.
36. Cardinal Cesare Baronius to Olivares, quoted in Pastor, *History of the Popes*, Vol. XXIII, p. 205.
37. Philip to Vargas, May 19, 1560; Ministerio de Asuntos Exteriores, Legajo 1, #87.

Habsburg empire.[38] Multiply this by forty years, and one senses the scale of the paperwork machine in the age of Philip II.

Other requests were of a more personal nature. In July 1591 Philip wrote to the count of Olivares, asking that Pope Gregory XIV bestow a high ecclesiastical office in Spain on the king's nephew, Archduke Albert of Austria. Philip mentioned the sees of Cuenca or Siguenza as possibilities, but he was not sure if they were open; he suggested that the pope should just give Albert the best position available.[39] Apparently Philip was not satisfied with the papal response: three years later he wrote again on Albert's behalf, this time to the duke of Sessa. Since the archbishop of Toledo had just died, Philip wrote, perhaps Albert could be named as a replacement. "Knowing by experience the great virtue and laudable habits God has seen fit to give Albert," Philip did not hesitate to recommend him for the position.[40] Not all such requests were so obviously nepotistic. In November 1560, Philip's sister Juana, princess of Portugal, wrote to Vargas on behalf of a scholar named Dr. Andrea Bello. Bello, it seems, was related to a member of Juana's household, and needed employment. The princess asked if the ambassador could recommend Bello to the pope for a secretarial position in Rome.[41] Here we see the early modern patronage system at work.[42]

Another favor which the king and his household often asked for on other people's behalf was marriage dispensations. The Church had strict rules about consanguinity, which resulted in many requests to break those rules. The Council of Trent decreed that marriages in the third degree (e.g. uncle and niece), and sometimes even closer kinship, were permissible given "sufficient cause." The Church viewed the granting of dispensations as a valuable tool for establishing control over the institution of marriage.[43] The Spanish Crown sent its ambassadors a steady stream of petitions for such dispensations. The count of Olivares, for example, between 1582 and 1591 received at least 150 letters from Philip asking permission for someone to marry.[44] Often the petitioner had a connection

---

38. Ministerio de Asuntos Exteriores, Legajo 1, #117–57. The actual number of requests was probably higher; forty letters are what have survived in this particular file.
39. Philip to Olivares, July 10, 1591; Ministerio de Asuntos Exteriores, Legajo 16, #54.
40. Philip to Sessa, November 7, 1594; Archivo Histórico Nacional (Madrid), Legajo 15,194 No. II, #13 (4). The pope approved of the request, but Albert spent very little time in Toledo. In April 1995 he was named the new governor of the Netherlands.
41. Juana to Vargas, November 16, 1560; Ministerio de Asuntos Exteriores, Legajo 1, #102.
42. Cf. the seminal work on early modern patronage networks: Sharon Kettering, *Patrons, Brokers, and Clients in Seventeenth-Century France* (Oxford, 1986).
43. Jack Goody, *The Development of the Family and Marriage in Europe* (Cambridge, 1983), pp. 145–46.
44. Ministerio de Asuntos Exteriores, Legajo 16, #81–231.

to the king. In January 1585, for instance, Philip asked for a dispensation for one Alonso Guerrero, who wanted to marry his cousin Maria; Alonso's father had served in the household of the king's sister, and so had been able to obtain royal backing.[45] A few months later, the king asked for a dispensation for a *letrado* (a university-trained scholar in government service) named Juan Montañes, who wished to marry the niece of his deceased wife.[46] Obviously, such matters did not hold the same importance as high politics or finance, yet it is noteworthy that the king of Spain took the time to write such letters, and expected the ambassador to spend time and effort fulfilling the requests.

While Philip's interest in the minutiae of governance was legendary, some of the requests he sent to his ambassadors in Rome show an amazing attention to detail. In 1560, for example, Philip sent several notes to Vargas concerning minor issues related to religion and the Church. In one letter, Philip explained that a monastery in the mountains near the city of Tarrazona (on the western edge of Aragon) needed funds for repair and upkeep. This ancient and holy establishment, the king wrote, could only be inhabited six months out of the year, because "it is located high in the mountains, where the land is infertile and cold, with much snow and ice." The monks who lived there thus could not be self-sufficient, and the maintenance costs were high. Philip asked that the pope grant this monastery "certain favors and indulgences" to help out.[47] This request reflects Philip's interest in reforming Spain's religious institutions, a campaign he began in the early 1560s.[48] Still, the king's knowledge of and concern for a remote monastery is remarkable. The request also highlights the mundane aspects of the Roman embassy, which routinely handled dozens of such cases annually.

In another interesting example from 1560, Philip sent a special request to Vargas on behalf of a man in Mexico named Don Juan Cano de Montezuma. The half-Spanish, half-Aztec name alerts us that we are here dealing with the clash of cultures that characterized New Spain at the time. And indeed, Philip himself explained a problem relating to race. Don Juan was the nephew of Montezuma, the deposed king of the Aztecs. Charles V had tried to bestow upon him membership in the Order of Alcántara, one of the three great military/religious orders of Spain. But as a son of pagans, Don Juan was barred from joining by the rules of the

45. Philip to Olivares, January 27, 1585; ibid., #81.
46. Philip to Olivares, March 30. 1585; ibid., #82.
47. Philip to Vargas, April 1, 1560; Ministerio de Asuntos Exteriores, Legajo 1, #100.
48. Bruce Taylor, *Structures of Reform: The Mercedarian Order in the Spanish Golden Age* (Leiden, 2000), pp. 140–42.

Order. So Philip wrote to Vargas asking for a papal dispensation allowing Don Juan in. The king ordered Vargas to assure the pope that Don Juan was fully qualified and deserving of the honor, notwithstanding his Indian blood.[49] Once again, Philip personally attended to an obscure detail of his vast empire. Unfortunately, there is no record of how the pope responded to either this petition or the request for the monastery; the important point, however, is that the ambassadors' responsibilities extended to even such small details as these.

Other special tasks entrusted to the ambassadors were more directly connected to the Habsburg quest for greatness. For one thing, Philip and his envoys lobbied relentlessly to get the papacy to canonize more Spanish saints. For centuries, almost no Spaniards had won official saintly status, a fact that hurt Spanish pride. Philip was determined to correct this state of affairs.[50] In particular, the king championed the case of Diego of Alcalá (1400?–1463), a Dominican friar revered in Spain as a local saint. Diego had long had a devoted local following, but he came to prominence in 1562. That year Philip's son Carlos suffered grave injuries after falling down a flight of stairs. He was in a coma, and the doctors despaired of his life. In desperation, the king ordered that Diego's body be brought to his son's bed; as soon as Carlos's hand was placed on the holy corpse, he was cured. A grateful Philip immediately petitioned the pope to have Diego canonized. His plea was successful, but only after he and his ambassadors badgered the papacy for twenty-five years.

The late sixteenth-century papacy tended to be cautious about the canonization process, because the practice had come under attack from the Protestants, who mocked the overabundance of medieval saints. On the other hand, Protestants developed their own martyrology, and the Catholic Church did not want to lose their control of the sacred. Diego of Alcalá would become the first Counter-Reformation saint.[51] The campaign began during Requeséns' tenure in Rome. In 1566, he wrote to Prince Carlos asking for information on Diego's life and death, so that the case for his canonization could be argued. At the time, no authorized hagiographical work on Diego existed, so Carlos ordered one to be written.[52] But Pope Pius V was not satisfied with the evidence. Gregory XIII would not be convinced either, and year after year Spanish ambitions were stymied.

---

49. Philip to Vargas, November 30, 1560; ibid., #95.
50. Dandelet, *Spanish Rome*, pp. 170ff.
51. Peter Burke, "How to Be a Counter-Reformation Saint," in *The Historical Anthropology of Early Modern Italy* (Cambridge, 1987), pp. 48–62.
52. Dandelet, *Spanish Rome*, p. 173.

In February 1585, for example, Olivares wrote to Philip about his stalled negotiations with Gregory concerning Diego's canonization. Soon after arriving in Rome, Olivares had petitioned for Diego's sainthood. The pope had demanded "proofs" of Diego's miracles, which the Spaniards provided. Then fourteen months passed, during which time Olivares spoke to the pope personally on the issue on three or four occasions, while holding an "infinite" number of debates with the papal officials in charge of the case. But there was no progress. Olivares speculated that a popular superstition in Rome, which held that popes who declared saints died soon afterward, might be partly to blame.[53] Two months after Olivares dispatched this letter, Gregory in fact died, but without having canonized Diego, perhaps disproving the theory. In any case Olivares immediately importuned the new pope, Sixtus V, about Diego's case. The ambassador reported that he had made greater headway in one conversation with Sixtus than he had in two years with Gregory.[54] Nonetheless it would still take three more years before the Church officially proclaimed Diego a saint.

In the late sixteenth and early seventeenth centuries, the Church acknowledged a number of Spanish saints. This could be interpreted as evidence of the growing influence of Spain on Rome and the papacy.[55] Yet the papacy never simply rubber-stamped the Spanish monarch's recommendations, much to the king's frustration. In 1593, for example, Philip wrote to the duke of Sessa, strongly advocating the canonization of Ignatius Loyola, founder of the Society of Jesus.[56] This was not Philip's first plea on behalf of Loyola, who had died in 1556. But Philip would not live to see Loyola canonized (it finally happened in 1622). Another Spaniard whom Philip championed, Ramón de Penyafort, would likewise be declared a saint only after Philip's death. In 1594, the king sent Sessa a fervent letter about Ramón, a thirteenth-century Dominican friar credited with helping to found the Mercedarians (a Spanish order dedicated to freeing Christians imprisoned by the Muslims). Philip exhorted Sessa to inform Pope Clement about Ramón's exemplary life and death, and the many miracles attributed to him; he ordered Sessa to do whatever he deemed necessary to get Ramón canonized.[57] But once again the process

53. Olivares to Philip, February 25, 1585; AGSE 946, #9.
54. Olivares to Philip, May 21, 1585; AGSE 946, #26.
55. Dandelet describes Diego de Alcalá's canonization as "possibly the strongest symbolic testimony to that time of the growing power and influence of the Spanish monarch in Rome" (*Spanish Rome*, p. 171).
56. Philip to Sessa, October 16, 1593; Ministerio de Asuntos Exteriores, Legajo 21, #263.
57. Philip to Sessa, December 19, 1594; ibid., #256.

took time: the Church did not proclaim Ramón a saint until 1601.[58] There is no question that the number of Spaniards canonized in the early modern period indicates Spain's influence in Rome, but Spanish control over the papacy must not be exaggerated.

The duke of Sessa did not spend all of his time arguing on behalf of Spanish saints. Sometimes he dealt with much more worldly matters. In December 1593, for example, he became involved in the unfortunate death of the marquis of Vasto (Francisco Fernández Avalos de Aquino), an important figure in Spanish-Italian relations. Sessa wrote to Philip informing him that the marquis had come to Rome to discuss family affairs with his uncle, the Cardinal of Aragon. Sadly, as he set out on the return journey, he suddenly fell into a swoon, as he had done several times before in recent weeks. This happened in the countryside, far from any cities, so no doctors could get to him in time. He was brought to a small local church, where he died that night. Or at least that was the story, so far as the Roman court knew. Sessa switched into code to explain the facts. The Cardinal of Aragon, he says, revealed the truth to him in great secrecy. The marquis had not in fact come to Rome to see his uncle, but rather to see a certain young lady, a relative of the Orsini (one of the ancient aristocratic families of Rome). This woman had been a lady-in-waiting to the marquis's wife, and the marquis had taken a fancy to her. The jealous wife had sent her rival away, and paid her to keep silent, but the marquis had not been able to forget the girl. He came to see her in secret, and had been in bed with her when he died. To avoid a scandal, the body had been removed from the young lady's house, and placed in the local church, which happened to be under the protection of the Cardinal of Aragon. The cardinal had then contacted the ambassador, and the two of them agreed on a more palatable account of the marquis's death.[59] Not all the ambassador's duties were routine.

Considering their tremendous workload, Spanish ambassadors were woefully underpaid. Renaissance European princes notoriously exploited their envoys.[60] The Spanish Habsburgs, to judge by their ambassadors' complaints, were no exception. Every Spanish ambassador in sixteenth-century Italy begged for money, often repeatedly; the Roman embassy, however, was an especially expensive post.[61] Ambassadors in Rome were

58. Taylor, *Structures of Reform*, pp. 402–3.
59. Sessa to Philip, December 19, 1593; AGSE 961, unnumbered.
60. Garrett Mattingly, *Renaissance Diplomacy* (reprint, New York, 1988), pp. 199–200.
61. Which is not to say the ambassadors in Venice were happier. In November 1530, Rodrigo Niño begged Charles V for money, claiming that expenses were higher than ever in Venice (AGSE 1308, #113). Diego de Mendoza and Diego Guzmán de Silva were no better off.

expected to maintain large households, and sponsor lavish demonstrations of wealth, as a reflection of the magnificence and power of their masters.[62] Luis de Requeséns, for example, employed a doctor, nine pages, and a cook during his time in Rome.[63] His brother, Juan de Zúñiga, founded a Spanish confraternity in 1579, which became a focal point for displays of Spanish piety and power in Rome.[64] In addition, Rome was a center of political news and gossip, which meant that ambassadors bore heavy expenses related to post and courier services.[65] In 1588, which as we have seen was a year that highlighted the importance of communications between Rome and Madrid, the count of Olivares complained that the costs of mail service had become prohibitively high, causing "chaos" in the embassy.[66]

The Spanish Crown did value its ambassadors' efforts: of all the Habsburg embassies, the one in Rome received the highest salary, at twelve thousand ducats annually (the second highest, in Vienna, only received eight thousand).[67] But it was never enough, or so the ambassadors claimed. Francisco de Vargas, for example, wrote Philip a peevish letter in 1561, complaining that his salary did not cover even a third of his annual expenses. As the ambassador in Rome, he said, he had to maintain a certain image, which did not come cheap.[68] Almost forty years later, the duke of Sessa wrote a similar letter to the royal secretary, Juan de Idiáquez, although Sessa was more apologetic than Vargas. The duke begged pardon for importuning the king and his ministers so often, but he just had to ask for more money. He had recently been denied credit, and so had been forced to pay the embassy's expenses out of his own pocket. It was embarrassing, he wrote, that the king of Spain's representative had been brought to such straits. Soon he would have to choose between sending mail and eating.[69] As dramatic as such entreaties were, however, they rarely brought results. There were a few exceptions, always followed by thank-you notes; Diego Hurtado de Mendoza, for instance, just after being appointed to the Rome embassy, wrote gratefully to Charles V to

---

62. Peter Partner, *Renaissance Rome 1500–1559: A Portrait of a Society* (Berkeley, 1976), pp. 52–53.

63. Adro Xavier, *Luis de Requeséns en el Europa del siglo XVI* (Madrid, 1984), pp. 500–503.

64. Dandelet, *Spanish Rome*, chap. 4.

65. See E. John B. Allen, *Post and Courier Service in the Diplomacy of Early Modern Europe* (The Hague, 1972). For more on ambassadors as news gatherers, see below, chapter 6.

66. Olivares to Philip, January 4, 1588; AGSE 950, #5.

67. Manuel Fernández Álvarez and Ana Díaz Medina, *Los Austrias mayores y la culminación del imperio (1516–1598)* (Madrid, 1987), p. 240.

68. Vargas to Philip, January 5, 1561; AGSE 889, #84.

69. Sessa to Idiáquez, October 29, 1597; AGSE 969, unnumbered.

acknowledge a gift of fifteen hundred ducats.[70] But no one took the job of ambassador to become rich.[71]

If the ambassadors did not personally profit, however, they were the source of riches for others in Rome. Perhaps the highest priority for Spain's Roman embassy in the early modern period was to create and strengthen the Spanish faction amongst the College of Cardinals and the Roman court.[72] The more supporters the ambassadors had, the more pressure they could apply on the papacy, and of course the greater the chances of getting pro-Spanish popes elected. The ambassadors used the arts of persuasion to win friends in Rome, but they also depended on the surer method of cold hard cash. Every Spanish ambassador in Rome made a point of locating and recruiting people in positions to help them, by offering pensions, benefices, or knightly honors. The ambassadors also kept tabs on their recruits, making sure they remained happy, and reminding them of the quid pro quo. The Spaniards seemed very matter-of-fact about buying the favors of Church officials. In 1591, for example, Olivares sent Philip a list of cardinals who either might accept, or had already been paid, some sort of financial inducement: the Cardinal of Santa Severina has a nephew who needs money; Cardinal Aldobrandino has pledged his goodwill in hopes of a pension; Cardinal Spinola received the thousand ducats we sent him; and so on for twenty other cardinals.[73] Requeséns, in a letter to Francisco de Eraso, secretary of Philip's Council of Finance, made an even more explicit statement about the uses of money in Rome: "In most of His Majesty's letters which go through Your Excellency's hands there are always recommendations for people [seeking money] . . . and I implore Your Excellency to have no doubt that one cannot negotiate here [in Rome] without gratifying these people, and that I never claim that I do so out of friendship, but only because [the recipients] may then perform well in His Majesty's service."[74] The ambassadors had no qualms or pretensions about what they were doing; it was just the cost of doing business. And the cost was high: one historian estimates that in 1591, the Spanish Crown spent thirty thousand ducats on pensions for cardinals.[75]

---

70. Mendoza to Charles, August 18, 1546; AGSE 873, #136.
71. The Roman embassy could often be a stepping-stone to more lucrative positions, however; Requeséns, after leaving the embassy, became governor of Milan, then governor of the Netherlands, while both Zúñiga and Olivares left Rome to become viceroys of Naples.
72. Dandelet, *Spanish Rome*, pp. 125–26.
73. Olivares to Philip, September 22, 1591; AGSE 958, unnumbered.
74. Requeséns to Eraso, March 12, 1564; AGSE 896, #35.
75. Dandelet, *Spanish Rome*, p. 138.

Of course, packing the College of Cardinals with Spaniards would have been cheaper and more reliable, but it was not easy to do. As long as popes were Italian, so would be the majority of cardinals they created. In 1529, Miguel Mai warned Charles V that the king had too few loyal servants in Rome (see chapter 2). In 1566, Requeséns said much the same thing to Philip. We cannot have too many Spanish cardinals, Requeséns wrote, because they are the only ones we can really trust. Besides, he continued, popes tend to fill the College with their friends and relatives, who turn out to be lazy or stupid; what we need are more pious and educated men (presumably Spaniards).[76] Requeséns' patriotic prejudice is obvious, yet he also noted that the four Spaniards currently in the College of Cardinals were not particularly effective at advancing Philip's program. The ambassadors were sometimes disappointed with their own colleagues.

And this raises another point: the size of the Spanish faction in Rome did not necessarily correspond to its relative power.[77] For one thing, internal unity was never guaranteed, and individual agendas sometimes outweighed wider concerns. Zúñiga discovered this, much to his chagrin, during the controversy over Cosimo de'Medici's bid to become the "Grand Duke of Tuscany." Zúñiga's attempts to block the granting of this title were hampered by a Spanish cardinal, Francisco Pacheco, bishop of Burgos (d. 1579). Pacheco was the Cardinal Protector of Spain, which meant he had the specific responsibility of representing Spain's interests among his fellow cardinals.[78] But Pacheco also had close personal ties to Cosimo de'Medici. In 1569, Zúñiga warned Philip that Pacheco would not be a good candidate for the papacy, because of his overdependence on the Duke of Florence.[79] A few years later the ambassador's opinion was confirmed when he tried to organize a campaign against Cosimo's new title. Pacheco actively opposed Zúñiga's efforts, even going so far as to advise Cosimo to ignore Zúñiga's threats and protests.[80] Cosimo did just that, and of course he got his title. Zúñiga complained that Pacheco's favoritism toward the duke of Florence was so blatant that those Italians who disliked Cosimo were never going to trust Philip.[81] Much to the

76. Requeséns to Philip, December 20, 1566; British Library, Additional Manuscripts 28.703*, ff. 5–7.

77. See Maria Antonietta Visceglia, "Factions in the Sacred College in the Sixteenth and Seventeenth Centuries," in *Court and Politics in Papal Rome, 1492–1700*, ed. Gianvittorio Signorotto and Maria Antonietta Visceglia (Cambridge, 2002), pp. 99–131.

78. The office of "Cardinal Protector" developed in the fifteenth century, but their functions were in large part assumed by resident ambassadors in the following century. *Enciclopedia universal ilustrada europeo-americana*, 70 vols. (Madrid, 1907–1930), Vol. XI, p. 832.

79. Zúñiga to Philip, September 28, 1569; *Correspondencia diplomática*, Vol. IV, pp. 159–60.

80. Zúñiga to Philip, July 3, 1571; ibid., pp. 378–79.

81. Ibid.

ambassador's relief, later that year Pacheco expressed a wish to return to Burgos, a move that Zúñiga fully supported.[82] In any case, this episode illustrates that the Spanish faction did not always function properly.

Nevertheless, Spanish ambassadors depended on the support network they built in Rome. Their feelings of insecurity, in fact, often made them desperate to find more friends, even as they doubted the loyalties of the ones they had. A remarkable letter from Requeséns to Philip written in December 1566 demonstrates this:

> Many times I have written to Your Majesty about how important it is for your service to give favors to many of the cardinals, and yet it is not to be believed how much they complain, as if we have not given them anything. . . . Your Majesty is negotiating many issues of great importance at this court, and if these people are not kept satisfied it will be impossible to accomplish anything. If for nothing else, we need [the cardinals] to be grateful to us during papal elections. Due to our sins, there is not enough Christian zeal amongst them to ensure they will do the right thing. Your Majesty should not trust in our recent success [i.e., the election of Pope Pius V], for this was a miracle and God does not perform them every day. For your service and for Christendom it is important that Your Majesty have [on your side] part, or even all [of the College]. . . . A restless, hostile pope would be a worse enemy than the Turks or the king of France, since against them Your Majesty could hope to win, while against popes you can only lose. . . . they could take away your states, or at least force you to spend millions defending them.[83]

Once again, at a moment when the Spanish ambassador in Rome should have felt confident, he clearly did not. Seven years after the Treaty of Cateau-Cambrésis, and eleven months after the election of a pope the Spaniards considered a gift of God, the ambassador felt no triumph, expressed no certainty of victory. Instead, he warned the king that much more work had to be done. The College of Cardinals, and thus the pool of potential popes, could not be trusted, in spite of all the money that had already been spent. Instead of proclaiming an invulnerable "pax hispanica," Requeséns called for help.

Why did Requeséns and his fellow ambassadors feel so insecure, in spite of Spanish imperial power? Much of the answer lies in what they

---

82. Zúñiga to Philip, August 11, 1571; ibid., pp. 404–5.
83. Requeséns to Philip, December 20, 1566; British Library, Additional Manuscripts 28.703*, ff. 4–5.

knew about the state of affairs, and the state of opinions, in Rome as well as the rest of Italy. In addition to all of their other responsibilities, the ambassadors acted as intelligence agents. In the words of Francisco de Vargas, they maintained "vigilance," watching for any potential threats (external or internal) to Spanish hegemony in Italy. And the more they learned, the less confident they felt. It is to this aspect of the ambassadors' lives that we turn next.

CHAPTER SIX

The Ambassadors as Intelligence Officers

Ever since the development of permanent embassies in the late Middle Ages, states and statesmen have understood that ambassadors act as political analysts, as well as outright spies.[1] The first thing an early modern ambassador reported was his assessment of the character and motivations of the host government, and the status of its relations with other states.[2] Over time, he would then attempt to uncover diplomatic secrets, especially concerning hostile intentions. Spanish ambassadors in sixteenth-century Italy tried to do all these things, but the fluid nature of Italian politics made their task difficult. As we will see, the ambassadors' attempts at intelligence gathering met with limited success. The one thing they all agreed on was that Spanish imperial might did not guarantee them many friends in Italy. In both Venice and Rome, the more the Spanish ambassadors learned about Italian politics and opinions, the less secure they felt. The Spaniards' spies and sources told them few things they wanted to hear; their vigilance convinced them only of the need for even greater vigilance, against enemies on both sides of the Alps. Once again, Spanish power did not necessarily translate into a Spanish peace.

The Habsburg campaign for control of Italy depended on accurate and timely information. Both Charles V and Philip II greatly valued their ambassadors' observations, and went to great lengths keeping this

---

1. Donald E. Queller, *The Office of Ambassador in the Middle Ages* (Princeton, 1961), pp. 82–84. This of course is still true of modern ambassadors.
2. John R. Hale, *The Civilization of Europe in the Renaissance* (New York, 1994), pp. 70–71.

information secret. Like most early modern princes, the Habsburgs employed elaborate codes and ciphers in all of their diplomatic correspondence.[3] They also periodically changed the codes, knowing that inevitably letters get intercepted and codes get broken. In April 1556, for example, the newly crowned Philip wrote to Francisco de Vargas in Venice, informing him that his ambassadors would no longer be using the emperor's codes. (This may have been an attempt to differentiate himself from his father as much as a security issue.) Philip sent Vargas two new ciphers, one for "general" correspondence amongst Spanish ministers of state, and the other to be used when sending urgent letters directly to the king. He stressed to his ambassador that he should vary which numbers stood for which letters or words, in order to maximize the codes' effectiveness.[4]

This system was typical for Philip's diplomatic corps. Sometimes it could be even more complex; Spanish ambassadors in Paris used up to five different codes simultaneously.[5] This level of security was understandable in enemy territory—but even the ambassadors to ostensibly friendly governments acted similarly. In 1570, for example, Philip instructed Antonio de Mendoza, a new ambassador to Genoa, on how to maintain secrecy. The Genoese were among Philip's closest allies in Italy, and yet the king made it clear Mendoza should keep his eyes open, and report what he saw in code. Mendoza, too, received one code for general correspondence, and "another particular one for those things which are so secret that it is advisable to use it."[6] So the ambassador to a "friendly" Italian state still proceeded as if he could not trust his hosts. But as concerned about intelligence from Genoa as the king may have been, it was nothing compared to what he wanted from the embassies in Venice and Rome.

Both Venice and Rome were nominally friendly with Spain, but also often befriended Spain's enemies; the ambassadors' primary intelligence objectives, therefore, were to divine Italian intentions, and anticipate betrayal. The unique nature of Venetian and papal governments, however, made analysis of their policies an arduous process. In the Republic of Venice, for example, the Doge was the nominal ruler, but much of the actual power lay in the hands of the Senate and various councils, which were often divided

3. Garrett Mattingly, *Renaissance Diplomacy* (reprint, New York, 1988), pp. 214–16.

4. Philip to Vargas, April 26, 1556; Archivo General de Simancas, Sección Estado (hereafter AGAS) 1323, #132. Actually, it was usually the ambassador's secretary who did the coding work, just as one of Philip's secretaries would then decode the message on the other end. The archives contain many examples of coded letters, together with decoded copies (*decifradas*).

5. De Lamar Jensen, *Diplomacy and Dogmatism: Bernardino de Mendoza and the French Catholic League* (Cambridge, Mass., 1964), pp. 122–23.

6. Philip to Antonio de Mendoza, October 1, 1570; AGSE 1401, #258.

into factions. In addition, while the Doge held his title for life, temporary officials and magistrates performed many government functions.[7] The actual formation of policy, therefore, was a complex and opaque process, hard to decipher by outsiders. The Venetians intended this to be the case. The *Signoria* hid its inner workings from foreign surveillance, and went so far as to set up a counterintelligence agency. This move produced mixed results.

Throughout the Renaissance, a profitable black market in state secrets existed in Venice, and in response the *Signoria* in 1539 created the State Inquisition to root out informants inside the government.[8] Three years later the *Signoria* passed a law forbidding any Venetian from visiting the house of a foreigner (including ambassadors) without express government permission.[9] Spanish ambassadors routinely complained about the difficulties in getting anybody to talk to them. Diego Guzmán de Silva, for instance, wrote that "Here [in Venice] they proceed so secretly and with such caution and reserve that not only do [government officials] keep silent . . . but even the other nobles, and thus it is dangerous for me to give opinions for I cannot say anything for certain."[10]

As a result, the ambassadors resorted to watching the *Signoria* closely, looking for indications of policy shifts, and gauging the relative power of individuals or factions inside the Senate. Rodrigo Niño, for instance, less than a month after arriving in Venice, sent Charles a hopeful report about a change of personnel in the Senate: "some left who I was glad to see go, and others entered who I would want to stay forever."[11] Diego Hurtado de Mendoza, by contrast, sent a more ambivalent description of the *Signoria* upon first arriving at his post:

> Here are two heads working together, and these are the persons whose hands presently govern the affairs of this Republic. One is [Senator] Marco Foscari, and the other is Gian Dolfin, who is the former's creature. This Marco Foscari is much too close to the French and the Turks [*françesissimo y turquissimo*]. He has a good knowledge of everything, and seems easygoing. He has a son, a bishop, whom he wants to make a cardinal and rich. It would not be difficult, if treated with skill, and promised Your Majesty's favor, to make him change sides, especially if he obtained some profit or Church benefice. If he came over to our side, so would his followers.[12]

7. See D. S. Chambers, *The Imperial Age of Venice, 1380–1580* (London, 1970), pp. 73–107.
8. Paolo Preto, *I servizi segreti di Venezia* (Milan, 1994), pp. 95–146.
9. Erica Spivakovsky, *Son of the Alhambra: Don Diego Hurtado de Mendoza, 1504–1575* (Austin, 1970), p. 120.
10. Guzmán to Philip, June 14, 1571; AGSE 1329, #64.
11. Niño to Charles, April 2, 1530; AGSE 1308, #22.
12. Mendoza to Francisco de los Cobos, September 3, 1539; *Algunas Cartas de Don Diego*

So according to Mendoza, the most powerful man in Venice was currently friendly with Spain's enemies, but he could be bought. As we will see, Spanish ambassadors often complemented espionage with bribery. But Mendoza never got a chance to test his theory: the following month, Foscari and Dolfin fell from power. Mendoza complained that the Venetian political scene shifted faster than he could he report it.[13]

Over the years Mendoza often supplemented his assessment of the *Signoria* with disparaging comments about Venetian avarice. In 1540, the ambassador warned Charles that the Venetians valued their business interests in the Levant more highly than defeating the Muslim enemy.[14] Two years later, soon after the Republic had signed a separate peace with the Turks, Mendoza complained, "the senators are all wealthy men, and when they anticipate war they raise money and cause shortages, but when they expect a period of peace, they deposit their money and devalue the currency."[15] Mendoza's final report on Venice, written in 1546, again emphasized that the Venetians' overriding concern was their commercial empire. According to Mendoza, of all the world powers, the Venetians feared only Charles and the Turks, respected only Charles, and wished everyone ill.[16] This last assertion may have been a projection of Mendoza's own anger and resentment toward Venice. Despite the ambassador's best efforts, the Venetians had abandoned their alliance with Charles and made peace with the Turks. The Venetians might respect the emperor, but not enough to place his interests above their own.

The Ottoman Turks, of course, scared everybody in the sixteenth century, and they were a particular concern for Spanish ambassadors in Venice. Their correspondence almost always began with a status report on the Turkish military situation, whatever the topic of the dispatch. The key question was always the same: Were the Turks about to attack? The usual answer was, nobody really knows, but everybody fears yes. Such

Hurtado de Mendoza, escritas 1538–1552, ed. Alberto Vazquez and R. Selden Rose (New Haven, 1935), pp. 11–12; also quoted in Spivakovsky, *Son of the Alhambra*, pp. 79–80. Both Foscari and Dolfin were descended from former doges of Venice; see John Julius Norwich, *A History of Venice* (reprint, New York, 1989), pp. 232–34, 334–40.

13. Spivakovsky, *Son of the Alhambra*, pp. 81–82.
14. Mendoza to Charles, December 19, 1540; *Algunas Cartas*, p. 60.
15. Mendoza to Charles, July 30, 1542; AGSE 1497, Libro 66, ff. 12–13.
16. Mendoza to Charles, December 29, 1546; AGSE 1318, #141–44. It is interesting that Mendoza's last report on Venice greatly resembled Venetian *relazioni*, i.e., the final reports that Venetian ambassadors wrote when they ended their terms. See Donald Queller, "The Development of Ambassadorial Relazioni," in *Renaissance Venice*, ed. J. R. Hale (London, 1973), pp. 174–96.

fears remained present even after the Turks ceased to be Spain's main concern. In December 1597, for example, twenty years after Philip signed a truce with the Turks, Iñigo de Mendoza wrote an urgent letter to the state minister Juan de Idiáquez, warning of rumors of war preparations in Constantinople, and signs of a large fleet massing for an attack.[17] Mendoza and his colleagues in Venice were usually the first Spaniards to hear about Turkish maneuvers, because of Venice's unique interaction with the Near East. Venetian colonies and commercial outposts extended throughout the eastern Mediterranean, and Venice itself stood at a crossroads between western Europe and the Levant.[18] Furthermore, Venice and Constantinople kept in remarkably close contact, each maintaining resident embassies in the other's city.[19] The Spanish Habsburgs thus relied on the Venetians for information on the Turks, even as they condemned their sometime ally for being too friendly with the enemy.[20] In 1530, for example, Rodrigo Niño wrote to the Empress Isabel that

> Your Majesty commands me to always advise you about the Turks, and I assure you that my greatest concern is to learn what is most important in this matter, and I always report what they know here in my letters. But as I have told Your Majesty before, [the Venetians] keep their relations with the Turks greatly secret, because of their concern for their commerce in the Levant. . . . The merchants who reside in Constantinople do not dare write about [political] matters, and the only ones who do are the [Venetian] ambassadors, and so we cannot get the latest news except through a torturous route, and I suspect we know nothing except what [the Venetians] wish to be known.[21]

Niño was obviously frustrated about being forced to depend on unreliable sources of information. Almost seventy years later, Iñigo de Mendoza expressed similar aggravation to Idiáquez: the one thing he found repugnant about his job, he said, was that his inability to state the truth about Venetian-Turkish relations threatened his reputation as an honest man.[22]

17. Mendoza to Idiáquez, December 13, 1597; AGSE 1676, unnumbered.
18. See William H. McNeill, *Venice, the Hinge of Europe 1081–1797* (Chicago, 1974).
19. See Maria Pia Pedani, *In nome del Gran Signore: Inviati ottomani a Venezia della caduta di Constantinopla alla Guerra di Candia* (Venice, 1994).
20. See Giovanni K. Hassiotis, "Venezia e i domini veneziani tramite di informazioni sui turchi per gli spagnoli nel sec. XVI," in *Venezia centro di mediazione tra Oriente e Occidente (secoli XV–XVI)*, ed. Hans-Georg Beck (Florence, 1977), pp. 116–36.
21. Niño to Isabel, November 20, 1530; AGSE 1308, #115.
22. Mendoza to Idiáquez, May 9, 1598; AGSE 1676, unnumbered.

As a matter of fact, Spanish ambassadors were routinely made to look like liars when it came to Venice's true relationship with the Turks. Diego Hurtado de Mendoza and Diego Guzmán de Silva, of course, suffered the worst, as it was on their respective watches that the Venetians abandoned alliances with Spain and made peace with the Turks. Although both were skilled diplomats, they both failed at their primary mission. In Mendoza's case, he was perhaps less to blame than his superiors; he provided good intelligence on the Venetians, but nobody listened. From his arrival in Venice in 1539, Mendoza made it clear that the Republic was in no condition to fight a prolonged war. Food supplies represented the most immediate problem: as he wrote, "in this city there is great need for wheat, and an even greater need of hope, because here as in the rest of Italy there have been very bad harvests, and they have nowhere to turn except for [our] Kingdoms of Naples and Sicily, or else the Turks, and this could force them into making peace."[23] For months, Mendoza repeated this basic message, emphasizing that the Venetians' continued participation in the Holy League depended on more generous grain shipments to Venice from Spanish Italy. But Charles, perhaps deluded by Venice's reputation as a commercial powerhouse, did little to alleviate his ally's misery.[24]

Still, Mendoza remained calm. He hoped that the Turks' obvious hostility, and the Venetians' sense of duty to Christendom, would keep them firmly allied with the emperor.[25] Yet he held few illusions about Venetian virtue. In the name of unity, Mendoza was willing to overlook uncomfortable facts. In September 1539, for example, Mendoza advised his superiors about how to react to the loss of the fortress of Castelnuovo, in Naples, to the infamous corsair Barbarossa. The Spaniards knew that one of the reasons for this defeat was that the Venetians had secretly agreed not to fight the Muslim pirate, but Mendoza recommended that the emperor should pretend ignorance in order to preserve the Holy League. As the ambassador wrote to the state secretary Francisco de los Cobos,

> You [in Spain] must always take care to show great confidence in these people here [in Venice]. This will allay their fears; they have believed that His Majesty [Charles] despises them ever since the fall of Castelnuovo, because they made a truce with the Turk. . . . [The Venetians] should be told, if you think it right, that His Majesty believes Barbarossa deceived them. . . . if this

23. Mendoza to Charles, August 7, 1539; AGSE 1315, #152.
24. Spivakovsky, *Son of the Alhambra*, p. 77.
25. Mendoza to Charles, November 28, 1539; AGSE 1315, #165.

is not done, I am afraid their fear of the Emperor—which is always stirred up by those [Venetians] who do not like us, and by the French, who never sleep—together with the poor food conditions . . . will fill them with despair and really make them join the Turk.[26]

So in this case, the ambassador advised his government on how best to lie to an ally, who had just betrayed them, in order to prevent even worse betrayals: a clear example of the art of diplomacy.

The Venetians, however, refused to play by Spanish rules. All the signs Mendoza could read pointed to disaster. In a long letter of October 1539, Mendoza reported that the *Signoria* had entertained Turkish ambassadors, who had been behaving "very confidently and insolently," in a secret room in the Ducal Palace. Furthermore, the Venetian ambassador in Constantinople (Lorenzo Gritti) had sent word that the king of France's agent in the Levant, Antonio Rincón, had spread rumors of growing discord between Venice and Charles. Even worse, Gritti encouraged these rumors, and complained to the Turks that neither the emperor nor any other Christian prince had answered Venice's plea for food supplies. Lastly, Mendoza warned that several key people in the Venetian government resented imperial power. "I do as much as I can," Mendoza concluded, "to keep the *Signoria* friendly with Your Majesty . . . or at least to prevent them from joining with the enemy. They assure me they will not do this for any reason, except if, as I have said before to Your Majesty, they are compelled by extreme necessity."[27] Once again, Mendoza stated unequivocally that without food, Venice would defect from the Holy League. However, the urgency of the ambassador's intelligence notwithstanding, Charles was unwilling or unable to offer help; within a year, Venice had signed a separate peace.

Thirty years later, Guzmán de Silva fared no better; indeed, if anything, he performed poorly. Before being assigned to Venice, Guzmán had been posted as ambassador in England, where by all accounts he did rather well.[28] In Venice, however, he often appeared befuddled, never sure what the Venetians really thought or intended. He did know from the beginning his cause was in trouble: from the moment he set foot in Venice in 1571, he faced an uphill battle over getting the Venetians to commit to the Holy League. Two weeks after his arrival, he reported that the *Signoria*

26. Mendoza to Cobos, September 3, 1539; *Algunas Cartas*, pp. 9–10, also quoted by Spivakovsky, *Son of the Alhambra*, pp. 76–77.
27. Mendoza to Charles, October 19, 1539; AGSE 1315, #124–27.
28. See Manuel Fernández Álvarez, *Tres embajadores de Felipe II en Inglaterra* (Madrid, 1951), pp. 137–90; and Mattingly, *Renaissance Diplomacy*, pp. 174–75.

was stalling both him and the papal legate sent to discuss the alliance. Furthermore, a sizable faction of the Venetian nobility favored peace negotiations with the Turks.[29] Three weeks later nothing had changed, as far as he could tell; he bemoaned Venetian indecisiveness, "because the Turk does not sleep, and could do much damage."[30] In the following weeks the ambassador's dispatches wavered between cautious optimism and total despair, and the official declaration of the Holy League in May came almost as a shock. But that pleasant surprise would be nothing compared to what happened two years later. The triumph of Christian might at Lepanto turned to disillusionment with astonishing speed.

In the afterglow of Lepanto, Guzmán could perhaps be excused for being lulled into a false sense of security. When news of the victory arrived in October 1571, Venice exploded in celebration, and the canals rang with praise for Spain (see chapter 1). As Guzmán wrote,

> [The Venetians] demonstrate nothing but great contentment and joy for this most happy success. Such are the praises for Your Majesty and their debt to you that no words can express them. They never stop thanking God for the favor He has done them by uniting them perpetually with Your Majesty. I have seen their gratitude in their tears of joy, and the delight with which they declare their allegiance. . . . In the streets and houses they say nothing else out loud except "Long live King Philip the Catholic!" and many add, "our lord."[31]

The ambassador's own emotions, of course, may have colored his account; we do not know if crowds of Venetians were actually proclaiming their allegiance to Philip.[32] Still, there is no doubt that both the Venetians and the Spaniards were in a jubilant mood. A few days after the celebrations, the French bishop of Aix, an important diplomat/spy, appeared in Venice. Ordinarily Guzmán would have been alarmed, as the bishop was known to be France's main agent in a long-standing campaign to drive a wedge between Spain and Venice.[33] At this moment,

29. Guzmán to Philip, March 30, 1571; AGSE 1329, #26. Unknown to Guzmán, the Venetians were in fact conducting simultaneous negotiations with Spain and Rome on one side, and the Turks on the other. Jack Beeching, *The Galleys at Lepanto* (New York, 1982), pp. 166–71; and for a recent description of the events leading up to Lepanto, see also Rafael Vargas-Hidalgo, *La Batalla de Lepanto, según cartas inéditas de Felipe II, Don Juan de Austria y Juan Andrea Doria e informes de embajadores y espías* (Santiago, 1998).
30. Guzmán to Philip, April 21, 1571; AGSE 1329, #31.
31. Guzmán to Philip, October 22, 1571; AGSE 1329, #106.
32. Setton quotes Venetian municipal records of the celebrations, which mention Don Juan of Austria's name, but not Philip's. Kenneth M. Setton, *The Papacy and the Levant (1204–1571)*, 4 vols. (Philadelphia, 1976–1984), Vol. IV, p. 1060 n. 54.
33. The bishop was in fact in Venice for just that purpose: see below.

however, he dismissed the Frenchman as harmless, now that the Venetians were so grateful to Philip. Yet even in this period of confidence, Guzmán sounded an oddly cautious note: "What I can say about this city [of Venice] is this, *unless they deceive me:* that one can be sure about them."[34] Did Guzmán have a premonition of disaster? He seems to be undermining his own intelligence report—and he was right to do so.

Over the next year and a half Guzmán would become increasingly anxious about Venice's commitment to the Holy League. His uncertainty reflected divisions within the city itself. In March 1572 he reported that the Council of Ten, a government body that debated "the most secret and important matters of state," had met for three straight days. An informant told Guzmán that an elder noble named Nicolò da Ponte (who would become Doge in 1578) had spoken in the meeting against staying in the League, and had castigated Spain for being insolent and imperialistic ever since Lepanto. Guzmán also warned that while some in the Council had defended the League, others had agreed with Da Ponte, and that French agents were spreading similar ideas throughout the city.[35] Later that year, anti-Spanish sentiment increased after the League fleet failed to accomplish anything. Guzmán reported much grumbling among the Venetians about Don Juan de Austria's performance as commander of the fleet; the ambassador remarked sarcastically that "these people who are in their houses and at their leisure fight very well by sea or by land . . . but those who understand [combat] speak more cautiously and moderately."[36] His irritation with Venice's armchair admirals no doubt reflects underlying anxiety; he sensed that Venice was inching toward a defection from the League.

Philip, perhaps in response to his ambassador's concerns, agreed to shoulder a greater proportion of League costs in an effort to keep the Venetians happy.[37] But the Venetian response was ambiguous at best. In January 1573, Guzmán reported that the *Signoria* had demonstrated "contentment" with Philip's offer, but the ambassador warned that such concessions did not guarantee support for the League. In fact, Guzmán admitted ignorance about the true state of Venetian-Turkish relations: "It pains me not to be able to clarify nor give any specifics about [Venice's] intentions in this business, as I have said before. I believe they could very well make peace with the Turks, as some lean that way, while

34. Guzmán to Philip, October 25, 1571 (emphasis added); AGSE 1329, #111.
35. Guzmán to Philip, March 19, 1572; AGSE 1331, #26.
36. Guzmán to Philip, September 10, 1572; AGSE 1331, #103.
37. Luciano Serrano, *La Liga de Lepanto entre España, Venecia y la Santa Sede (1570–1573),* 2 vols. (Madrid, 1918–1920), Vol. II, chap. 9.

others the contrary."[38] This is a remarkable acknowledgment of clueless-
ness. Guzmán concluded the letter by relaying the Doge's assurances to
him that Venice would stay in the League, which he says he believed, and
yet noted that "it is fitting that Your Majesty should make provisions so
that whatever happens . . . you will be prepared." In other words, the
ambassador had no idea what was going to happen, and hoped for the
best, but feared the worst.

The next few months were particularly trying for Guzmán, as he desperately sought to determine Venetian intentions. His opinion on
whether Venice would stay in the League changed from week to week. In
February 1573 so many rumors of peace negotiations were flying around
the city that Guzmán wanted to confront the *Signoria* with them, but a
Venetian noble talked him out of it, arguing that a display of mistrust
would offend too many people.[39] A few weeks later Guzmán vented his
frustration to the king: "on the twenty-fifth when I spoke to the *Signoria*
on Your Majesty's behalf it seemed to me that they were happy and content; today I could judge the contrary. . . . Please God the devil does not
deceive them. I am acting with the required care, but also with the distress of not knowing the truth about what is happening."[40] Despite his evident fear, however, on March 17 Guzmán wrote a surprisingly positive
letter, reporting that the Venetians had declared themselves to be "totally
determined to remain in the League."[41] He did not say why Philip should
believe the Venetians, in the face of so much contrary evidence; perhaps
Guzmán was all too eager to grasp at straws. Soon he would realize how
wrong he had been.

The first sign of catastrophe occurred on April 3, 1573, with the arrival
of two mysterious messengers from Constantinople. Guzmán's description of events gives us a fascinating view of the cloak-and-dagger atmosphere surrounding the Venetian-Turkish peace negotiations:

> This morning I was advised that yesterday at nightfall there arrived two men
> in a ship which came from Ruvino, who did not want to present themselves
> before the ministers of the city, as is the custom for all foreigners, as they
> wished to go directly to the Doge. . . . Having been given permission, they

38. Guzmán to Philip, January 2, 1573; AGSE 1332, #2.
39. Guzmán to Philip, February 17, 1573; AGSE 1332, #19.
40. Guzmán to Philip, February 27, 1573; AGSE 1332, #26. Guzmán was not the only one
who was worried: on March 19, Pope Gregory XIII issued a papal bull threatening to excommunicate any League member who defected, and he clearly had Venice in mind. Setton, *The
Papacy and the Levant*, Vol. IV, pp. 1090–91.
41. Guzmán to Philip, March 17, 1573; AGSE 1332, #30.

were taken from the ship in a covered gondola so they would not be seen. They went by a somewhat isolated canal to St. Mark's, and afterwards they returned there, and according to what I was told they had been with the Doge. The more important of the two men came dressed in crimson damask, and the other in black, both in Levantine style.

Guzmán does not say who tipped him off to these developments, but he does describe how he investigated:

The Papal nuncio was in the College this morning. I went to his house to ask if he knew anything about these events. He told me [the Venetians] had told him nothing. . . . But the emperor's ambassador had sent to him to say that the son of the *bailo* [the Venetian ambassador to Constantinople] had arrived, and had brought with him a signed peace treaty with the Turks. I went to look for the [imperial] ambassador and met him on the street that leads to the nuncio's house and from there to my residence. I asked him what he knew, and he told me a highly placed source had told him the *bailo's* son had come with a signed peace treaty. I asked him if he knew anything more specific, but he said no. I asked him to try to discover more, and I will do the same.[42]

We see here the diplomatic community in Venice at work, as the various foreign ambassadors combined their resources to uncover the truth. Unfortunately, the truth was exactly what Guzmán had feared: Venice had abandoned the League.

In the aftermath, Guzmán sought to discover what had happened. As best as he could determine, the Council of Ten, and specifically Nicolò da Ponte, had initiated the peace negotiations. Significantly, they blamed Spain for forcing them into a separate peace, by failing to support League operations. The *Signoria* pointed to Don Juan's tardiness in joining the League fleet, and the subsequent failure of the 1572 campaign (see chapter 1). Or at least this was the "story" (*ficción*) the *Signoria* published. Guzmán claimed that many Venetians grieved over the defection, and refused to meet his eye, "like embarrassed and ashamed people."[43] Yet Guzmán himself also appeared somewhat embarrassed. Over the next few months various Venetian nobles, including many who had supported the League, accused Spain of being unwilling to fight, and thus causing the

42. Guzmán to Philip, April 3, 1573; AGSE 1332, #36. This document was originally encoded, and deciphered by a secretary.
43. Guzmán to Philip, April 8, 1573; AGSE 1332, #39.

disintegration of the League.[44] And Guzmán had no retort. In truth, Philip had indeed ordered Don Juan not to proceed to the Levant, although it is unclear if Guzmán knew that.[45] In any case, Venice's defection should not have come as a surprise, either to Guzmán or to Philip.[46] For the next three years, Guzmán tried to atone for his failure, and bring the Venetians to their senses, but he never really understood them. In April 1575, he admitted, "it pains me not to be able to advise Your Majesty with certainty about what [the Venetians] know about Constantinople."[47] To the end, Guzmán mourned his failures as an intelligence agent, as did many of his colleagues in Venice. Guzmán had been vigilant, but in the end he had no power, and no control over Venetian policy.

The Spanish ambassadors in Rome faced a different set of challenges. Instead of trying to decipher the actions of various councils and senators, in Rome the ambassadors focused on understanding one man, the pope. They analyzed the pontiff's every move and word, and speculated on what they could not see. Two key questions dominated the Roman embassy's attentions: Would the pope favor Spain or its enemies? And how long before the next papal election? The latter issue produced some rather startling comments from the ambassadors; they reported the pope's physical condition in minute detail, including his eating and urination habits.[48] In January 1564, for example, Requeséns described at length how Pope Pius IV had for some time been suffering stomach pains and lack of appetite. For days, Pius had eaten too little and drunk too much, and the Roman court buzzed with rumors about possible papal ailments.[49] Twenty years later, Olivares noted that Pope Gregory XIII's relatives were concerned that the pope should not exert himself too much during Rome's stifling summer months; in fact, on the advice of his doctors, Gregory had begun to take afternoon siestas in the nude.[50] The pope's privacy, it seems, was limited.

As much time as the ambassadors spent discussing papal physiology, however, they were even more interested in the pontifical psychology.

44. Guzmán to Philip, June 20, 1573; AGSE 1332, #63.
45. Serrano, *Liga de Lepanto*, Vol. II, p. 270–71.
46. The Venetian ambassadors in Madrid who broke the news of the defection to Philip reported that the king claimed to be surprised, although he clearly was not. See *Pursuit of Power: Venetian Ambassadors' Reports on Spain, Turkey, and France in the Age of Philip II, 1560–1600*, ed. James C. Davis (New York, 1970), p. 104.
47. Guzmán to Philip, April 9, 1575; AGSE 1334, #27.
48. On April 6, 1591, Olivares reported on Pope Gregory XIV's trouble urinating, which his doctors feared could mean the presence of gallstones. AGSE 957, unnumbered.
49. Requeséns to Philip, January 13, 1564; AGSE 896, #13.
50. Olivares to Philip, July 13, 1583; AGSE 944, #95.

The ambassadors took great care to construct psychological profiles of
the different popes. Sometimes their reports could be pithy, like
Requeséns' description of Pius IV: "the pope's humor is to be taken for a
soldier and a man of great vision, and to be remembered as such."[51] Similarly, Requeséns quickly summarized Pius V as a man who knew nothing
of politics, and seemed to think of himself as an Old Testament figure, so
sure was he of God's support for his policies.[52] Other times, the ambassadors' reports could go into great detail, as Zúñiga did with Gregory XIII:

> In all of the letters I have written to Your Majesty after the pope's election I
> have related how he conducts business, and [described] the people who
> have a say in his decisions, and now . . . I will say that the pope has always
> shown himself to be man of good intentions. In affairs of state he has done
> much to demonstrate how little experience he has in such matters. As
> regards the issue of Church reform, it was thought that having been raised
> at this court, he would favor a more relaxed atmosphere, but after discover-
> ing this belief he has been very careful to follow the example of Pius V. Car-
> dinal Borromeo has been very influential on him in this matter. . . . With
> princes he desires to be strictly neutral, and it seems that most of all he will
> want peace.[53]

Thus the ambassador analyzed the pope's character, and theorized how
Gregory would most likely handle political and religious issues. This is the
kind of assessment of leaders that has been the goal of political analysts
throughout the history of diplomacy.[54]

So Zúñiga and his colleagues closely studied the current popes; at the
same time, they always had an eye toward the next pope. Handicapping
the College of Cardinals has always been the favorite pastime of the Roman
court, and the Spanish ambassadors played the game with intensity.[55] They
evaluated every cardinal: What were his chances? Would he be good or bad
for Spain? And how could the odds be improved? Requeséns, for example,

---

51. Requeséns to Philip, January 6, 1564; AGSE 896, #10.
52. Requeséns to Philip, March 16, 1567; *Correspondencia diplomática entre España y la Santa
Sede durante el pontificado de S. Pío V*, ed. Luciano Serrano, 4 vols. (Madrid, 1914), Vol. II, p.
65.
53. Zúñiga to Philip, August 11, 1572; AGSE 919, #63.
54. For an analysis of the development of modern diplomatic theory, see James Der Derian,
On Diplomacy: A Genealogy of Western Estrangement (Oxford, 1987).
55. Of course, it was not just the Spaniards who did this, but everyone. The cardinals
watched each other, for one thing, and the Italians at court loved to guess who was *papabile*
(literally, "papable," or likely to be elected pope). See *Court and Politics in Papal Rome,
1492–1700*, ed. Gianvittorio Signorotto and Maria Antonietta Visceglia (Cambridge, 2002).

dispatched a number of massive reports on this subject. One such document, written in January 1565, ran to forty-eight pages. Requeséns himself
felt rather overwhelmed by his task, as he suggested:

> Your Majesty commanded me to describe very particularly what I under-
> stood in Rome about the personality of each of the competing cardinals,
> and the strengths and weaknesses of each as a possible pope. . . . In this
> matter Your Majesty must presuppose that nothing in the world is more
> difficult than to really know people, and there is nothing in which decep-
> tions are more common. And if this is generally true of all people, then it
> is even more so of the clerics and cardinals of Rome. One need look no
> further for an example of this than the last two pontiffs to be elected, one
> of whom [Paul IV] was thought to be very holy, but turned around to set
> fire to all of Christendom, and the other [Pius IV] who was Your Majesty's
> servant and vassal and who was made Pope with your help, but [after being
> elected] attended to Your Majesty's needs not at all . . . and besides, there
> is no business in the world whose outcome is harder to predict than a
> papal election.[56]

Requeséns thus warned the king that his assessments were no more
than educated guesses, which could be disastrously wrong. Even if the
Spanish faction got its first choice elected, the ambassador pointed out,
there were no guarantees about how that pope would act once on the
throne.

That being said, Requeséns then launched into a detailed description
of over fifty cardinals. His analyses of individual figures varied in length,
but typically he would state a cardinal's age, physical condition, birth-
place, financial status, education, work experience, political affiliations,
friends and enemies in the College, reputation (both political and religious), potential agenda if elected pope, and relative chances of being
elected. Not every cardinal received such a thorough vetting; Requeséns
had little to say about Spaniards and Frenchmen, for example, although
for different reasons. Obviously, he expected the king to be familiar with
the Spanish cardinals, and the opposition to them; on Francisco Pacheco,
for instance, he merely wrote that "Your Majesty knows him and his many
good qualities, but as he is Spanish, he has no chance [to be elected]."[57]
Conversely, since the Spaniards automatically opposed any French candidate, Requeséns spent no time on them either. He was careful to note,

56. Requeséns to Philip, January 5, 1565; AGSE 900, #43.
57. Ibid.

however, sometimes in scathing terms, which Italian cardinals were members of the French faction. Of the Cardinal of Ferrara, Requeséns said, "está lleno de mal Francés en el alma y en el cuerpo," which roughly translated meant the man belonged to the French body and soul, but with the added implication that the Cardinal suffered from the "French disease," namely syphilis.[58] Early modern politics could be rough.

Requeséns devoted more space to those Italian cardinals who favored Spain, or at least had the potential to do so. Some he dismissed as candidates because they lacked experience, or intelligence, or in one case (the Cardinal of San Clemente) because "he is so ill-tempered that countless times he has exploded at people for no good reason." Ultimately what the ambassador looked for was a pro-Spanish cardinal who stood a chance of getting elected. One individual Requeséns singled out was an obscure ex-Dominican friar, Cardinal Alessandrino:

> He is sixty years old, but seems older because of very poor health. He is a theologian and a very good man of exemplary lifestyle, and greatly zealous in matters of faith. In my judgment he is the cardinal most fitting to be pope in these times, but I think he will get no votes, because he is considered rigid, and the other cardinals want a pope who would be a good companion. Although it may not yet be time to support him, he seems to me to be very worthy of nomination by Your Majesty.[59]

A year later, Requeséns would be pleasantly surprised when this unpopular, doctrinaire cardinal was elected as Pope Pius V. On this occasion, the ambassador's intelligence report was faulty due to being overly pessimistic. But this would hardly be the Spanish ambassadors' worst failure. In 1592, Ippolito Aldobrandini was not the Spaniards' first choice for pope (in fact he was last among the acceptable candidates), but they did support him in the end.[60] As it turned out, this was a terrible mistake, as Clement VIII proved to be the most anti-Spanish pope since Paul IV. Sessa and Olivares did not foresee this outcome, and it cost the Spaniards dearly.

Still, most of the Spanish ambassadors' assessments of cardinals seem accurate, which raises a question: How did they know so much? Part of the answer lies in how seriously the ambassadors took their duties as intelligence agents. They watched everybody, but subjected the pope to especially intense surveillance, and reported whatever they saw. This was true

58. My thanks to Geoffrey Parker for his help translating this pun.
59. Requeséns to Philip, January 5, 1565; AGSE 900, #43.
60. Ludwig von Pastor, *The History of the Popes from the Close of the Middle Ages*, trans. Ralph Francis Kerr, 40 vols. (London, 1891–1953), Vol. XXIII, pp. 8–17.

even in times of relative peace. In October 1530, for example, only a few months after Charles's coronation ceremony in Bologna, Miguel Mai described how he would not let Pope Clement VII out of his sight. The pope had recently entered into an alliance with Charles, but Mai remained suspicious. When the pope decided to travel to the countryside on a hawking and hunting expedition, Mai feigned interest in joining him, so he could "observe him in everything he did." Unfortunately, when the party arrived in Ostia, it rained so hard the hunt had to be cancelled, and Mai had no opportunity to mingle.[61] Fifty years later, the count of Olivares carefully noted that Gregory XIII (a relatively pro-Spanish pope) often went horseback riding for his health, and when in the countryside, he stayed in the house of Cardinal Este of Ferrara.[62] Clearly, the ambassadors kept tabs on who spoke to the pope and when, and worried about what such meetings could mean.

But the ambassadors did not work alone, and this is where observation shaded into actual espionage. Just as happens today, Spanish diplomats in Italy paid for information from anyone who would sell. This does not necessarily reflect the level of corruption in Rome or any other court. In early modern Europe, the giving of gifts in return for favors was an accepted part of the patronage system.[63] Ambassadors oversaw cash payments to cardinals in the Spanish faction (see chapter 5); but they also channeled funds to lesser functionaries in the Roman court, often in return for information. In 1564, after Requeséns had left Rome following the precedence fiasco, he remained in contact with a secretary in a senior cardinal's household. He recommended that the king offer a pension to this man to keep him happy, and also forwarded the names of two other men in similar positions, whom he believed to be open to offers.[64]

Evidence suggests that the Roman embassy regularly paid for such informants, as well as other useful men. An expense account report (*gastos*) for the years 1568–1579, for example, suggests that Requeséns and Zúñiga gave "gifts" of silverwork and altar plate to numerous Church officials.[65] In 1571, the embassy spent 395 escudos on a silver candelabra and altar plate for the Apostolic Datary, the office which supervised the granting of ecclesiastical posts, pensions, and financial concessions. Was this

61. Mai to Charles, October 10, 1530; AGSE 850, #108.
62. Olivares to Philip, June 25, 1582; AGSE 943, #36.
63. Sharon Kettering, *Patrons, Brokers, and Clients in Seventeenth-Century France* (Oxford, 1986), pp. 192–206.
64. Requeséns to Philip, October 10, 1564; AGSE 896, #107.
65. Archivo General de Simancas, Contaduría Mayor, Segunda Epoca, Legajo 1241, sección 3, compiled in November 1582.

gift meant to grease the wheels of the papal bureaucracy? We can only speculate. In the same year the embassy also sent gifts of silver to a papal postmaster and his lieutenant for "the good news they brought of the victory over the Turkish fleet [at Lepanto]." Considering the critical value of timely information, making friends in the papal postal service would have been a top priority. Obviously, none of these expenses were listed as "bribes," but that is probably what they were. The most blatant example in this particular report was a gift of silver plate to "the chamberlain of His Holiness most dedicated to the service of His Majesty." Chamberlains controlled access to the pope's apartments, so they were definitely targets for bribery—and in this case, the man in question was already pro-Spanish.

The ambassadors in Venice likewise recruited informants inside the *Signoria,* in an attempt to pierce the mysteries of Venetian policymaking. In 1540, for example, Diego de Mendoza wrote a remarkably candid letter to Charles about how best to set up a spy system in Venice. The emperor had evidently suggested that his ambassador should offer money to certain high officials, but Mendoza was hesitant. He pointed out that people's true allegiances were difficult to determine. If a secretly anti-imperial senator were offered a bribe, he might go public, which would be a "great danger and risk to Your Majesty's credit and authority."[66] Mendoza promised that he would approach ranking members in the Venetian government, if a safe opportunity presented itself. In the meantime, however, he suggested an alternative plan: "In my opinion what would be most advantageous would be to buy a pair of secretaries who will advise [us] of events [in the *Signoria*] quickly and reliably." Such well-placed sources, the ambassador wrote, would be of great help when negotiating with the Venetians. Charles agreed, so Mendoza suborned two secretaries, paying them an annual salary of six hundred escudos each. In later years Mendoza was so pleased with his purchases that he encouraged the emperor to spend four thousand escudos a year, twice the ambassador's own salary, on recruiting more informants.[67] Guzmán de Silva wrote similar letters to Philip; in 1576, he recommended that a salary be offered to a certain Venetian noble, "Because I understand that he could be very useful, and it is appropriate that he be rewarded."[68]

The ambassadors in Venice did not limit their espionage activities to the Venetian government; in fact, they ran an entire network of spies that spanned the eastern Mediterranean. In July 1543 Charles wrote to his

66. Mendoza to Charles, February 9, 1540; AGSE 1316, #15.
67. Spivakovsky, *Son of the Alhambra*, pp. 94–95.
68. Guzmán to Philip, May 5, 1576; AGSE 1335, #26.

state minister Francisco de los Cobos concerning Diego de Mendoza's finances, specifically referring to money earmarked for "spies and intelligences which [Mendoza] has in the Levant and other places, as well as dispatches and other important matters done in our service." Mendoza had requested five thousand escudos for such expenses, in addition to the six thousand he had already been allotted; the emperor approved of the request, half to be paid in cash, the other half in a letter of credit to be paid by the viceroy of Naples.[69] Two years later, Mendoza boasted to a Church secretary at the Council of Trent that he had received news of Turkish military maneuvers from "his own spy" on the Bosporus.[70] In addition to his other duties, Mendoza was a spymaster.

Mendoza's successors in Venice operated similarly. In February 1555 Francisco de Vargas reported to Charles that he had a spy in the household of an important Turkish official, who kept the ambassador informed about the sultan's dealings with both Venice and France.[71] Sixteen years later, Diego Guzmán de Silva, just two days after arriving at his post in Venice, wrote to Juan de Zúñiga in Rome concerning the urgent necessity of developing new intelligence sources on Venetian-Turkish relations.[72] As we have seen, Guzmán would spend his entire tenure in Venice wondering what was really going on, but his ignorance was not for lack of trying. The *Signoria* shared some of its intelligence reports with Guzmán, but they obviously did not tell him everything. In a conversation with the Doge in January 1572, Guzmán relayed a request from Don Juan de Austria, commander of the League fleet, that the Venetians should increase their espionage campaign against the Turks. The Doge promised he would dispatch more agents into the field, and suggested the Spaniards should do the same, perhaps with the aid of Jews, or of Christians pretending to be Jews.[73] Given Spanish sensitivity about Jewish ancestry, this well may have been an insult.[74] Yet Guzmán apparently took the Doge at his word, and hired Jewish spies.

The Ottoman Turks were relatively tolerant of Jews living in their lands, and Jewish merchants traded and traveled freely throughout the eastern

69. Charles to Cobos, July 7, 1543; Archivo General de Simancas, Consejo y Juntas de Hacienda, Legajo 16, #154.

70. Setton, *The Papacy and the Levant*, Vol. III, pp. 487–88.

71. Vargas to Charles, February 4, 1555; AGSE 1323, #57. Vargas mentions that the spy was in danger of being beheaded if he was discovered.

72. Guzmán to Zúñiga, March 17, 1571; AGSE 1500, #3.

73. Guzmán to Philip, January 8, 1572; AGSE 1332, #2.

74. In 1573, the Venetian ambassador to Spain, Leonardo Donà, wrote a contemptuous report about the Spaniards, who claimed to be more Catholic than anyone else, but in reality were all "so many baptized Jews and Moors." *Pursuit of Power,* p. 97.

Mediterranean.[75] As a result, these Jews saw and heard quite a lot, and many came through Venice with valuable information. Guzmán took advantage of this, so we have the fascinating spectacle of a Spanish ambassador (and a cleric to boot) working closely with Levantine Jews in late Renaissance Venice. Sometimes these men remain anonymous, like a Jewish member of a Turkish ambassador's entourage, who discussed the current state of Turkish-Venetian relations with Guzmán in June 1574.[76] Guzmán described other sources in great detail, such as a man named David Passi, who volunteered his services in the summer of 1573. Passi was a diplomat and a career spy, who worked for both Christian and Muslim masters.[77] Guzmán's initial report on Passi illustrates the ambassador's thorough research:

> A Jew named David has arrived here from Ragusa, who was in that republic during the recent conflict with the Turks. According to my sources, he is the nephew of the Jewish doctor who negotiated peace [between Venice and the Turks]. He speaks Spanish, and claims to be a native Spaniard, and to have debts there, and as a Spaniard desires to enter Your Majesty's service. He has been serving the Venetians, but claims to be dissatisfied with them because they have not paid him; but you cannot trust Jews. . . . He tells me he knows for certain that the Venetians always intended to seek peace [with the Turks], and that no one would know better than he, because he handled many of the negotiations.[78]

Despite his distrust, Guzmán was impressed by Passi's depth of knowledge, and accepted his offer of service. Over the next two years Guzmán's correspondence with Philip contained numerous references to Passi and the intelligence he gathered on the Turks. At one point Guzmán passed on the king's personal thanks to Passi for his work.[79] Evidently even Philip did not let religious prejudice get in the way of using a good spy.

Spanish ambassadors in Venice remained in charge of espionage on the Turks long after the Venetians defected from the League, and indeed long after Philip himself signed a truce with the sultan. The Ottoman Empire remained a threat, so the intelligence network was maintained.

---

75. See Daniel Goffman, *The Ottoman Empire and Early Modern Europe* (Cambridge, 2002), chap. 6.
76. Guzmán to Philip, June 11, 1574; AGSE 1333, #48. Guzmán mentions that this Jew was a native of Milan, and thus one of Philip's subjects, which may explain why he was willing to spy for Spain.
77. Paolo Preto, *I servizi segreti de Venezia* (Milan, 1994), pp. 100–105.
78. Guzmán to Philip, August 13, 1573; AGSE 1332, #78.
79. Guzmán to Philip, March 26, 1574; AGSE 1333, #31.

Iñigo de Mendoza's expense reports from 1597 to 1598, for example, itemize 150 escudos spent on a "secret person who serves Your Majesty in the Levant."[80] All of the ambassadors knew that if the network were compromised, the results could be catastrophic. This fact explains the panic evident in a letter from another ambassador in Venice, Francisco de Vera y Aragon, to the duke of Sessa in Rome in October 1593. De Vera warned Sessa that one of their best sources on the Turks, a certain Greek merchant, might in fact be a double agent. De Vera had turned up evidence that this Greek was playing both sides (*que haze a dos manos*), and had been corresponding with a known Turkish spymaster. De Vera was not certain about the man's treachery, but thought it likely, since "Greeks are avaricious."[81] Unfortunately, no other records of this episode have survived, so we do not know how the situation was resolved. But it is clear that the Spanish embassy in Venice was a command center for espionage in the Mediterranean.

One focus of the ambassadors' espionage activities was the Turks; the other was France. Often the two were related: as we have seen, French diplomacy aimed at separating Venice from Spain, and successfully facilitated both Venetian-Turkish peace treaties. The Spanish ambassadors were aware of French plots, and so kept a wary eye on any French diplomat who visited the Republic. Both Rodrigo Niño and Diego de Mendoza, for example, tracked every movement of Antonio Rincón, the renegade Spaniard and French agent who flitted between Venice and Constantinople (see chapter 1). As early as 1530, Niño warned Charles that Rincón was secretly offering to broker a truce between the Venetians and the Turks, as well as enticing the Turks to declare war on the emperor.[82] And Niño's fears were warranted: Rincón was in fact instrumental in the signing of the 1540 peace treaty. When imperial troops assassinated Rincón in 1541, the ambassadors no doubt celebrated, quietly.

A generation later, Guzmán de Silva fought a similar losing battle against François Noailles, the French bishop of Aix. Like Rincón before him, Noailles facilitated peace negotiations between Venice and the Turks, and thus directly opposed Guzmán's efforts to keep Venice in the Holy League.[83] From 1571 to 1573 Noailles made periodic appearances

---

80. *Relacion de gastos,* dated January 1598; AGSE 1676, unnumbered. Another item lists 72 escudos spent on servants and secretaries inside the *Signoria.*

81. De Vera to Sessa, October 30, 1593; Instituto de Valencia de Don Juan, Envio 9, Caja 15, #400.

82. Niño to Charles, May 18, 1530; AGSE 1308, #59.

83. See Noailles' correspondence in *Négociations de la France dans le Levant,* ed. E. Charrière, 4 vols. (reprint, New York, 1966), Vol. III, pp. 221–22, 240–44.

in Venice, and each time Guzmán reported it to Philip. The Spanish ambassador's fear and hatred of his rival are clear in his letters; he often refers to Noailles as "that dangerous heretic," and makes sneering references to the bishop's friendship with Gaspard de Coligny, leader of the French Protestants.[84] Guzmán knew very well what Noailles was up to: the Spanish intelligence network tracked the bishop's travels back and forth from Constantinople. The papacy was also aware of this rogue bishop: in July 1572, the papal nuncio in France reported that Noailles, who was "much in the confidence of the Venetians," had "put the negotiation for peace between the Venetians and the Turk on an excellent footing."[85]

Yet knowing what the French were doing and being able to stop them were separate issues. In July 1573, a few months after the announcement of the truce, one of Guzmán's spies inside Ottoman territory confirmed earlier reports that Noailles had been directly involved in the peace negotiations.[86] Once again French diplomacy had bested the Spaniards. Two years later, David Passi informed Guzmán that the bishop was currently trying to arrange an anti-Spanish alliance amongst Venice, France, and the Turks.[87] So not only had Noailles helped dissolve the Holy League, now he was attempting to turn Venice into an enemy!

Whatever hostility Guzmán may have felt toward the French, however, in July 1574 he had to dissimulate. That month Venice played host to no less a personage than Henry III, the new king of France. Henry, who had been in Poland (where he had also been—briefly and unhappily— king), was touring northern Italy on his way back to France. Venice honored him with a week-long series of celebrations and feasts.[88] The circus-like atmosphere was matched by the whirlwind of diplomatic activity that accompanied the visit. Various Italian princes came to see Henry, and Guzmán watched with a jaundiced eye. As Spain's representative in Venice, he participated in the festivities and played the gracious courtier, but he could not help but be nervous and resentful of the attention the Venetians lavished on the French king. The intelligence he sent back to Spain about these events boded ill for Habsburg hegemony in Italy.

84. See for example Guzmán to Philip, October 26, 1571; AGSE 1329, #111.

85. Antonio Maria Salviati to Cardinal Boncampagno, July 16, 1572; *Calendar of State Papers, Relating to English Affairs, Preserved Principally at Rome, in the Vatican Archives and Library*, ed. J. M. Rigg, Vol. II (London, 1926), pp. 28–29.

86. Guzmán to Philip, July 16, 1573; AGSE 1332, #72. Guzmán also noted that this particular agent was a Neapolitan who had fled Naples on suspicion of murdering his own mother. As any modern intelligence agent knows, saints do not make good spies.

87. Guzmán to Philip, January 22, 1575; AGSE 1334, #10.

88. Norwich, *History of Venice*, pp. 492–94.

Guzmán reported in great detail the excitement in Venice about the royal visit. Three weeks before the event he remarked on the grand apartments the Venetians had decorated for the king's use, and the ten gondolas covered with scarlet satin they had prepared to convey Henry and his entourage.[89] From the moment Henry arrived, the Venetians heaped honors on his head. The Doge met the king on the outskirts of the city, and accompanied him personally on his way to the Ducal Palace; according to Venetian civic ritual, this was the highest compliment possible.[90] Guzmán waited for the king with the other foreign ambassadors, and greeted him courteously, as he told Philip: "I said to him in a few words what seemed fitting for the occasion. The king responded graciously in Italian, that being what I spoke to him, knowing he understands no languages other than that and French."[91] Clearly Guzmán had done his homework in preparation for this meeting. The king and the ambassador exchanged pleasantries, and Guzmán noted that Henry doffed his hat when speaking to him—a signal mark of respect for the king of Spain's representative.

As good-natured as this initial meeting appeared to be, however, this was a deadly serious situation for the Spanish ambassador. He watched the proceedings, and described to Philip the magnificence of the reception, because of the event's political ramifications. Signs of friendship between Venice and France were not innocent to Spanish eyes.[92] Even apparently comic moments had ominous overtones. One spectacle the Venetians created for the king's amusement involved a traditional mock battle, where two "armies" fought over possession of a bridge.[93] Guzmán explained to Philip that this game had been banned for some years, because too many people had gotten maimed or killed, but in Henry's honor the *Signoria* had reinstated it. According to Guzmán, the king greatly enjoyed the spectacle, "because many people were knocked into the water."[94] The interesting thing about Guzmán's account is that it disagrees with the Venetian memory of the event. According to Venetian sources, the *Signoria* was

89. Guzmán to Philip, July 2, 1574; AGSE 1333, #57.

90. Edward Muir, *Civic Ritual in Renaissance Venice* (Princeton, 1981), p. 235.

91. Guzmán to Philip, July 22, 1574; AGSE 1333, #65.

92. Edward Muir suggests that the Venetians purposely designed their decorations around the theme of "courting French favor at the expense of the Spanish." "Images of Power: Art and Pageantry in Renaissance Venice," *American Historical Review* 84 (1979), pp. 43–45.

93. For details on this event, see Robert C. Davis, "The Spectacle Almost Fit for a King: Venice's *Guerra de'canne* of 26 July 1574," in *Medieval and Renaissance Venice*, ed. Ellen E. Kittell and Thomas F. Madden (Urbana, 1999), pp. 181–212; and idem, *The War of the Fists: Popular Culture and Public Violence in Late Renaissance Venice* (New York, 1994).

94. Guzmán to Philip, undated; AGSE 1333, #68.

embarrassed because the "fake" fight got out of hand (nine people were killed); worse, Henry actually got bored, and supposedly said that if the battle was in play, then it was too much, but if it was real, then it was too little.[95] Guzmán, it seems, overestimated how greatly the Venetians had impressed Henry. In his eyes, the Venetians had been entirely too successful at endearing themselves to the king of France.

Guzmán also noted other disquieting signs of a growing rapprochement between Henry and the Venetians. The *Signoria* added Henry's name to the Book of Gold, the list of Venetian families recognized as nobility—a much-treasured and jealously guarded privilege.[96] Henry also conducted a number of closed meetings with the Doge and the Senate. Guzmán had no way to know what they discussed, but he knew it could not be good for Spain; and in fact, the Doge spoke to Henry about how Lepanto had increased Spain's imperial arrogance, and encouraged the king to counter Spanish expansion.[97] Furthermore, various Italian princes, including the dukes of Savoy and Ferrara, also took the opportunity to cozy up to Henry.[98] Guzmán himself led a Spanish delegation to talk with Henry, but this meeting did nothing to reduce the ambassador's general alarm about French-Italian relations. A year later, Guzmán was further provoked when the *Signoria* erected a monument to commemorate Henry's visit. Although some Venetians expressed suspicion about Henry's intentions, Guzmán wrote, the monument illustrated how many in Venice bore fond memories of the king of France.[99] The Spanish ambassador did not share this sentiment.

The French, of course, were a source of worry for the entire Spanish diplomatic system in Italy. Spanish ambassadors watched for any hint of French involvement in the peninsula, or of Italian inclinations toward France, with ceaseless vigilance. Even supposed allies such as the Republic of Genoa had to be monitored. Philip's instructions to Antonio de Mendoza, the ambassador he appointed to Genoa in 1570, make this clear:

> Although that Republic is as you know very devoted to my service . . . still, since the French are so clever about meddling with any negotiation or activity within their reach, and since they will have opportunities to gain supporters in that Republic, it is appropriate that you seek to discover which of

95. Davis, "The Spectacle Almost Fit for a King," p. 204.
96. Guzmán to Philip, undated; AGSE 1333, #66. On the Book of Gold and the Venetian aristocracy, see Chambers, *Imperial Age of Venice*, chap. 3.
97. Norwich, *History of Venice*, p. 493.
98. Guzmán to Philip, July 22, 1574; AGSE 1333, #65.
99. Guzmán to Philip, June 10, 1575; AGSE 1334, #45.

those people [in Genoa] favor our affairs, and which do not, and which belong to France. But this must be done with great care and skill, and without causing anyone to become suspicious, because what is most important . . . is that you proceed in all your actions so pleasantly and sweetly that no one could suspect your methods, but instead should perceive you to be totally honest and desirous of pleasing everyone.[100]

Modern historians have emphasized how closely tied to Spain Genoa had become by the late sixteenth century.[101] Yet Philip specifically told his ambassador to Genoa to assume that he had enemies there, and that they conspired with France. The king also told his representative to maintain a benign image, even as he spied on his hosts. Renaissance Italian diplomats specialized in the practice of "honorable dissimulation," or lying for a diplomatic purpose.[102] Now Spanish diplomats turned those same skills on the Italians, even those most friendly to Spain.[103] Even Philip's own relatives were not immune to dissimulation. In October 1569, the king ordered Guzmán de Silva to visit the duke of Savoy on his way to Venice, to convey the king's good wishes. The duke was Philip's cousin; nonetheless, Philip commanded his ambassador to scrutinize Savoy, "with total dissimulation and secrecy and without anyone understanding that you have other business besides the visit."[104] So much for a "pax hispanica" in Italy if Philip felt it necessary to spy on his own cousin!

If the duke of Savoy was not above suspicion, neither of course was the pope. Spanish ambassadors in Rome were more alert than any of their colleagues for signs of French influence. A papal alliance with France against Spain was the nightmare scenario every ambassador feared, especially since it sometimes came true, as happened with Paul IV. Afterwards, the Spaniards saw every Frenchman who set foot in Rome as a potential harbinger of disaster. The ambassadors took special note if a high-ranking French official met with the pope. In 1561, for example, Francisco de Vargas flew into a rage when Pius IV agreed to meet with an envoy from Antoine de Vendôme, the titular king of Navarre, from the French noble house of Bourbon. Vendôme's religious faith and pretensions to the

100. Philip to Mendoza, October 1, 1570; AGSE 1401, #258.
101. See for example Geoffrey Parker, *The Grand Strategy of Philip II* (New Haven, 1998), p. 82.
102. J. R. Woodhouse, "Honorable Dissimulation: Some Italian Advice for the Renaissance Diplomat," *Proceedings of the British Academy* No. 84 (Oxford, 1993), pp. 25–50.
103. On early modern Spanish theories of lying and statecraft, see J. A. Fernández-Santamaría, *Reasons of State and Statecraft in Spanish Political Thought, 1595–1640* (Lanham, 1983), chap. 3.
104. Philip to Guzmán, October 24, 1569; AGSE 1398, #250.

throne were both questionable, and he hoped to obtain papal recognition as a legitimate Catholic prince.[105] Vargas strongly objected to the pope meeting with Vendôme's ambassador, which would give him just such legitimacy, but Pius hoped he could save the prince from heresy. Vargas argued with Pius that Vendôme was beyond hope, and should be treated as an enemy. According to the ambassador, welcoming this envoy "was not the road to preventing war as His Holiness believed, but rather would incite one."[106] Vargas railed at the pope, accusing him of blindly ignoring the danger of legitimizing a Huguenot prince (whom Vargas referred to as a "seed of Satan"). But Pius became enraged in turn, and threw Vargas out of his chambers. During this episode Vargas seems to have thought the pope to be guilty of idiocy, if nothing more sinister; but the longer he stayed in Rome, the more he suspected Pius of favoring France over Spain. When Pius refused to grant Spain precedence, Vargas had all the proof he needed.

Every Spanish ambassador in Rome reacted with similar concern whenever the papacy appeared too friendly with France. Requeséns, of course, left Rome in protest against Pius IV's decision in favor of French precedence. Zúñiga did not even try to continue that battle; instead, he concentrated on bombarding Pope Pius V with anti-French propaganda. In March 1568, an emissary from King Charles IX of France arrived in Rome to beg for financial aid in the war against the Huguenots. Pius was willing to consider the request, but Zúñiga counseled against it, because the French could not be trusted. He urged the pope to send his own envoy to France to gauge the king's policies, and to give money only if Charles "progressed in an appropriate manner" against the Protestants.[107] Zúñiga's skepticism was apparently well founded: later that week Charles signed the Peace of Longjumeau, which granted limited tolerance to the Huguenots.[108] Over the next few months Zúñiga triumphantly reported that Pius, disgusted by the French king's treachery, now sided with Spain.[109] His declaration of victory, however, was premature; in January 1569 a Roman news bulletin announced that another French envoy had asked Pius for money, and this time the pope showed

105. Pastor, *History of the Popes,* Vol. XVI, 161–62.
106. Vargas to Philip, September 30, 1561; AGSE 892, #72.
107. Zúñiga to Philip, March 19, 1568; *Correspondencia diplomática,* Vol. II, pp. 326–32.
108. Robert Knecht suggests that Charles signed this peace merely to lull the Protestant leaders into a false sense of security, although many French Catholics did not know this. *The French Civil Wars, 1562–1598* (London, 2000), pp. 142–43.
109. See for example Zúñiga to Philip, July 15, 1568; *Correspondencia diplomática,* Vol. II, pp. 411–13.

"much readiness to afford help of every kind."[110] Even the saintly Pius V never disavowed the French as the Spaniards wanted.

But at least Pius V did not appear to want the French in Italy. With Gregory XIII, Zúñiga was not so sure. In June 1573, the ambassador sent the following assessment of Gregory's personality:

> The Pope does not have the courage to start wars, although he may desire to aid the intentions of the French; [he is prevented from doing this by] the sainted memory of Pius V, and the common understanding that he must aid Your Majesty if the French should move armies into Italy, and that he must dissuade any of the powers of this province from their known inclinations toward France. For my part, I do what I can to reinforce these ideas.[111]

Once again, the ambassador in Rome hardly sounded confident about a "pax hispanica" if all that prevented the pope from aiding France was the example of a past pope and a vague sense of political tradition. In 1582, Olivares sounded no more confident about Gregory's political allegiances; instead, he warned that Rome was suspiciously full of young French nobles, who no doubt conspired against Spain.[112] Fifteen years later, things would get even worse: during the Ferrara crisis, the duke of Sessa feared that the pope was on the brink of inviting the king of France into Italy.[113] The overall message is clear: Philip's ambassadors in Rome never felt safe from a French invasion of Italy, or from papal plotting.

The ambassadors also worried about Italian princes plotting with each other. Venice and the Papacy, of course, were the powers the Spaniards most worried about, so they had to be watched for signs of collusion. In the early 1540s, for example, Diego de Mendoza chronicled an intensive campaign by Pope Paul III to seduce the Venetians into an alliance with him against Charles.[114] In June 1541, Mendoza reported that the Venetian ambassador in Rome had told the *Signoria* of an offer from the pope to join forces, in order to strengthen themselves against imperial expansion. According to Mendoza, Paul had made the same offer twice before, but the Venetians had refused to respond. They feared that Paul

---

110. *Avvisi* dated January 29, 1569; *Calendar of State Papers, Relating to English Affairs, Preserved Principally in Rome, in the Vatican Archives and Library*, ed. J. M. Rigg, Vol. I (London, 1916), pp. 296–97.
111. Zúñiga to Philip, June 19, 1573; AGSE 922, #112.
112. Olivares to Philip, July 23, 1582; AGSE 943, #45.
113. Sessa to Philip, December 18, 1597; AGSE 969, unnumbered.
114. This contradicts Pastor, who claimed that Paul maintained strict neutrality in this period, and did his best to prevent "unholy strife" between Charles and Francis I. *History of the Popes*, Vol. XII, pp. 146ff.

intended to invite the French into the alliance, thus ensnaring Venice in another anti-imperial war, such as the one that had resulted in disaster for the Republic a generation earlier.[115] Mendoza does not say how he discovered this plot, but it is exactly the kind of information the Spanish ambassadors sought, yet feared to find. In this case the Venetians seemed unwilling to join, but that made the news only slightly less alarming. A nominally friendly pope had revealed himself as a potential enemy.

Over the next few years, Mendoza reported repeated attempts by Paul to get the Venetians to ally with him against the emperor. Each time the pope stressed the danger Charles presented to Italy in general, and to Venice in particular, and offered the Venetians eternal friendship and mutual support. In January 1543 Mendoza mentioned that a person "who should know well" (but who is otherwise unidentified) had informed him of another such overture. This source assured the ambassador that Venice was still turning a deaf ear to the pope's proposal.[116] The following month, however, Mendoza learned that Paul had increased the stakes: he told the Venetians that Charles consorted with Protestants, "who may invade Italy, which the *Signoria* may see as very dangerous for Christendom and for the Apostolic See; and thus [Venice] ought to join with [the pope] in defense, and if they do so he will give them Cervia and Ravenna."[117] So the pope applied pressure on the Venetians, using the classic carrot-and-stick method. It seemed fantastic to the Spaniards that the pope would go to such lengths, but Mendoza later confirmed that Paul was trying to scare Venice into an alliance, by raising the specter of Protestant armies (commanded by Charles) overrunning Italy. Paul may have genuinely feared such an event; after all, imperial soldiers had in fact sacked Rome not many years earlier.[118] The pope might also have been cynically using such fears for his own ends. According to Mendoza, the Venetians regarded Paul as deceitful and irreligious—but was he projecting his own feeling onto them? In any case, the ambassador asserted that Venice would never risk antagonizing Charles, because they feared him, and also recognized in him their only hope against the Turks.[119] Given the Venetian defection from the Holy League three years earlier, this reassurance rings hollow.

Philip's ambassadors were equally wary of Italian conspiracies against Spain. In 1573, for example, a mere four months after the collapse of the Holy League, Guzmán de Silva reported hearing rumors of an anti-Spanish

115. Mendoza to Charles, June 30, 1541; AGSE 1497, Libro 67, ff. 178–80.
116. Mendoza to Charles, January 23, 1543; AGSE 1317, #181–83.
117. Mendoza to Charles, February 13, 1543; AGSE 1317, #205–7.
118. For the impact of the 1527 Sack of Rome on the Italian imagination, see André Chastel, *The Sack of Rome, 1527*, trans. Beth Archer (Princeton, 1983).
119. Mendoza to Charles, February 13, 1543; AGSE 1317, #205–7.

alliance being negotiated between Venice, Pope Gregory XIII, and France.[120] Three days later Juan de Zúñiga wrote an almost identical letter, reporting the same rumor.[121] Neither ambassador appeared overly alarmed; Guzmán called the idea "rubbish," while Zúñiga dismissed the rumor as a "big joke." Yet both men felt it necessary to tell Philip about what they had heard, and it surely must have raised eyebrows in Madrid when two independent intelligence reports mentioned this "ridiculous" rumor.[122] Two years later Guzmán informed Philip that the same rumor had resurfaced. This time he had interrogated one of his sources, a Venetian ambassador to Rome, who "swore to me with the faith of a Christian and a gentleman that this alliance had not been made or discussed, nor would it be in the future."[123] Guzmán does not say if he believed the man, but the fact that the Spanish ambassador had even asked the Venetian such a question demonstrates how seriously he took the possibility.[124]

The Spaniards feared Italian alliances with France so much that they opposed the idea even when they had been invited to join. In 1568, Philip specifically instructed Juan de Zúñiga to quash any discussion of a multinational League headed by the papacy. The king had learned that the papal nuncio in France had raised the issue of an alliance of all Christian states against the Turks, but Philip did not approve.[125] Any alliance between Rome and France had to be prevented, even if Spain participated in the union. Zúñiga in turn argued against such a league with the pope and his advisers. He told Cardinal Morone, who had encouraged Pius V to pursue this course, that "for the defense of Christendom, and particularly of Italy, it is not appropriate to obligate [Philip] with a league."[126] The Spaniards may have wanted to preserve their freedom of action, but they also simply

120. Guzmán to Philip, August 18, 1573; AGSE 1332, #81.
121. Zúñiga to Philip, August 21, 1573; AGSE 922, #136.
122. The rumor was partially correct. The previous year Pope Gregory had in fact sent a legate to France with an offer of a military alliance against the Turks, which was rejected. Gregory did not intend the alliance to be anti-Spanish, however, as he was trying to keep peace between France and Spain. Pastor, *History of the Popes*, Vol. XIX, pp. 515–16.
123. Guzmán to Philip, July 16, 1575; AGSE 1334, #55.
124. The Venetian ambassador, Paolo Tiepolo, never mentioned such an alliance in his *relazione* of 1576, so it seems he told the truth. *Le relazioni degli ambasciatori veneti al Senato durante il secolo decimosesto*, ed. Eugenio Àlberi, 15 vols. (Florence, 1839–1863), Series II, Vol. X, pp. 215–30.
125. Philip to Zúñiga, October 12, 1568; *Correspondencia diplomática*, Vol. II, p. 480. Much of the king's intelligence on France came from the Spanish ambassador in Paris; see Jensen, *Diplomacy and Dogmatism*, chap. 5; and Valentin Vázquez de Prada, "La embajada española en Francia en la época de Felipe II," in *Política, religión, e inquisición en la España moderna*, ed. P. Fernández Albaladejo, J. Martínex Millán, and V. Pinto Crespo (Madrid, 1996), pp. 671–90.
126. Zúñiga to Philip, November 23, 1568; *Correspondencia diplomática*, Vol. II, pp. 507–10.

did not trust either France or the papacy. In 1582, Olivares dismissed yet another offer to join a French-Italian league, on the grounds that both Pope Gregory and France had ulterior (and anti-Spanish) motives.[127] And in April 1598, the duke of Sessa reported that Pope Clement VIII had reacted to the news of the Peace of Vervins by promoting a new Christian alliance against the Turk, combining Spanish, French, papal, and Venetian forces.[128] Sessa does not state his opinion on the matter, but his very silence perhaps suggests his assumption that there was nothing to say. At that moment, Spain was not in a condition to join any military alliance, let alone one with France and a pro-French pope.

Why did the Spaniards mistrust the Italians so much? National prejudices may be one factor, but more importantly, they were convinced that the Italians mistrusted them. All of the ambassadors' intelligence reports led up to this conclusion. Why did Pius IV rule against Spain in the precedence dispute? According to Requeséns, it was because he feared and resented Spanish power.[129] Why did the Venetians abandon the Holy League? According to Guzmán de Silva, it was because they feared and resented Spanish power.[130] This was the paradox of Spanish hegemony in Italy. To recall Francisco de Vargas's words, Spain needed to maintain "vigilance and power" in Italy if it was going to establish control. But the vigilant ambassadors discovered that it was their own power that guaranteed they would never establish complete control. The ambassadors functioned as the eyes and ears of Spain in Italy, but they did not like what they saw or heard. The more the ambassadors learned as intelligence agents, the less secure they felt. They never concluded their reports by stating "we have total control of Italy." As diplomats, the ambassadors dreamed of establishing a "pax hispanica," but as intelligence officers, they knew it was only a fantasy. Moreover, the limits of Spanish imperial power in Italy reflected the more general failure of the Spanish Habsburgs' grand strategies in early modern Europe. In 1644, the count-duke of Olivares, despondent over the collapse of his life's work, complained bitterly to his secretary of Spain's inability to remake the world according to its desires. The one certain thing about the world, he said, "is its instability and inconstancy and lack of gratitude."[131] The count-duke's father, and all of his fellow ambassadors in sixteenth-century Italy, would have understood perfectly.

127. Olivares to Philip, July 23, 1582; AGSE 943, #45.
128. Sessa to Philip, April 26, 1598; AGSE 970, unnumbered.
129. Requeséns to Philip, April 6, 1564; AGSE 896, #53.
130. Guzmán to Philip, March 19, 1572; AGSE 1331, #26
131. Quoted in J. H. Elliott, *Richelieu and Olivares* (Cambridge, 1984), p. 172.

CHAPTER SEVEN

The Ambassadors as Cultural Contacts

In addition to diplomacy and espionage, Spanish ambassadors were also responsible for exploiting Italy's cultural and material resources. Italy, after all, was not only a political unit in the Habsburg system, but also the center of Renaissance culture and a rich mine of art and artifacts. The ambassadors often acted as middlemen or procurers of merchandise for their monarchs or peers, or else took personal advantage of the opportunities arrayed before them. They thus served as conduits of Renaissance Italian culture into the Spanish kingdoms, or what I would call cultural contacts between Italy and Spain. Of course, ambassadors were not the only Spaniards in Italy who served this function; viceroys, governors, soldiers, and Spaniards simply passing through the peninsula acted similarly.[1] The ambassadors, however, appeared to serve a unique function as official intermediaries between Spaniards and Italian artists, craftsmen and merchants. Their attitude toward Italian cultural wealth is also significant, as it highlights the Spanish imperial mind-set, and the arrogance that so repelled Italians, friends and enemies alike.

Ambassadors in Venice kept particularly busy as liaisons with the Republic's great painters like Titian, Tintoretto, and Jacopo Bassano. Titian's work was especially beloved by both Charles V and Philip II, and their ambassadors negotiated commissions and prices with the master for

---

1. Cardinal Granvelle, a great patron of Italian art and literature, was one prime example. See *Les Granvelle et l'Italie au XVIe Siècle: Le mécénat d'une famille,* ed. Jacqueline Brunet and Gennaro Toscano (Besançon, 1996).

over thirty years.[2] Diego Hurtado de Mendoza, for example, enjoyed both a professional and a personal relationship with Titian, as well as with other members of the Venetian cultural scene like Pietro Aretino and the sculptor Jacopo Sansovino.[3] The Emperor Charles sent a number of requests for paintings from Titian through Mendoza. On April 17, 1545, for instance, Charles wrote to Mendoza inquiring if Titian's famous portrait of the Empress Isabella had been finished yet, and instructing that if so the ambassador should have it sent to Spain as soon as possible.[4] Mendoza did not send the portrait until October, with the excuse that "Titian is old and works slowly."[5] Mendoza praised the portrait, and relayed the artist's request for criticism from Charles so that any flaws in Isabella's likeness could be corrected (she had died in 1539, so Titian never saw her in person). Mendoza noted that he had told Titian what he personally liked and disliked about the painting, although we have no indication whether Titian cared what Mendoza thought. Titian also painted at least one portrait of Mendoza himself, perhaps indicating the ambassador's status in the Venetian art world as well as in politics. In a surviving portrait (which may or may not be Titian's), now in the Pitti Palace Gallery in Florence, Mendoza appears as a proud Spanish gentleman, with a classical frieze in the background reflecting his interest in art and archeology.[6] In any case, Mendoza's main role was to relay instructions and commissions, monitor the artist's progress, and arrange for the transportation of the works back to Spain.

We can see the passing of the patron's torch from Charles to his son Philip in the correspondence of Francisco de Vargas a decade later. In March 1555 Vargas wrote to Charles that he had spoken with Titian about more commissioned work, "for which he is very pleased and content, and kisses Your Majesty's feet and hands. He will proceed to make a portrait of

2. Fernando Checa Cremades, *Tiziano y la monarquía hispánica: Usos y funciones de la pintura veneciana en España (siglos XVI y XVII)* (Madrid, 1994), p. 21.
3. Erica Spivakovsky, *Son of the Alhambra: Don Diego Hurtado de Mendoza, 1504–1575* (Austin, 1970), pp. 87–88.
4. Archivo General de Simancas, Sección Estado (hereafter AGSE) 1318, #93.
5. Mendoza to Charles, October 5, 1545; AGSE 1318, #40. Ambassadors would still be complaining of Titian's age and slowness thirty years later! In this letter Mendoza also says that Titian had recently finished a mythological painting for Charles, "which they say is the best he has ever done," but there is no indication which painting he is referring to.
6. See R. Foulché-Delbosc, "Le portrait de Mendoza," *Revue Hispanique* 23 (1910), pp. 310–13. Giorgio Vasari praised a Titian portrait of Mendoza in his *Lives of the Artists* (trans. George Bull, Vol. I (reprint, London, 1987), pp. 453–54), and art historians have traditionally identified this painting with the one in Florence. Recently, however, this identification has been disputed: see Matteo Mancini, *Tiziano e le corti d'Absburgo nei documenti degli archivi spagnoli* (Venice, 1998), pp. 33–34.

Our Lady, and I will solicit him to do it with brevity."[7] The following year Philip wrote back that the paintings had been received in Spain, and that both he and his father were pleased.[8] He also informed Vargas that the different paintings he and Charles had ordered would be paid for in one lump sum. With Charles's abdication, Philip evidently took over as Titian's patron—and ambassadors in Venice now answered to him as well.

Twenty years later, Diego Guzmán de Silva was still negotiating commissions between Philip and Titian—a testament to the painter's longevity (he died in 1576 at the age of eighty-five). Like all his predecessors in this post, Guzmán had many responsibilities. Yet in August 1571, in the midst of Holy League negotiations, he still found time to tell Philip that Titian had asked him to arrange for transport of a painting of Tarquin and Lucretia, and had shown him the preliminary drawings for a St. Lawrence and other works.[9] "He is old," Guzmán wrote, "but he still works, and is a very good servant of Your Majesty who merits all grace and favor . . . and as it seems these [works] now are already the last fruits of his art, I have taken care that they may be sent quickly." His recommendation that Titian deserved a reward received a positive response: Philip awarded Titian a pension of a thousand ducats as proof of his affection, and sent his assurance that he was Titian's "very good friend."[10]

Guzmán also sometimes coordinated visits by Spanish painters to see Titian and other Venetian masters. In 1575 he wrote to Philip that "when Hieronymo Sanchez brother of Alonso Sanchez, Your Majesty's painter, passed through here in order to converse and communicate with Titian, he copied a great painting which he had done of St. Peter Martyr . . . which they say is one of the greatest works done by Titian . . . and when he left here for Rome, he asked me to send it to Your Majesty."[11] "Alonso Sanchez" is presumably Alonso Sanchez Coello (c. 1531–1588), official court painter of Philip II after 1555.[12] Hieronymo Sanchez is less well known, but he appears in Guzmán's correspondence several times. On a few occasions he aided Guzmán in searching for "colors," presumably special paints or dyes, which Philip had specially ordered from Venetian merchants.[13] Sanchez also evidently went

---

7. Vargas to Charles, March 7, 1555; AGSE 1323, #47.
8. Philip to Vargas, September 7, 1556; AGSE 1323, #127.
9. Guzmán to Philip, August 2, 1571; AGSE 1329, #79.
10. *Tiziano e la corte di Spagna nei documenti dell'Archivio generale di Simancas* (Madrid, 1975), p. 11.
11. Guzmán to Philip, September 24, 1575; AGSE 1234, #84.
12. See Jonathan Brown, *The Golden Age of Painting in Spain* (New Haven, 1991), pp. 54–55; and Fernando Checa Cremades, *Felipe II, mecenas de las artes* (Madrid, 1992), passim.
13. *Tiziano e la corte di Spagna*, p. 113.

to Rome to study the great works there, and again the resident Spanish ambassador provided support. In April 1576 the secretary of state Antonio Pérez wrote to Juan de Zúñiga that a copy of Raphael's *Galatea,* which Sanchez had made and left in Zúñiga's care, should be shipped to Spain.[14]

Sometimes the ambassadors took a more active role in finding painters who might please the king. Philip intended the Escorial, the great palace-monastery forever associated with him, to be the focal point for his artistic patronage and a monument to his aesthetic tastes.[15] Philip's ambassadors knew this, and tried to help. In January 1574 Guzmán reported that he had recently heard of a painter named Bassano, who was highly esteemed in Venice for his naturalistic work. Guzmán had acquired one of this artist's works, *The History of Jacob,* and he sent it to Philip "so that Your Majesty may see his manner of painting."[16] This painter was in fact Jacopo Bassano, who would become famous, in part as a result of the works Philip later commissioned from him for the Escorial.[17] In this one case, the Spanish ambassador in Venice was directly responsible for discovering a painter and launching his career as a client of the Spanish crown.

Other times, the ambassadors simply arranged for the passage of Italian artists to Spain. In 1577 Philip wrote to Juan de Zúñiga in Rome, inquiring about artists who might be suitable (and available) to decorate the Escorial. Philip wanted an established Italian artist, but the two most famous Venetian masters of the time, Veronese and Tintoretto, were unwilling to leave Venice.[18] Zúñiga replied that Federico Zuccaro, while not the best painter in Italy, might be the best the king could get.[19] Over the next decade the embassies in Rome and Venice exchanged a series of letters about luring Zuccaro into Philip's service.[20] In 1585 Zuccaro finally agreed to go, after being promised a salary of two thousand escudos a year. Interestingly, although the painter was from Venice, Philip ordered the Rome embassy to pay Zuccaro's initial salary and travel

---

14. Pérez to Zúñiga, April 17, 1576; Archivo de Zabálburu, Caja 74, #221.

15. Checa Cremades, *Felipe II, mecenas de las artes,* p. 14. For more on the significance of the Escorial, see George Kubler, *Building the Escorial* (Princeton, 1982), and Catherine Wilkinson-Zerner, *Juan de Herrera, Architect to Philip II of Spain* (New Haven, 1993).

16. Guzmán to Philip, January 21, 1574; AGSE 1510, #114.

17. Checa Cremades, *Tiziano y la monarquía hispánica,* pp. 67–70.

18. Jonathan Brown, *Painting in Spain 1500–1700* (New Haven, 1998), p. 57.

19. Rosemarie Mulcahy, "Philip II Lover of the Arts," in *Philippus II Rex,* ed. Pedro Navascués Palacio, Vol. II (Barcelona, 1998), p. 42.

20. Copies of these letters are in the Ministerio de Asuntos Exteriores (Madrid), Embajada de Santa Sede, Legajo 19, #330–38.

expenses.[21] The ambassador also had to mollify Pope Gregory XIII, who had already hired Zuccaro for a project of his own.[22] It seems the Spaniards were not above stealing artists from the pope if Philip wanted to hire them.

The monarchs were not the only Spaniards to take advantage of the ambassadors' connections to artists. Charles's minister of state, Francisco de los Cobos, received a marble bust of Apollo courtesy of the resident ambassador in Rome, Miguel Mai.[23] When the marquis del Vasto arrived in Venice in 1539, Mendoza introduced him to all of his acquaintances among the cultural elite, in a series of festivals whose magnificence was recorded by Pietro Aretino.[24] A generation later, the marquis de Ayamonte, governor of Milan from 1573 to 1580, established a rather more mercenary relationship with Guzmán de Silva. During the first three years of his tenure in Milan Ayamonte sent at least twenty letters to Venice giving exact instructions about what he wanted from Titian.[25] He often complained impatiently about the delays involved in getting finished works out of the aged painter, and sometimes even grumbled that Titian's hand was not as steady as it had once been.[26]

Nonetheless, Ayamonte's orders for more works kept coming, mostly for religious scenes. In January 1575 he told Guzmán he wanted a Birth of Jesus and an Adoration of the Kings.[27] In another letter he gave specific instructions about the composition of the painting he wanted: a Crucifixion, with "the mother at his feet looking at him with sorrow."[28] The next month he wrote twice to Guzmán saying that he expected his wife to arrive in Milan very soon, and he wanted the paintings done before then.[29] Ayamonte's autocratic attitude is very interesting—he knew what he wanted, and he expected Guzmán to get it for him, with little regard for Titian's sensibilities. He expressed his feelings clearly to Guzmán later that same month, stating that he hoped to finish his tenure in Milan "rich

21. Philip to Olivares, February 1586; AGSE 946, #291. After all the haggling, Zuccaro ended up completing only a small amount of work in the Escorial; see Fernando Collar de Cáceres, "Arte y rigor religioso: Españoles e italianos en el ornato de los retablos del Escorial," in *Felipe II y el arte de su tiempo* (Madrid, 1998), pp. 112–13.
22. Olivares to Philip, October 25, 1582; AGSE 942, unfoliated.
23. Hayward Keniston, *Francisco de los Cobos, Secretary of the Emperor Charles V* (Pittsburgh, 1960), p. 151.
24. Spivakovsky, *Son of the Alhambra*, pp. 87–88.
25. Mancini, *Tiziano e le corti d'Absburgo*, p. 81
26. Ayamonte to Guzmán, January 5, 1575; AGSE 1514, #1.
27. Ibid.
28. Ayamonte to Guzmán, February 27, 1575; AGSE 1514, #5. Also quoted by Checa Cremades, *Tiziano y la monarquía hispánica*, p. 21.
29. March 3, 1575 (AGSE 1514, #10), and March 10, 1575 (AGSE 1514, #11).

in relics and painting of Italy."[30] Guzmán, in his view, was thus a tool in his quest to enrich himself at Italy's expense.

Paintings were not the only commodities the ambassadors routed from Venice to Spain. The Venetian trading empire extended throughout the Mediterranean and beyond, and the Spanish monarchs and nobility eagerly sought to profit from it. In 1530, for example, Rodrigo Niño assured the Empress Isabella that he was diligently seeking silks and other cloths on her behalf, and sent some samples of green, blue, and red damask for her inspection.[31] Similarly, Diego de Mendoza supplied his friend and colleague Francisco de los Cobos with oriental rugs, special Venetian-made eyeglasses, and jewelry made from shells.[32] On one occasion, Mendoza sent a letter to Prince Philip informing him that he had met a merchant who was offering a number of pearls, "the best I have ever seen of orientals and the roundest, medium clear and fresh."[33] He asked whether he should purchase the gems in the prince's name, to which Philip agreed, indicating that they would make a fine present for his new bride, María Manuela of Portugal.[34] We should also note that sometimes the ambassadors themselves took advantage of the Venetian market. In 1579 Juan de Zúñiga wrote to the secretary in the Venetian embassy asking about buying tapestries, and later sent a thousand ducats for the purchase of some particularly fine specimens.[35]

Of all the ambassadors in Venice, Guzmán de Silva supplied an especially broad range of artifacts to various clients, reflecting the remarkable breadth of the Venetian markets. On at least one occasion, he purchased musical instruments (including cornets, trumpets, and flutes) and scores for Don Juan of Austria.[36] He also received a large number of requests for Venetian glassware and crystal, especially from the island of Murano,

30. Ayamonte to Guzmán, March 24, 1575; AGSE 1514, #12.

31. Niño to Isabella, December 1, 1530; AGSE 1308, #105.

32. Spivakovsky, *Son of the Alhambra*, p. 101; letters from Mendoza to Cobos describing the eye-glasses printed in *Algunas Cartas de Don Diego Hurtado de Mendoza, escritas 1538–1552*, ed. Alberto Vázquez and R. Selden Rose (New Haven, 1935), pp. 41–44.

33. Mendoza to Philip, October 6, 1544; AGSE 1318, #19. Mendoza reported that the asking price was six thousand escudos for sixty-eight pearls, and he was probably hesitant to spend that amount without permission.

34. Philip to Mendoza, December 19, 1544; quoted by Eugenio Sarrablo Aguareles, "La cultura y el arte venecianos, en sus relaciones con España, a traves de la correspondencia diplomática de los siglos XVI al XVIII," *Revista de Archivos, Bibliotecas y Museos* 52 (1956), p. 645. Aguareles provides an exhaustive list of exactly the kind of commercial interactions I discuss here.

35. Zúñiga to Christoval de Salazar, August 1 and September 19, 1579; Instituto de Valencia de Don Juan, Envío 20, Caja 29, #704–5.

36. The invoice is dated. Feb. 20, 1572, AGSE 1330, #124–25,

which was famous (as it still is) for the skill of its glassblowers. In 1570, while Guzmán was still in Genoa, he arranged for a quantity of stained glass [*vidrieras*] to be sent from Venice to Philip in Spain.[37] A few months later the king's secretary Antonio Pérez sent the ambassador a letter ordering another batch from the same source, and instructed Guzmán to ship them with "the same care and diligence" as he had used the last time.[38] Once Guzmán settled into his post in Venice, he received a steady stream of such orders; in 1571 alone he arranged for the purchase of over thirteen hundred pieces of Murano crystal for his king.[39] Don Juan likewise used Guzmán as a middleman for the purchase of glassware, as a 1572 invoice shows.[40]

Guzmán and his fellow ambassadors also facilitated Philip's interests as a collector.[41] They scoured Italy for two items in particular: books and relics. First of all, Philip wanted to create a magnificent library as part of the Escorial.[42] In April 1572 Philip wrote to Guzmán that "because I wish to assemble a copious library of all manner of good books, in all languages and faculties, and the principal part of it . . . should be of handwritten and rare [books] of some antiquity, in both Greek and Latin and other tongues, many of which it is believed can be found in that city [of Venice] . . . I charge you to inform yourself from knowledgeable people of what is or may be there, and then to advise me of all the particulars, and of what steps may be taken to obtain some of these books."[43] He further instructed Guzmán to pursue his search for books with "secrecy and dissimulation," but he does not say why; perhaps he sought to keep the prices down, or else he wanted to avoid trouble with the Roman Inquisition, which had begun clamping down on the printing of heretical works.[44]

Guzmán acknowledged Philip's orders in May, and remarked that his predecessor Diego Hurtado de Mendoza had already purchased a number

37. Guzmán to Philip, June 2, 1570; AGSE 1400, #63.
38. Pérez to Guzmán, September 10, 1570; AGSE 1499, #131. Pérez instructed that the order should be sent ahead to Venice, and that more requests would come once Guzmán took up his post there.
39. Invoice of glassware purchased in 1571; AGSE 1501, #180. The document states that the crystal cost a total of 462 escudos.
40. AGSE 1330, #110.
41. On Philip's interests see Henry Kamen, *Philip of Spain* (New Haven, 1997), pp. 188–91.
42. Checa Cremades, *Felipe II, mecenas de las artes*, pp. 380ff.; *Documentos para la historia del Monasterio de San Lorenzo el real de El Escorial*, ed. Gregorio de Andrés, Vols. V–VIII (Escorial, 1962–1965), Vol. VII; and Fernando Bouza Álvarez, "La biblioteca de El Escorial y el orden de los saberes en el siglo XVI o la fama de Felipe II y la 'claridad' de sus libros," in *Imagen y propaganda: Capítulos de historia cultural del reinado de Felipe II* (Madrid, 1998), pp. 168–85.
43. Philip to Guzmán, April 20, 1572; AGSE 1503, #138.
44. See Paul Grendler, *The Roman Inquisition and the Venetian Press, 1540–1605* (Princeton, 1977).

of books "of the quality that Your Majesty desires."[45] Mendoza's library was in fact one of the most famous in sixteenth-century Spain. During his career in Italy he collected many manuscripts on his own, and employed scholars to buy or copy other works throughout the Mediterranean.[46] He even got permission from Duke Cosimo de'Medici in Florence, a bitter rival, to have copies made of a number of manuscripts in the Florentine collections.[47] After Mendoza's death in 1575, Philip bought his library and added it to the Escorial collection.[48] Evidently Mendoza had done such a thorough job collecting manuscripts that later ambassadors sometimes had trouble finding anything new. Juan de Zúñiga, who also received instructions to look for books, responded that Mendoza had already snapped up most of the good ones in Rome.[49] More importantly, however, his letter illustrates that Philip had ordered a systematic search throughout Italy, using his ambassadors as agents.[50]

Guzmán enjoyed much more success finding books in Venice. From the beginning he displayed remarkable enthusiasm for the task, calling it "a project worthy of Your Majesty and of great importance, for matters of religion as well as learning."[51] Two months after receiving Philip's orders he sent a crate of books to Spain, along with the usual glassware and other Venetian merchandise.[52] Meanwhile, Philip appointed a secretary named Antonio Gracián to oversee the efforts to build the library, who maintained a busy correspondence with Guzmán and other ambassadors.[53] Gracián wrote to Guzmán in July 1572 asking for catalogues from Venetian booksellers, so he could check for gaps in the library.[54] Guzmán

45. Guzmán to Philip, May 22, 1572; AGSE 1507, #99.

46. Spivakovsky, *Son of the Alhambra*, p. 73.

47. Letters Mendoza to Cosimo, dated October 5, 1541 and November 17, 1544; Archivio di Stato di Firenze, Mediceo 2964, f. 95r, and Mediceo 2965, f. 199r.

48. Antonio Gracián to Guzmán, 1575; AGSE 1516, #126. See also *Vida y obras de Don Diego Hurtado de Mendoza*, ed. Ángel González Palencia and Eugenio Mele, 3 vols. (Madrid, 1941–1943), Vol. II, pp. 393–95, for the sale of the library, and Vol. III, pp. 481–564, for an inventory.

49. Zúñiga to Philip, June 13, 1572; Instituto de Valencia de Don Juan, Envío 61 (II), f. 300r. Zúñiga asked to be sent an inventory of the Escorial collection, so he would not spend money on copying what they already had, but there is no record if he received it.

50. Philip sent out another such letter to all of the ambassadors and ministers in Italy (as well as those at the imperial court) in October 1583. For the copy received in Rome, see AGSE 944, #168.

51. Guzmán to Philip, June 14, 1572; quoted by Sarrablo Aguareles, "La cultura y el arte venecianos, en sus relaciones con España," p. 659.

52. Invoice dated June 20, 1572; AGSE 1331, #135.

53. Checa Cremades, *Felipe II, mecenas de las artes*, p. 386; and Gregorio de Andrés, *Documentos para la historia del Monasterio de San Lorenzo el real de El Escorial*, Vols. V, pp. 7–17, and VIII, pp. 7–9.

54. AGSE 1504, #94.

quickly complied, much to Philip's delight; he wrote to the ambassador that "I have seen the diligent efforts you have made to obtain ancient and rare books, and the catalogue of them which you bought . . . all of which seems to me very well, and your purchases very shrewd, and thus I thank you."[55] That Philip should take the time to personally thank his ambassador demonstrates his keen enthusiasm for books.

It is easy to see why Philip was so pleased with Guzmán's performance. The ambassador negotiated with various booksellers in Venice, and collected information about libraries throughout Italy. One 1572 invoice, for example, lists a merchant from Corfu as the source of sixty-four handwritten Greek manuscripts.[56] In the same year Guzmán received a letter from an (anonymous) Italian source that a certain monastery in Sicily had a collection of over three hundred "very ancient books," including works in Greek, Latin, Hebrew, and Arabic.[57] In some cases we have the names of scholars whom Guzmán hired to help him search for books. A certain Dr. Giovanni Rasario, who held a chair in Latin and Greek studies at the University of Padua, figured prominently in Guzmán's correspondence. Guzmán praised his "learning, ability, and good qualities" to Philip, and recommended he be given a pension as a reward for his services.[58] We do not know if Rasario received such a pension, but he assisted Guzmán in at least a semiofficial capacity for a number of years. He sent Guzmán a number of lists of available books he had found, along with prices and evaluations of their quality.[59] In one letter, after describing some books of saints' lives he had found, he told Guzmán that he had no other intention but to serve and satisfy the ambassador. Perhaps he was merely being courteous, but his words sound sincere.[60] In any case we see that the search for books was a truly international effort.

Over the period 1572–1576, Guzmán sent dozens of crates of books back to Spain. Gracián reported that Philip's pleasure increased with each shipment, and the secretary boasted that before long the Escorial's library "will be one of the best in Christendom."[61] In addition to encouragement Gracián also sent specific requests. In March 1575, for example, he reminded Guzmán not to forget to look for manuscripts of St. Isidore of Seville, whom Philip especially wanted to honor. Scholars were combing

55. Philip to Guzmán, July 16, 1572; AGSE 1503, #211.
56. ASGE 1503, #211. The books cost three hundred escudos.
57. AGSE 1507, #136.
58. Guzmán to Philip, August 28, 1573; AGSE 1332, #86.
59. Letters dated August 25 and 30, 1575; AGSE 1516, #124–25.
60. September 8, 1575; AGSE 1514, #123.
61. Gracián to Guzmán, February 25, 1573; AGSE 1509, #95.

Spain for such works, but surely Guzmán could find many more in the libraries of Italy.[62] Guzmán produced quick results: a few months later Gracián wrote again, praising the ambassador for his diligence in finding works by St. Isidore, and added that Guzmán "wins the prize . . . for buying good and cheap books."[63] Guzmán apparently became well known for his shopping skills. At one point Gracián reported a conversation with a Venetian bookseller visiting Spain, who was upset that Guzmán had bought so many manuscripts at bargain prices. The irate merchant asked if Guzmán would be staying in Venice much longer, to which Gracián replied affirmatively, and that while there he would buy every last book in Italy. The Venetian was not amused.[64]

The invoices and catalogues of books in Guzmán's correspondence show a wide range of literature earmarked for the Escorial. In May 1573 he sent sixteen boxes of books, including works in Greek, Latin, and Hebrew.[65] We have a much more detailed invoice dated 1576, which lists several hundred individual titles and their prices.[66] It is an impressive collection, representing the best Renaissance humanist scholarship could offer. The Greek works included Aristotle, Plato, Homer, Thucydides, Demosthenes, and Sophocles; classical Latin authors were equally well represented by Cicero, Catullus, Julius Caesar, Horace, Juvenal, and Virgil. The list also includes works by Greek and Latin Church Fathers, various biblical commentaries, and historical accounts. Nor were all the works of strictly literary value: one section of the invoice notes "thirty escudos for twenty-six books on alchemy or the Great Art, handwritten in Latin and Italian." This intriguing entry includes several works by the medieval mystic Raymond Lull, as well as books with titles like *The Key to Wisdom, The Idea of Solomon,* and *The Means of Reducing Natural Silver into its Pristine Substance.* These particular finds must have especially pleased Philip, who had a fascination for magic and alchemy.[67] In any case it is clear that Guzmán's efforts to procure books were highly successful, and that while such duties may have been secondary to his diplomatic responsibilities, they were not minor. It should also be noted that in the late 1570s, when the post of resident ambassador to Venice was temporarily empty, the embassy secretary Christoval de Salazar continued to send books to Spain.[68]

62. Gracián to Guzmán, March 25, 1575; AGSE 1515, #87.
63. Gracián to Guzmán, May 15, 1575; AGSE 1514, #111.
64. Gracián to Guzmán, July 26, 1574; AGSE 1513, #100.
65. AGSE 1509, #246.
66. AGSE 1549, #44–45.
67. Geoffrey Parker, *Philip II*, 3d ed. (Chicago, 1995), pp. 49–51.
68. AGSE 1550, #403.

The Roman embassy produced less spectacular results, but it too was involved in the bibliophilic quest. As already noted, Juan de Zúñiga had low expectations of finding anything at first, but he searched diligently nonetheless, aided by the embassy's archivist Juan de Verzosa.[69] He got further assistance from Benito Arias Montano, the Escorial's first head librarian.[70] Montano made several trips to Rome, where he managed to find a number of works that Diego de Mendoza had missed. He even hired a Jewish scholar to buy or copy Hebrew manuscripts, and sent dozens of such works back to Spain.[71] It is a remarkable story: His Catholic Majesty's librarian buying Jewish books in Counter-Reformation Rome! But Montano seems quite matter-of-fact about his work. He also routinely enlisted the resident ambassador to help him ship his purchases back to Spain. In the 1580s, the count of Olivares found the time to oversee a number of such consignments. At one point Philip wrote to Olivares directly about acquiring the library of a recently deceased cardinal who was known for his taste in Greek manuscripts.[72] Olivares complied, and sent Philip a catalogue of works for sale. Philip replied excitedly about the possibility of filling gaps in the Escorial's collection, and ordered Olivares to buy whatever he could.[73]

Philip may have been a passionate bibliophile, but he had an even greater mania for relics. The deeply religious king amassed a collection of over seven thousand of them, many of which would be housed in the Escorial on permanent display.[74] Many of these artifacts and assorted body parts came from Italy, again provided by the resident ambassadors. And once again, Guzmán de Silva led the way, perhaps sharing in his king's devout enthusiasm. In January 1574 he wrote to Philip that he wanted to offer something from Venice to be placed in the Escorial as a memorial to the victory of Lepanto, and he could not think of anything "more fitting for Your Majesty's great devotion to the service of Our Lord than some part of these saints and relics" from the many Venetian churches.[75]

---

69. Zúñiga to Gracián, September 12, 1572; Instituto de Valencia de Don Juan, Envío 20, Caja 29, #498.

70. Kamen, *Philip of Spain,* p. 188; see also B. Rekers, *Benito Arias Montano (1527–1598)* (London, 1972).

71. Montano to Gabriel de Zayas, October 1583; Ministerio de Asuntos Exteriores, Embajada de la Santa Sede, Legajo 14, #374–75. The list of books he sent includes a number of midrashim (rabbinical commentaries on the Scriptures) as well as books on Gematria, or works of numerology and mysticism.

72. Philip to Olivares, January 2, 1586; Ministerio de Asuntos Exteriores, Embajada de la Santa Sede, Legajo 49, #324.

73. Philip to Olivares, November 13, 1587; Ministerio de Asuntos Exteriores, Embajada de la Santa Sede, Legajo 49, #327.

74. Parker, *Philip II,* p. xv.

75. Guzmán to Philip, January 21, 1574; AGSE 1510, #144.

Apparently on his own initiative, the ambassador had procured papal permission to remove certain relics from their previous resting places in
Venice and its territories, and send them to Spain. Eighteen sealed boxes of
relics accompanied this letter to Madrid. On receiving this bounty Philip
expressed much pleasure, having personally overseen the unpacking of the
relics. He promised Guzmán that the relics would be transferred immediately to the Escorial, where they would be "seen and displayed with all due
respect."[76]

   This would not be the only shipment of relics Guzmán engineered. We
have in his correspondence an invoice of all the relics he sent from
Venice to Spain over the period 1574–1576, and it is an impressively long
list.[77] The catalogue, written in Latin, runs to thirteen manuscript pages,
and lists several hundred items. Most of the artifacts were earthly remains
of saints, such as fingers from the right hand of John the Baptist, the skull
of St. Vitus, and an unidentified bone from St. Barbara. Other items
include "a piece of the flagellation column" and an "ampoule of blood
from the forty martyrs." Perhaps the greatest prizes, listed on page four,
were "Spinam Coronae et Fragmentum Ligni . . . Verae Crucis," a thorn
from the Crown of Thorns and a piece of the True Cross. Certainly Philip
seemed excited about them; Gracián wrote to Guzmán that the king was
very pleased, and of all the relics at the Escorial, these would be "the
greatest treasure and the most esteemed by His Majesty."[78]

   Of course, in matters of religious artifacts, the papacy had a large say,
and thus the ambassadors in Rome were much involved in the building of
the Escorial. In 1566, when Philip first conceived the project, he wrote to
Luis de Requeséns about getting papal permission to annex the monastery
of San Lorenzo and transfer it to royal jurisdiction.[79] Soon thereafter
Requeséns became embroiled in a battle with the canons of the Cathedral
of St. John Lateran, who refused to relinquish relics of St. Lawrence which
Philip wanted translated to the Escorial. After appealing to the pope for
support, Requeséns managed to arrange for the relics to be shipped to
Spain, and Philip sent compensation in the form of two silver statues
worth two thousand ducats.[80] Philip was not satisfied, however, as twenty

76. Philip to Guzmán, April 14, 1574; AGSE 1510, #82.

77. AGSE 1514, #231. The document is titled "Index of relics of male and female saints,
which certain bishops, abbots, abbesses, priors, rectors, and preferred churches and monasteries . . . bequeathed to Don Diego Guzmán de Silva."

78. Gracián to Guzmán, July 26, 1574; AGSE 1513, #124.

79. Philip to Requeséns, May 10, 1566; Instituto de Valencia de Don Juan, Envío 61 (II), ff.
230r–31r.

80. Carlos M. N. Eire, *From Madrid to Purgatory: the Art and Craft of Dying in Sixteenth-Century
Spain* (Cambridge, 1995), p. 267.

years later he wrote to the count of Olivares again asking about obtaining relics of St. Lawrence. The king specifically requested an arm or a hand, or "something similar," depending on what was available.[81] Nor was this his last request for pieces of that particular saint. In 1592 the duke of Sessa wrote a short note to Philip "concerning what Your Majesty commanded me in one of your letters . . . about informing myself if in this city there may be a head of St. Lawrence or part of it."[82] He promised he would search diligently, but a week later he wrote again to say that after consulting various "intelligent and knowledgeable people" about the head, he had little to report.[83] Nonetheless Philip remained undeterred. In January 1598, mere months before his death, he was still writing letters to Sessa about transferring relics of St. Lawrence from Italy to the Escorial.[84]

The Spanish ambassadors may have plundered Italy for its artistic, scholarly, and religious wealth, but they also exploited its human resources. There were many Italians of various professions willing to be hired by Spanish masters, and the embassies often served as employment agencies. In one example, Luis de Requeséns recommended a Genoese historian of his acquaintance to the state secretary Antonio Pérez: "In Spain His Majesty is greatly lacking men who write histories in good stylistic Latin as Your Excellency knows. In Italy there are many who do write them, but in order that they remain truthful . . . it behooves us to pay them, as they are base people. . . . Here in Rome resides a Genoese cleric named Oberto Foglieta who is one of the best writers . . . I believe His Majesty ought to give him a pension, and I will charge him to write the ancient and modern history of Spain."[85] Philip, however, did not favor the writing of such chronicles, and so the commission never materialized.[86] Nonetheless it is interesting that a proud Spaniard like Requeséns would suggest an Italian writer to produce a history of Spain.[87] He may have

81. Philip to Olivares, January 2, 1586; Ministerio de Asuntos Exteriores, Embajada de la Santa Sede, Legajo 19, #43.
82. Sessa to Philip, April 27, 1592; AGSE 959, unfoliated.
83. Sessa to Philip, May 3, 1592; AGSE 959, unfoliated.
84. Philip to Sessa, January 8, 1598; Ministerio de Asuntos Exteriores, Embajada de la Santa Sede, Legajo 19, #90.
85. Requeséns to Pérez, March 12, 1572; AGSE 918, #78.
86. Richard L. Kagan, "Philip II, History, and the *Cronistas del Rey*," in Palacio, *Philippus II Rex*, p. 23. Foglieta did, however, publish a history of the "Holy League against Selim II" in 1598. *British Museum General Catalogue of Printed Books*, Vol. LXXIV (London, 1961), pp. 935–37.
87. To compare the two national traditions, see Eric Cochrane, *Historians and Historiography in the Italian Renaissance* (Chicago, 1981); and Richard L. Kagan, "Clio and the crown: writing history in Habsburg Spain," *Spain, Europe and the Atlantic World*, eds. Richard L. Kagan and Geoffrey Parker (Cambridge, 1995), pp. 73–99.

wanted an Italian to help write a convincing piece of propaganda, to help counter the anti-Spanish works of such chroniclers as Paolo Giovio, who he mentions as one of the "base people" who "had not been bought off" by the Spanish Crown.[88]

In addition to Italian writers, the Spaniards also showed interest in Italian printers. Venice in particular was a center of early modern print culture, and a great deal of business came its way through the literary interests of Spain and Spanish Italy.[89] Guzmán de Silva, among other ambassadors to Venice, received a number of requests from various Spanish officials to act as a middleman with Venetian presses. The state secretary Antonio Pérez, for example, arranged for Guzmán to find a Venetian printer for his father's Castilian translation of Homer's *Odyssey*.[90] Similarly, a scholar named Alvar Gómez wrote from the University of Alcalá, requesting that Guzmán find a publisher for a biography of the university's founder, Cardinal Francisco Ximénez de Cisneros.[91] A different kind of commission came to Guzmán from the bishop of Segorbe, who sent the ambassador a letter of credit worth a thousand ducats to buy "some quantity of the new Roman prayerbook for His Majesty."[92] He must have been happy with the results, as a month later he wrote again asking for the purchase of a number of "breviaries, missals, and books of new prayers" which were scarce in Spain, France, and the Netherlands.[93] This particular request seems a little odd, since Philip had specifically ordered that Christopher Plantin's press in Antwerp would have a monopoly on printing editions of the new Roman breviaries to be used in the Spanish territories.[94] In any case, as a man of the Church, Guzmán was no doubt quite happy to comply with the bishop's wishes.

Men of letters were not the only Italians who found employment through the Spanish ambassadors; military engineers and soldiers also found themselves in great demand. Spanish *tercios* may have been the

88. For more on Giovio, see T. C. Price Zimmermann, *Paolo Giovio: the Historian and the Crisis of Sixteenth-Century Italy* (Princeton, 1995).
89. See Augustus Pallotta, "Venetian Printers and Spanish Literature in Sixteenth-Century Italy," *Contemporary Literature* 43 (Winter 1991), pp. 20–42.
90. Diego de Fuyca (chief deputy to Antonio Pérez) to Guzmán, October 11, 1575; AGSE 1514, #128.
91. Gómez to Guzmán, October 18, 1573; AGSE 1509, #105.
92. June 20, 1574; AGSE 1573, #99.
93. July 28, 1574; AGSE 1510, #67.
94. See Robert M. Kingdon, "Patronage, Piety, and Printing in Sixteenth-Century Europe," *Festschrift for Frederick B. Artz,* ed. David H. Pinckney and Theodore Ropp (Durham, 1964), pp. 31–36; and idem., "The Plantin Breviaries: A Case Study in the Sixteenth-Century Business Operations of a Publishing House," *Bibliothèque d'Humanisme et Renaissance* (1960), pp. 133–50.

most feared infantry of the time, but they looked to Italy for expertise in the technological arts of war.[95] For example, Diego de Mendoza, himself a soldier, on hearing that Charles needed military engineers, recommended the prior of Barletta.[96] This individual had sent Charles "a design for a fortress," presumably an example of the *trace italienne,* or new system of fortifications which revolutionized siege warfare in this period.[97] Later, during Mendoza's tenure as governor of Siena, he mentioned several times that he had hired a certain engineer named Giovambattista Romano to help him build a great castle.[98] Romano was one of a group of engineers who visited Siena in 1550, and designed a model of the city's fortifications.[99] Mendoza's plans for a magnificent castle in Siena would be ill-fated, but it is significant that he turned to Italian experts for help.[100]

While Mendoza hired an Italian engineer on his own initiative, Luis de Requeséns was commanded to look for one, with interesting consequences. In June 1572 Requeséns wrote from Milan to Guzmán de Silva, saying that he had received orders from Philip to find a "capable and soldierly" engineer and send him to Spain.[101] After doing some research, Requeséns determined that Venice was the best place to locate such men, and so he asked Guzmán to "do me the favor of ordering one to be procured directly." He even informed Guzmán of the name of an engineer he had heard about, one Vicencio Locatelo Cremones, who seemed to fit the bill. Unfortunately, this fellow was also a local bandit. Requeséns suggested that Guzmán make some quiet inquiries into what crimes Locatelo Cremones may have committed, which were rumored to be grave. He should also see if he could interview the man personally, and "with dissimulation discuss with him if he might find himself employed in the service of the king." Evidently Requeséns was more concerned about getting entangled with local authorities than about whether his new hire had a clear conscience. Three weeks later Requeséns acknowledged Guzmán's positive evaluation of Locatelo Cremones, and suggested sending him to

95. See L. A. Maggiorotti, *Architetti e architetture militare,* 3 vols. (Rome, 1933–1939), Vol. III, *Gli architetti militari italiani nella Spagna, nel Portogallo e nelle loro colonie.*
96. Mendoza to Charles, August 16, 1540; AGSE 1497, Libro 67, ff. 101v–3r.
97. See Geoffrey Parker, *The Military Revolution: Military Innovation and the Rise of the West, 1500–1800,* 2d ed. (Cambridge, 1996); and Michael E. Mallett and J. R. Hale, *The Military Organization of a Renaissance State: Venice c. 1400 to 1617* (Cambridge, 1984), chap. 14. A copy of the prior's design is in AGSE 1316, #73.
98. Mendoza to Charles, October 14, 1550 (AGSE 876, #59–1), and April 3, 1552 (AGSE 877, #34.
99. Simon Pepper and Nicholas Adams, *Firearms and Fortifications: Military Architecture and Siege Warfare in Sixteenth-Century Siena* (Chicago, 1986), p. 60.
100. See Spivakovsky, *Son of the Alhambra,* chap. 11.
101. Requeséns to Guzmán, June 25, 1572; AGSE 1503, #72.

Spain with the title of captain and a salary of fifty escudos a month, as well as the possibility of a pardon for his crimes.[102] Locatelo Cremones was in fact wanted on a murder charge, but Requeséns indicated that Guzmán might "close his eyes" to this uncomfortable truth. Despite his religious calling, Guzmán did just that, and Locatelo Cremones found himself shipped to Spain, and then to the Netherlands.[103] Nor is there any doubt Philip knew about this bending of the laws. In August 1572 Requeséns informed Philip about Locatelo Cremones, and confirmed that he was facing a death sentence for murder and highway robbery—but he was available, as he had been charged in absentia and had not yet been captured.[104] So the king was at least indirectly complicit in aiding a fugitive to flee from Venetian justice; the Spanish empire's military needs outweighed any ethical considerations.

The ambassadors were not always so eager to sign up Italian engineers and military men. In 1575 Guzmán complained to Philip about how inventors constantly pestered him with "clever secret machines of war," which were either impractical or absurd.[105] Most of the time, however, the Spanish officials in Italy were happy to accept offers of service, which helped bind the Italian aristocracy closer to the Crown.[106] Often such appointments were made for political reasons as much as for the applicant's military expertise. In 1572, for example, Requeséns informed Philip that Paolo Orsino, a commander of the papal forces and a member of one of the oldest aristocratic families in Rome, had inquired about entering the king's service. The ambassador recommended that the offer be accepted, noting that Orsino "is a man of brains and valor, and has much influence in this city and court."[107] A month later Zúñiga wrote a similar letter, saying that Orsino greatly desired employment, and should be given an appointment "in order to conserve him in devotion to Your Majesty."[108] Both brothers believed it would be politically expedient to give Orsino a job.

102. Requeséns to Guzmán, July 16, 1572; AGSE 1504, #54.
103. On July 28, 1572, Locatelo Cremones signed a receipt for two hundred escudos for his journey to Spain (ASGE 1507, #85), and on January 9, 1574, Requeséns wrote to Guzmán from Antwerp that the engineer had arrived in that city (AGSE 1511, #37). He also mentioned that the duke of Alba disapproved of their hiring a criminal.
104. Requeséns to Philip, August 3, 1572; AGSE 1235, #124.
105. Guzmán to Philip, January 8, 1575; AGSE 1334, #3. The Simancas archives contain a number of plans for just such fantastic machines, so Guzmán and others must have listened occasionally.
106. See Manuel Rivero Rodríguez, "Felipe II y los 'Potentados de Italia,'" *Le dimensione europea dei Farnese, Bulletin de L'Institut Historique Belge de Rome* 63 (1993), pp. 337–70; and Angelantonio Spagnoletti, *Principi italiani e Spagna nell'età barocca* (Milan, 1996).
107. Requeséns to Philip, February 28, 1572; AGSE 918, #68.
108. Zúñiga to Philip, March 1572; AGSE 918, #161.

In another case, Zúñiga recruited an aristocrat from a family of known French supporters. In a letter to Philip Zúñiga explained that although Onorato Caetani's family had traditionally been loyal to France, he would be an excellent candidate for a pension and a military appointment. He was an experienced soldier, a veteran of the wars against the Turk, and came with excellent references from both Requeséns and Don Juan de Austria. He was also very well connected, the nephew of a cardinal and the brother-in-law of Marc Antonio Colonna, admiral of the papal fleet. Finally, he was wealthy, and owned heavily fortified properties in important strategic locations on the road from Rome to Naples. Zúñiga asserted that Caetani was "a very good man and I have never seen an Italian of better customs nor a better Christian."[109] The ambassador suggested that as Caetani had offered his services, it would be convenient to accept them, "because as I have said his lands are considerable, and he is quite useful, and his uncle would be of great service in conclaves and other affairs here." Philip agreed, and authorized Zúñiga to offer Caetani a pension of fifteen hundred ducats.[110]

In such interactions between the Italian aristocracy and the Spanish monarchy, the resident ambassadors played a key role. As we have seen, the ambassadors acted as intermediaries between Italian and Spanish societies, the bridge between two cultures. The relationship was not always fair or equal; the Spaniards often took what they wanted, or at least felt entitled to do so. From the point of view of the Spanish nobility, Italy was a resource to be exploited, not a partner to be respected. And the ambassadors themselves were often the worst offenders in this regard. Their arrogance helps to explain Italian resentment against Spanish Habsburg power. To cite one example, when the ex-ambassador Juan de Zúñiga died in 1586, the Venetian ambassador in Madrid reported the event without the slightest regret. Instead, he remarked on how Zúñiga believed that "all princes, including the pope, were as nothing, and depended entirely on the king of Spain. It was enough for the latter to indicate his wishes to have them obeyed."[111] Obviously, not all Italians hated the Spaniards; many quite willingly entered into the king's service, or enjoyed Spanish patronage. Nonetheless Spanish ambassadors often focused on what they perceived as negative Italian attributes and attitudes. While they searched Italy for art and artifacts, they also looked nervously for signs of disaster.

109. Zúñiga to Philip, February 1, 1572; AGSE 920, #55.
110. AGSE 920, #55.
111. Quoted in J. N. Hillgarth, *The Mirror of Spain, 1500–1700: The Formation of a Myth* (Ann Arbor, 2000), p. 21.

CONCLUSION

Novedades, No Peace

Several generations of historians have asserted that the peace treaty of Cateau-Cambrésis of 1559 marked the beginning of a "pax hispanica" in Italy, which lasted through the early seventeenth century. Yet Italy during the reigns of Philip III (1598–1621) and Philip IV (1621–1665) was no more peaceful than it had been under Charles V or Philip II—in fact, less so. Wars involving Spain, France, and various Italian states erupted over possession of the northern Italian territories of Saluzzo (1598–1601), Monferrato (1613–1617), and Mantua (1628–1631).[1] In addition, the election of Pope Urban VIII (1623–1644) led to the most anti-Spanish papacy since Paul IV. For over twenty years he would blatantly favor French interests, while Spaniards could only look on with impotent rage.[2] Even "Spanish Italy" proved unstable: both Naples and Sicily experienced periodic unrest, climaxing in major revolts against Spanish rule in 1647.[3]

1. See Jose Luis Cano de Gardoquí, "España y los estados italianos independientes en 1600," *Hispania* 23 (1963), pp. 524–55; Paul C. Allen, *Philip III and the Pax Hispanica, 1598–1621* (New Haven, 2000), chap. 3; Antonio Bombín Pérez, *La cuestión de Monferrato, 1613–1618* (Vitoria, 1975); J. H. Elliott, *The Count-Duke of Olivares* (New Haven, 1986), chaps. 9–10.

2. Dandelet acknowledges the decline of Spanish influence in Rome under Urban VIII: *Spanish Rome 1500–1700* (New Haven, 2001), chap. 6. See also Laurie Nussdorfer, *Civic Politics in the Rome of Urban VIII* (Princeton, 1992).

3. See Rosario Villari, *The Revolt of Naples,* trans. James Newell with John A. Marino (Oxford, 1993); and Luis Antonio Ribot García, *La revuelta antiespañola de Mesina: Causas y antecedentes (1591–1647)* (Valladolid, 1982).

So Spanish control of Italy in the seventeenth century was even more problematic than it had been in the sixteenth. To be sure, throughout this period Italian opinions about the Spaniards were divided. Many among the Italian aristocracy benefited from Spanish imperialism. As we have seen, Charles V and Philip II both cultivated a Spanish faction in Rome, as well as several generations of "Hispanicized" Italian nobles. On the other hand, many Italians condemned what they perceived as Spanish oppression. From 1494 on, Italian writers mourned over the humiliation of their country at the hands of foreign princes, and particularly Spaniards.[4] The two greatest Italian chroniclers of the period, Machiavelli and Guicciardini, both declared that resisting Charles V's power in Italy should be the highest priority for Italian princes.[5] As the sixteenth century progressed, Italian resentment against Spain intensified. In 1588, a Florentine ambassador expressed his opinion of Spaniards to the Grand Duke of Tuscany: "to tell the truth to Your Lordship, these pigs wish to tyrannize the world, and [King] Philip thinks to make himself monarch [over everyone], having pretensions to every throne in the world."[6] This was hardly an isolated outburst. In fact, the "Black Legend" of Spain, which painted early modern Spaniards as cruel and domineering, in large part originated in Italy, before being polished and sharpened by English and Dutch Protestants.[7]

Debate and protest continued through the following centuries. In the eighteenth century, for example, several Neapolitan intellectuals such as Paolo Mattia Doria wrote "searing indictment[s] of the two hundred or so years of Spanish domination of southern Italy."[8] In the late nineteenth and early twentieth centuries, the rise of Italian nationalism further blackened the memory of Spanish rule. In the wake of the creation of

4. Denys Hay, "Italy and Barbarian Europe," in *Italian Renaissance Studies*, ed. E. F. Jacob (London, 1960), pp. 48–68.
5. Felix Gilbert, *Machiavelli and Guicciardini: Politics and History in Sixteenth Century Florence* (reprint, New York, 1984), p. 241.
6. *Négociations diplomatiques de la France avec la Toscane*, ed. Abel Desjardins, 6 vols. (Paris, 1859–1886), Vol. IV, p. 761. My thanks to Geoffrey Parker for this reference.
7. Sverker Arnoldsson, "La Leyenda Negra: Estudios sobre sus origines," *Goteborg Universitets Arsskrift* 66 (1960), pp. 7–147. Of course, Spaniards like Bartolomé de las Casas also criticized their country's imperial brutality, leading to the development of the "Black Legend" in the Americas. See also William Maltby, *The Black Legend in England: The Development of Anti-Spanish Sentiment, 1558–1660* (Durham, 1971); and J. N. Hillgarth, *The Mirror of Spain, 1500–1700: The Formation of a Myth* (Ann Arbor, 2000).
8. Anthony Pagden, *Spanish Imperialism and the Political Imagination: Studies in European and Spanish-American Social and Political Theory 1513–1830* (New Haven, 1990), p. 75; and see also the published results of a recent conference on anti-Spanish sentiment in eighteenth- and nineteenth-century Italy: *Alle origini di una nazione: Antispagnolismo e identità italiana*, ed. Aurelio Musi (Milan, 2003).

Italy as a modern unified nation-state, Italian historians looked to Renaissance Italy for signs of protonationalism, and identified Spain with foreign rule and tyranny. One such figure, Benedetto Croce, promoted "modern" Italian cultural identity, and rejected "foreign" hegemony over Italy.[9] In 1922, Croce published a highly influential work titled *La Spagna nella vita italiana durante la Rinascenza* (Spain in Italian Life During the Renaissance). Croce described late Renaissance Italy as a region dominated by the foreign tyranny of Spain, to its great detriment; according to him, sixteenth-century Italians (under Spanish influence) were "decadent," lacking the moral force to throw out Spanish overlords.[10] Croce also suggested that Italy derived some benefits from Spanish rule, such as protection from the Turks and the self-serving Italian aristocracy, but the vision of early modern Italy suffering under Spanish imperialism remained a powerful influence among Italian historians for decades.[11]

Croce and his disciples stressed the importance of Renaissance Italian protests against Spanish rule as evidence of *Italianità*, but historians of Spain tend to be more dismissive. For example, Henry Kamen argues, "much of the wholly unfavorable image of Spanish rule in Italy rests on uncritical acceptance of the savage portrait painted by anti-Spanish diplomats from [various] Italian states."[12] Similarly, Thomas Dandelet states that papal resentment of Spanish imperial power, particularly after 1559, was more than offset by the benefits popes derived from friendship with Spain.[13] But what did Spain's representatives in Italy think at the time? Evidence suggests they did not share this cavalier attitude toward Italian expressions of hatred and resentment. Indeed, as we have seen, the Spanish ambassadors in Rome and Venice took Italian anti-Spanish sentiment very seriously. They perceived Italian hostility as a real threat to Spanish hegemony, and doubted the stability of a "Spanish peace." For one thing, they insisted that Italians, by their nature, could not be trusted.

Antipathy among different ethnicities and regions, of course, has always existed in Europe. The connection between such sentiments and the idea of "nationalism," however, is difficult to define. Many historians trace the modern "nation" to the rise of centralized states in

9. See Edmund E. Jacobitti, "Hegemony before Gramsci: The Case of Benedetto Croce," *Journal of Modern History* 52 (1980), pp. 66–84.
10. Benedetto Croce, *La Spagna nella vita italiana durante la Rinascenza* (Bari, 1922), chaps. 11–12.
11. See for example Vittorio di Tocco, *Ideali di indipendenza in Italia durante la preponderanza spagnola* (Messina, 1926); and from a later generation, Romolo Quazza, *Preponderanza spagnola (1559–1700)* 2d ed. (Milan, 1950).
12. *Empire: How Spain Became a World Power, 1492–1763* (New York, 2003), p. 367.
13. *Spanish Rome*, pp. 216–17.

the Renaissance.[14] The Italians led the way in this area, as in so much else during the period.[15] But historians disagree about whether Renaissance "Italy" (as opposed to individual city-states like Florence or Venice) really existed as more than a geographical expression.[16] The same is true about contemporary "Spain."[17] It is perhaps the interrelationship between the two entities that can provide some answers.[18] Spanish imperialism in Italy helped crystallize both national identities; Italians and Spaniards defined themselves in opposition to each other.[19] Or at least, that is what the Spanish ambassadors seemed to think. They had definite ideas about what it meant to be "Italian," as well as "Spanish."

From the sixteenth century on, many literate Europeans identified Italians with Machiavelli, or more precisely with his popular image. "Machiavellism," a supposedly Italian trait, involved the amoral manipulation of politics and religion for personal gain, combined with skill (and delight) in deception.[20] In England, for example, dramatists like Marlowe and Shakespeare routinely depicted Italians as scheming villains, or designed their villains around "Machiavellian" behavior.[21] Similarly, early modern Spaniards often characterized Italians as being *ingenioso,* which can mean ingenious, clever, or tricky.[22] So Spanish ambassadors tended to be wary and mistrusting of Italians before they even arrived. Once they settled in their posts, their prejudices were usually confirmed: Italians, they complained, are deceitful and care only for themselves. The Spaniards did not seem to perceive any differences between Florentines, Romans, or Venetians in this regard; those of "the Italian nation" all behaved this way. So at least from the Spanish point of view, "Italy" existed, as did an "Italian" national character.

14. See for example Perry Anderson, *Lineages of the Absolutist State* (London, 1974); and Richard Bonney, *The European Dynastic States 1494–1660* (Oxford, 1991).

15. See *The Origins of the State in Italy 1300–1600,* ed. Julius Kirshner (Chicago, 1995).

16. See Felix Gilbert, "Italy," in *National Consciousness, History, and Political Culture in Early-Modern Europe,* ed. Orest Ranum (Baltimore, 1975), pp. 21–42.

17. See H. G. Koenigsberger, "Spain," ibid., pp. 144–72.

18. Several recent works have used this approach to examine early modern nationalism: see Peter Sahlins, *Boundaries: The Making of France and Spain in the Pyrenees* (Berkeley, 1989), and Henry Heller, *Anti-Italianism in Sixteenth-Century France* (Toronto, 2003).

19. Dandelet suggests that a stronger sense of national identity existed in the Spanish community in Rome than in the Iberian Peninsula itself; *Spanish Rome,* pp. 118–19.

20. See the classic work by Friedrich Meinecke, *Machiavellism: The Doctrine of Raison d'Etat and Its Place in Modern History,* trans. Douglas Scott (London, 1957).

21. There is a large body of literature on this topic; see for example John L. Lievsay, *The Elizabethan Image of Italy* (Ithaca, 1964); and more recently, John Roe, *Shakespeare and Machiavelli* (Cambridge, 2002).

22. Julio Caro Baroja, *Fragmentos italianos* (Madrid, 1992), pp. 16–19. The equivalent word in Italian, *furbo,* tended to have more positive connotations.

The ambassadors' obsession with *novedades* further illustrates their beliefs about Italian flaws. Of course, fear of instability and suspicion of change were not unique to early modern Spanish diplomats. Such expressions were common in contemporary European political discourse, as well as in diplomatic correspondence through the ages. But the word *novedades,* as used by Spanish ambassadors in late Renaissance Italy, was fraught with special meaning. As we have seen, the ambassadors complained with remarkable regularity about the Italians' fondness for *novedades.* Interestingly, the Italians themselves sometimes agreed with this characterization. Guicciardini, for example, says of the Neapolitans, "among all the peoples of Italy [they] are most noted for their instability and thirst for innovations."[23] Ironically, this passage refers to the difficulties King Charles VIII of France experienced trying to conquer and pacify Naples in the 1490s, and how the Neapolitans became nostalgic for their former Aragonese overlords; but it also foreshadows future problems in "Spanish Italy."

For the Spaniards, the Italian predilection for upsetting the status quo represented a major threat, as the ambassadors warned repeatedly throughout the sixteenth century. In 1530, mere weeks after Charles V's coronation at Bologna, Miguel Mai cautioned the emperor not to relax too much, as "the Italians catch fire at the least spark . . . because they always want *novedades.*"[24] In 1547, just after Charles's victory at Mühlberg, Diego Hurtado de Mendoza wrote a similar warning about Pope Paul III's political policies. The pope's ambitions threatened the peace of Italy, especially if Paul "intends to cause some *novedad.*"[25] Both of these ambassadors were writing at moments of relative peace and security, and yet they demonstrated anxiety, and fear of what the Italians might do.

The peace treaty of Cateau-Cambrésis in 1559, despite its importance in the eyes of modern historians, apparently did little to soothe these fears. In 1560, Francisco de Vargas alerted Philip that the Italian political situation was dangerously unstable, because Italians were fond of *novedades.*[26] Four years later, Luis de Requeséns loudly criticized Pope Pius IV and the College of Cardinals, because "besides being of that nation [i.e. Italian], and therefore extremely restless and fond of *novedades,* they

23. *The History of Italy* (1561), ed. and trans. Sidney Alexander (reprint, Princeton, 1984), p. 90. Guicciardini also makes a general statement about human nature, that people are always "dissatisfied with the present state of affairs." I am grateful to John Marino for pointing out this passage.
24. Mai to Charles, July 31, 1530; Archivo General de Simancas, Sección Estado (hereafter AGSE) 851, #52–53.
25. Mendoza to Charles, May 3, 1547; AGSE 874, #56.
26. Vargas to Philip, August 22, 1560; AGSE 886, #59.

want nothing more than war, which they believe will improve their situation."[27] Five years after that, Juan de Zúñiga raged about how many Italians seemed gleeful at religious and political chaos in France, "because of the desire they have for *novedades,* and it seems to some of them that the best way to have more [trouble] would be if the king of France came here with an army and waged war with [us]."[28] Six years after that, while reporting to Philip a rumor that various Italian princes were discussing the formation of an alliance, Zúñiga emphasized that "*novedades* in Italy are less desirable for Your Majesty than for anyone else."[29] Jump forward yet another eight years, and we find the count of Olivares warning Pope Gregory XIII that Italy is full of "unquiet people who desire *novedades* in every Italian state."[30] Finally, just to demonstrate that the monarchy was as anxious as its representatives, in 1591 King Philip himself commanded the duke of Sessa to make sure papal elections did not cause any *novedades* in pontifical policy.[31]

Clearly, Spanish ambassadors, as well as their king, regarded *novedades* with great trepidation. They also believed that *novedades* could happen at any moment—with good reason. Italian politics did indeed catch the ambassadors off guard, repeatedly throughout Philip II's reign: the Carafa War, the precedence controversy, the Venetian defection from the Holy League, the absolution of Henry IV, the Ferrara conflict. Their fear of *novedades* was actually well founded. Thus they did not express confidence in their imperial power or their control of the situation. Instead, the ambassadors' correspondence reflects deep insecurity. Anxiety often turns into anger, which also surfaced in their letters. Requeséns, for example, included quite a few indignant outbursts in his dispatches. In October 1573, he wrote a letter to the state secretary Antonio Pérez, in which he vented his frustration with Archbishop Carlo Borromeo (who had just excommunicated Requeséns over a jurisdiction dispute in Milan).[32] After excoriating Borromeo, Requeséns then extended his diatribe to all Italians: "the Italians are like hats, or rather the soles of shoes, which is to say the only way to avoid them hurting us is for us to break them in first."[33] So Requeséns expressed a desire to establish undisputed

27. Requeséns to Philip, April 29, 1564; AGSE 896, #58.
28. Zúñiga to Philip, April 24, 1569; *Correspondencia diplomática entre España y la Santa Sede durante el pontificado de S. Pío V,* ed. Luciano Serrano, 4 vols. (Madrid, 1914), Vol. III, p. 62.
29. Zúñiga to Philip, September 30, 1575; AGSE 925, #195.
30. Olivares to Philip, June 19, 1583; AGSE 944, #88.
31. Philip to Sessa, November 8, 1591; AGSE 958, unnumbered.
32. See José M. March, *Don Luis de Requeséns en el gobierno de Milan, 1571–1573* (Madrid, 1943).
33. Requeséns to Pérez, October 4, 1573; AGSE 1236, #214. A decade earlier, Antonio's

dominance over the Italians, but he knew it was only a wish, not an accomplished fact. Machiavelli said that fortune is a woman, who must be beaten into submission.[34] He was writing to Italian princes, encouraging them to unite and expel the foreign invaders; Requeséns turned Machiavelli's metaphor around, and exhorted his superiors to help him crush the Italian will to resist.

Requeséns's wrath could be dismissed as a reaction to the stress of the moment, except that he said similar things throughout his years in Italy. In fact, the anger he and his fellow ambassadors expressed is significant, because it reveals their intellectual paradigm: that of disappointed imperialists. The Spanish ambassadors dreamed of a submissive Italy, happy to be under Spanish rule, but instead they found resentment, plotting, and *novedades*. No wonder they were so upset. One last letter from Requeséns should illustrate this point. He wrote it to Antonio Pérez's father Gonzalo, Philip II's private secretary, in March 1565. Requeséns was in Genoa at the time, seven months after leaving Rome in protest against Pius IV's ruling on precedence—so once again, he had reason to be angry and frustrated. It is such a remarkable letter, revealing so much of the sixteenth-century Spanish imperial point of view, that it deserves to be quoted at some length:

> It may be that there are old men there in Castile who believe we were better off when we had no more than that realm . . . in that we had more peace and sold off fewer royal rents . . . and in truth if they could [they would] return things to that time when there was a king in Aragon and another in Naples, and a lord in Flanders and another in Burgundy, and a duke in Milan, and would likewise distribute what the King of France now has joined together. I confess that would be better for the kingdoms, although not for the authority and greatness of the kings; but supposing that the world, or at least Christendom, did come to be reduced [and divided] into only His Majesty's possessions and those of the King of France, and what is ours could not be otherwise unless it belonged to our enemy, it [would be necessary] to conserve [our lands], which requires having allies. And we cannot keep our allies in Italy except either by doing them many favors, or by kicking them often, and to choose a middle way is to do nothing, which in my opinion would be the worst choice. These people are by nature restless and fond of *novedades*,

---

father, the state secretary Gonzalo Pérez, told Philip II that "it is not well [to leave] Italy solely to the power and trust of the Italians." Quoted in Angel González Palencia, *Gonzalo Pérez, secretario de Felipe II*, 2 vols. (Madrid, 1948), Vol. I, p. 259.

34. Niccolò Machiavelli, *The Prince* (1516), ed and trans. David Wootton. Indianapolis, 1995) chap. 25.

especially when they find themselves in a position that they think could be improved. Not only do they complain in Rome and in other parts of Italy that they are not favored, but they also have come to persuade themselves that they need not remain loyal or serve the king [Philip] our lord. . . . I seek to persuade them to the contrary but they are not people who are guided by words alone, and it seems to me I have often said this to Your Excellency, who [already] believes the same thing. In this case it is my opinion, and I do not hold it to be friendly with Italians, who are the people I most hate in the world, and if God had not done me the favor of making me Spanish, I would wish to be Tartar before being Italian. Yet it is necessary for us to have some of them as allies, for the preservation of what we have here.[35]

We have here the heartfelt declaration of a proud sixteenth-century Spaniard, a man acutely aware of Spain's unique position of power at this time. He looked back to the previous century, before Spain ruled an empire, and indeed before "Spain" existed as a unified kingdom, but with pride rather than nostalgia. Requeséns clearly identified himself as "Spanish," and thus favored by God. Ever since the Catholic Kings Ferdinand and Isabella consolidated Spain as a Christian kingdom, a sense of divine mission permeated Spanish foreign policy.[36] This belief intensified in the sixteenth century, as Charles V and Philip II created a world empire.[37] Requeséns was of course an aristocrat, and his elitism may have been partly an expression of his noble status, but he was also a representative of the Spanish monarchy and nation, and as such he practically declared membership of a master race.

Yet Requeséns' pride was tinged with doubt and fear. He knew that becoming a world power meant being surrounded by enemies, which in turn meant needing friends. This was particularly true in Italy, a crucial part of the Habsburg empire. Requeséns himself flatly stated, "The preservation, peace, and grandeur of Spain depend on the affairs of Italy being well ordered."[38] Obviously, however, the Italians refused to be well

35. Requeséns to Gonzalo Pérez, March 3, 1565; AGSE 1394, #138.
36. See Ramón Menéndez Pidal, "The Significance of the Reign of Isabella the Catholic, According to Her Contemporaries," in *Spain in the Fifteenth Century 1369–1516*, ed. Roger Highfield (London, 1972), pp. 380–404; and Peggy K. Liss, *Isabel the Queen: Life and Times* (Oxford, 1992), chaps. 9–10.
37. See John M. Headley, "The Habsburg World Empire and the Revival of Ghibellinism," in *Theories of Empire, 1450–1800*, ed. David Armitage (Aldershot, 1998), pp. 45–79; and Geoffrey Parker, "David or Goliath? Philip II and His World in the 1580s," in *Success Is Never Final: Empire, War and Faith in Early Modern Europe* (New York, 2002), pp. 16–38.
38. Requeséns to Philip, November 7, 1574; quoted by Geoffrey Parker, *The Grand Strategy of Philip II* (New Haven, 1998), p. 82.

ordered. In fact, they often refused to take orders at all. Many felt no loy-
alty to Spain, indeed quite the opposite. Even the papacy rebuffed the
Spaniards. Requeséns had proclaimed Spain's greatness to Pope Pius IV,
in defense of Spanish precedence. But the pope had rejected his arguments. From Requeséns' point of view, the pope was Italian first and fore-
most, and for that reason threw Spanish claims of preeminence back in
the ambassador's face. Now, in the aftermath of that defeat, Requeséns
confided his anger and mistrust. He is arrogant, but he is not triumphant.
And he certainly is not at peace.

The Spanish ambassadors in sixteenth century Italy believed in their
own greatness, and yet discovered the limits of their power. Try as they
might, they never turned Italy into an unassailable fortress, or converted
the Italians into unshakeable allies. Despite the obvious military strength
of the Spanish Habsburgs, Venice and the papacy remained stubbornly
independent, and the "pax hispanica" was in some ways an illusion. Spanish hegemony in Italy was never absolute, and the ambassadors knew it.
That is why Francisco de Vargas warned Philip II that the Italian political
situation, while it appeared stable, could change at any moment. Italians,
he asserted, like change for its own sake, and also fear and resent the
Spanish imperial presence in Italy. The stronger the Spaniards became,
the more anti-Spanish sentiment they inspired. Power and anxiety were
thus two sides of the same Spanish coin.

The paradoxical weakness of Spanish imperialism in Italy reflects its
more general failure throughout Europe: the Netherlands successfully
revolted against Spanish rule, England turned back the Armada, France
recovered from civil war and became ascendant. Europe rejected Spanish
rule, even more forcefully than Italy did. The very size and power of the
Spanish empire guaranteed that its rivals would oppose it. Spanish ambassadors argued, threatened, pleaded, and lied for the sake of their country, but they never imposed their will on the world. And yet they came
tantalizingly close. For a brief time, the Spanish empire was the greatest
the world had ever seen, the first on which the sun never set.[39] The ago-
nizing sense of having victory not quite within one's grasp explains much
of the frustration expressed in Spanish diplomatic correspondence.
Machiavelli suggested that we control half of our lives, and that fortune
rules the other half.[40] The Spanish Habsburgs and their ambassadors well
understood this idea. They exercised what power they had, and remained
vigilant for what they could not control. In the end, however, Spanish
virtù proved insufficient, and *fortuna* overwhelmed their empire.

39. Ibid., p. 3.
40. Machiavelli, *The Prince*, chap. 25.

Bibliography

MANUSCRIPT COLLECTIONS

Archivio di Stato di Firenze
  Mediceo del Principato
Archivio di Stato di Venezia
  Collegio (Lettere Principi)
Archivio Segreto Vaticano
  Nunziatura Spagna
Archivo de Zabálburu (Madrid)
Archivo General de Simancas
  Consejo y Juntas de Hacienda
  Contaduría Mayor de Cuentas
  Estados Pequeños de Italia
  Patronato Real
  Secretaría de Estado (AGSE)
  Visitas de Italia
Archivo Histórico Nacional (Madrid)
Bibliothèque Publique et Universitaire de Genève
  Collection Edouard Favre
British Library, Department of Western Manuscripts (London)
  Additional Manuscripts
Instituto de Valencia de Don Juan (Madrid)
Ministerio de Asuntos Exteriores, Archivo General (Madrid)
  Embajada a la Santa Sede

PUBLISHED PRIMARY SOURCES

Algunas Cartas de Don Diego Hurtado de Mendoza, escritas 1538–1552. Ed. Alberto Vazquez and R. Selden Rose. New Haven: Yale University Press, 1935.

Calendar of State Papers and Manuscripts, Relating to English Affairs, Existing in the Archives and Collections of Venice, and in Other Libraries of Northern Italy. Ed. Rawdon Brown and G. Cavendish Bentinck. Vols. IV–VII. Nendeln: Kraus Reprints, 1970–1971.

Calendar of State Papers, Relating to English Affairs, Preserved Principally at Rome, in the Vatican Archives and Library. Ed. J. M. Rigg. Vols. I and II. London: Hereford Times, 1916, 1926.

"Cartas de Don Diego Hurtado de Mendoza." Ed. R. Foulché-Delbosc. *Archivo de Investigaciones Históricas* 2 (1911), pp. 155–95, 270–75, 463–75, 537–600.

Colección de documentos inéditos para la historia de España. 112 vols. Madrid: Impres. de la viuda de Calero, 1842–1895.

Correspondance du cardinal de Granvelle, 1565–1583. Vols. I–III. Ed. Edmond Poullet. Brussels: F. Hayez, 1877–1881.

Correspondance du Cardinal de Granvelle, 1565–1583. Vol. IV. Ed. Charles Piot. Brussels: F. Hayez, 1884.

Correspondencia diplomática entre España y la Santa Sede durante el pontificado de S. Pio V. Ed. Luciano Serrano. 4 vols. Madrid: Junta para ampliación de estudios é investigaciones científicas, 1914.

Documentos para la historia del Monasterio de San Lorenzo el Real de El Escorial. Ed. Gregorio de Andrés. Vols. V–VIII. Escorial: Imprenta del Real Monasterio, 1962–1965.

Guicciardini, Francesco. *The History of Italy* (1561). Ed. and trans. Sidney Alexander. Princeton: Princeton University Press, 1969; reprint, 1984.

Hurtado de Mendoza, Diego. *De la Guerra de Granada* (1571–1572). Ed. Bernardo Blanco-González. Madrid: Castilia, 1970.

La Lega di Lepanto nel carteggio diplomatico di Don Luys de Torres, nunzio straordinario di S. Pio V a Filippo II. Ed. A. Dragonetti de Torres. Turin: Fratelli Bocca, 1931.

Letters and Papers, Foreign and Domestic, of the Reign of Henry VIII. Preserved in the Public Record Office, the British Museum, and Elsewhere in England. Vol. XVII. Ed. James Gairdner and R. H. Brodie. Vadus: Kraus Reprints, 1965.

Machiavelli, Niccolò. *The Prince* (1516). Ed, and trans. David Wootton. Indianapolis: Hackett, 1995.

Négociations de la France dans le Levant. Ed. E. Charrière. 4 vols. Paris: Collection de Documents Inédits, 1853; reprint, New York: Burt Franklin, 1966.

Négociations diplomatiques de la France avec la Toscane. Ed. Abel Desjardins. 6 vols. Paris: Imprimerie National, 1859–1886.

El Papado y Felipe II: Colección de breves Pontificios. Ed. José Ignacio Tellechea Idígoras. Vols. I and II. Madrid: Fundación Universitaria Española, 1999–2000.

Pio IV y Felipe Segundo: Primeros diez meses de la embajada de Don Luis de Requeséns en Roma, 1563–1564. Ed. "F. del V." and "S. K." Madrid: Rafael Marco, 1891.

Pursuit of Power: Venetian Ambassadors' Reports on Spain, Turkey, and France in the Age of Philip II, 1560–1600. Ed. James C. Davis. New York: Harper and Row, 1970.

Le relazioni degli ambasciatori veneti al Senato durante il secolo decimosesto. Ed. Eugenio Àlberi. 15 vols. Florence: Tipografia e calcografia all'insegna di Clio, 1839–1863.

Relazioni di ambasciatori veneti al Senato. Ed. Luigi Firpo. 13 vols. to 1996. Turin: Bottega d'Erasmo, 1965–.

Sixte-Quint. Ed. Baron de Hübner. Vol. III. Paris: Catholic Publication Society, 1873.

Tellechea Idígoras, J. Ignacio. *El ocaso de un rey: Felipe II visto desde la nunciatura de Madrid 1594–1598.* Madrid: Fundación Universitaria Española, 2001.

Tiziano e la corte di Spagna nei documenti dell'Archivio generale di Simancas. Madrid: Istituto Italiano di Cultura, 1975.

Vasari, Giorgio. *Lives of the Artists* (1550, 1568). Trans. George Bull. Vol. I. London: Penguin, 1965; reprint, 1987.

Wiquefort, Abraham van de. *The Embassador and His Functions.* Trans. John Digby. London: n.p., 1716.

SECONDARY SOURCES

Allen, E. John B. *Post and Courier Service in the Diplomacy of Early Modern Europe.* The Hague: Martinus Nijhoff, 1972.

Allen, Paul C. *Philip III and the Pax Hispanica, 1598–1621.* New Haven: Yale University Press, 2000.

Anderson, John, ed. *The Princely Courts of Europe: Ritual, Politics, and Culture under the Ancien Regime 1500–1700.* London: Weidenfeld and Nicolson, 1999.

Anderson, M. S. *The Rise of Modern Diplomacy 1450–1919.* London: Longman, 1993.

Anderson, Perry. *Lineages of the Absolutist State.* London: NLB, 1974.

Antonovics, A. V. "Counter-Reformation Cardinals: 1534–90." *European Studies Review* 2 (1972), pp. 301–27.

Arnoldsson, Sverker. "La Leyenda Negra: Estudios sobre sus origines." *Goteborg Universitets Arsskrift* 66 (1960), pp. 7–147.

Baumgartner, Frederic J. "Henry II and the Papal Conclave of 1549." *Sixteenth Century Journal* 16 (1985), pp. 301–14.

———. *Henry II, King of France 1547–1559.* Durham: Duke University Press, 1988.

———. *France in the Sixteenth Century.* New York: St. Martin's Press, 1995.

Beeching, Jack. *The Galleys at Lepanto.* New York: Scribner's, 1982.

Bell, Gary M. "Elizabethan Diplomacy: The Subtle Revolution." *Politics, Religion, and Diplomacy in Early Modern Europe: Essays in Honor of De Lamar Jensen.* Ed. Malcolm R. Thorp and Arthur J. Slavin. Kirksville: Sixteenth Century Essays and Studies, 1994. Pp. 267–88.

Bernardi, Tiziana. "Analisi di una cerimonia pubblica: L'incoronazione di Carlo V a Bologna." *Quaderni storici* 61, April 1986, pp. 171–99.

Bitossi, Carlo. *Il governo dei magnifici: Patriziato e politica a Genova fra Cinque e Seicento.* Genoa: Edizioni Culturali Internazionali Genova, 1990.

Black, Christopher F. *Early Modern Italy: A Social History.* London: Routledge, 2001.

Bombín Pérez, Antonio. *La cuestión de Monferrato, 1613–1618.* Alava: Colegio Universitario de Alava, 1975.

Bonney, Richard. *The European Dynastic States 1494–1660*. Oxford: Oxford University Press, 1991.

Borromeo, Agostino. "España y el problema de la elección papal de 1592." *Cuadernos de investigación histórica* 2 (1978), pp. 175–200.

Bouza Álvarez, Fernando. "La biblioteca de El Escorial y el orden de los saberes en el siglo XVI o la fama de Felipe II y la 'claridad' de sus libros." *Imagen y propaganda: Capítulos de historia cultural del reinado de Felipe II*. Ed. Fernando Bouza Álvarez. Madrid: Akal, 1998, pp. 168–85.

Boyden, James M. *The Courtier and the King: Ruy Gómez de Silva, Philip II, and the Court of Spain*. Berkeley: University of California Press, 1995.

Brandi, Karl. *The Emperor Charles V*. Trans. C. V. Wedgwood. London: Jonathan Cape, 1939.

Braudel, Fernand. *The Mediterranean and the Mediterranean World in the Age of Philip II*. Trans. Siân Reynolds. 2 vols. New York: Harper and Row, 1973.

——. "L'Italia fuori d'Italia: Due secoli e tre Italie." *Storia d'Italia: Dalla Caduta dell'Impero romano al secolo XVIII*. Vol. II. Turin: Giulio Einaudi, 1974.

British Museum General Catalogue of Printed Books. Vol. LXXXIV. London: The Trustees of the British Museum, 1961.

Brown, Jonathan. *The Golden Age of Painting in Spain*. New Haven: Yale University Press, 1991.

——. *Painting in Spain 1500–1700*. New Haven: Yale University Press, 1998.

Brunet, Jacqueline, and Gennaro Toscano, eds. *Les Granvelle et l'Italie au XVIe siècle: Le mécénat d'une famille*. Besançon: Cêtre, 1996.

Burke, Peter. *The Historical Anthropology of Early Modern Italy*. Cambridge: Cambridge University Press, 1987.

Calabria, Antonio. *The Cost of Empire: The Finances of the Kingdom of Naples in the Time of Spanish Rule*. Cambridge: Cambridge University Press, 1991.

Cano de Gardoquí, José Luis. "España y los estados italianos independientes en 1600." *Hispania* 23 (1963), pp. 524–55.

Cantagalli, Roberto. *Cosimo I de' Medici, granduca di Toscana*. Milan: Mursia, 1985.

Caro Baroja, Julio. *Fragmentos italianos*. Madrid: Ediciones Istmo, 1992.

Carter, Charles Howard. *The Secret Diplomacy of the Habsburgs, 1598–1625*. New York: Columbia University Press, 1964.

——. "The Ambassadors of Early Modern Europe: Patterns of Diplomatic Representation in the Early Seventeenth Century." *From the Renaissance to the Counter-Reformation: Essays in Honor of Garrett Mattingly*. Ed. Charles H. Carter. New York: Random House, 1965. Pp. 269–95.

Casado Quintanilla, Blas. "La cuestión de la precedencia España-Francia en la tercera asamblea del Concilio de Trento." *Hispania Sacra* 36 (1984), pp. 195–214.

Càstano, D. Luigi. *Gregorio XIV (Nicolò Sfondrati) 1535–1591*. Milan: Centro Ambrosiano di Documentazione e Studi Religiosi, 1993.

Chambers, D. S. *The Imperial Age of Venice, 1380–1580*. London: Thames and Hudson, 1970.

Chastel, André. *The Sack of Rome, 1527*. Trans. Beth Archer. Princeton: Princeton University Press, 1983.

Checa Cremades, Fernando. *Carlos V y la imagen del héroe en el Renacimiento.* Madrid: Taurus Ediciones, 1987.

——. *Felipe II, mecenas de las artes.* Madrid: Editorial Nerea, 1992.

——. *Tiziano y la monarquía hispánica: Usos y funciones de la pintura veneciana en España (siglos XVI y XVII).* Madrid: Nerea, 1994.

Clark, Peter, ed. *The European Crisis of the 1590s: Essays in Comparative History.* London: Allen and Unwin, 1985.

Cochrane, Eric. *Historians and Historiography in the Italian Renaissance.* Chicago: University of Chicago Press, 1981.

——. *Italy 1530–1630.* Ed. Julius Kirshner. London: Longman, 1988.

Collar de Cáceres, Fernando. "Arte y rigor religioso: Españoles e italianos en el ornato de los retablos del Escorial." *Felipe II y el arte de su tiempo.* Madrid: Fundacion Argentaria, 1998. Pp. 79–117.

Cozzi, Gaetano. "Venezia dal Rinascimento all'Età barocca." *Storia di Venezia.* Vol. VI, *Dal Rinascimento al Barocco.* Ed. Gaetano Cozzi and Paolo Prodi. Rome: Istituto della Enciclopedia italiano, 1994. Pp. 3–125.

——, and Michael Knapton, eds. *Storia d'Italia,* Vol. XII, *La Repubblica di Venezia nell'età moderna: Dal 1517 alla fine della Repubblica.* Turin: UTET, 1986.

Croce, Benedetto. *La Spagna nella vita italiana durante la Rinascenza.* Bari: Gius. Laterza & Figli, 1922.

Dandelet, Thomas James. *Spanish Rome 1500–1700.* New Haven: Yale University Press, 2001.

Davis, James C. "Shipping and Spying in the Early Career of a Venetian Doge, 1496–1502." *Studi veneziani* 16 (1974), pp. 97–108.

Davis, Robert C. *Shipbuilders of the Venetian Arsenal: Workers and Workplace in the Preindustrial City.* Baltimore: Johns Hopkins University Press, 1991.

——. *The War of the Fists: Popular Culture and Public Violence in Late Renaissance Venice.* New York: Oxford University Press, 1994.

——. "The Spectacle Almost Fit for a King: Venice's *Guerra de'canne* of 26 July 1574." *Medieval and Renaissance Venice.* Ed. Ellen E. Kittell and Thomas F. Madden. Urbana: University of Illinois Press, 1999. Pp. 181–212.

Delumeau, Jean. *L'Alun de Rome XVe–XIXe siècle.* Paris: SEVPEN, 1962.

Der Derian, James. *On Diplomacy: A Genealogy of Western Estrangement.* Oxford: Basil Blackwell, 1987.

Diccionario de historia de España. 2d ed. 3 vols. Ed. Germán Bleiberg. Madrid: Revista de Occidente, 1967–1979.

Dickinson, Gladys. *Du Bellay in Rome.* Leiden: E. J. Brill, 1960.

Dietrich Fernández, Henry. "The Papal Court at Rome c. 1450–1700." Anderson, *The Princely Courts of Europe.* Pp. 141–63.

Eire, Carlos M. N. *From Madrid to Purgatory: The Art and Craft of Dying in Sixteenth-Century Spain.* Cambridge: Cambridge University Press, 1995.

Elliott, J. H. *Imperial Spain 1469–1716.* London: Edward Arnold, 1963; reprint, London: Penguin Books, 1990.

——. *Europe Divided 1559–1598.* London: Fontana Press, 1968; reprint, 1985.

——. *Richelieu and Olivares.* Cambridge: Cambridge University Press, 1984.

——. *The Count-Duke of Olivares: The Statesman in an Age of Decline.* New Haven: Yale University Press, 1986.

——. *Spain and its World 1500–1700.* New Haven: Yale University Press, 1989.

Enciclopedia universal ilustrada europeo-americano. 70 vols. Madrid: Espasa-Calpe, 1907–1930.

Fantoni, Marcello. "Carlo V e l'Immagine dell'Imperator." Fantoni, *Carlo V e l'Italia.* Pp. 101–18.

——, ed. *Carlo V e l'Italia.* Rome: Bulzoni Editore, 2000.

Fasano Guarini, Elana. "'Rome, Workshop of All the Practices of the World': From the Letters of Cardinal Ferdinando de'Medici to Cosimo I and Francesco I." Signorotto and Visceglia, *Court and Politics in Papal Rome, 1492–1700.* Pp. 53–77.

Fenlon, Dermot. *Heresy and Obedience in Tridentine Italy: Cardinal Pole and the Counter Reformation.* Cambridge: Cambridge University Press, 1972.

Fenlon, Iain. "Lepanto: Le arti della celebrazione nella Venezia del Rinascimento." *Crisi e rinnovamenti nell'autumno del Rinascimento a Venezia.* Ed. Vittore Branca and Carlo Ossola. Florence: Leo S. Olschki, 1991. Pp. 373–406.

Fernández Álvarez, Manuel. *Tres embajadores de Felipe II en Inglaterra.* Madrid: Consejo Superior de Investigaciones Científicas, 1951.

——. *Charles V: Elected Emperor and Hereditary Ruler.* Trans. J. A. Lalaguna. London: Thames and Hudson, 1975.

——. *Carlos V, el césar y el hombre.* 4th ed. Madrid: Espasa, 2000.

——. *Felipe II y su tiempo.* 10th ed. Madrid: Espasa, 2000.

——, and Ana Díaz Medina. *Los Austrias mayores y la culminación del imperio (1516–1598).* Madrid: Editorial Gredos, 1987.

Fernández-Armesto, Felipe. *The Spanish Armada.* Oxford: Oxford University Press, 1988.

Fernández Collado, Angel. *Gregorio XIII y Felipe II en la nunciatura de Felipe Sega (1577–1581).* Toledo: Estudio Teologico de San Ildefonso, 1991.

Fernández-Santamaría, J. A. *Reason of State and Statecraft in Spanish Political Thought, 1595–1640.* Lanham: University Press of America, 1983.

Fernández Terricabras, Ignasi. "El episcopado hispano y el patronato real: Reflexión sobre algunas discrepencias entre Clemente VIII y Felipe II." Martínez Millán, *Felipe II (1527–1598): Europa y la Monarquía Católica.* Vol. III, pp. 209–23.

Fichtner, Paula Sutter. "Dynastic Marriage in Sixteenth-Century Habsburg Diplomacy and Statecraft: An Interdisciplinary Approach." *American Historical Review* 81 (1976), pp. 243–65.

——. *Emperor Maximilian II.* New Haven: Yale University Press, 2001.

Finlay, Robert. "Prophecy and Politics in Istanbul: Charles V, Sultan Sūlayman, and the Habsburg Embassy of 1533–1534." *Journal of Early Modern History* 2 (1998), pp. 249–72.

Firpo, Massimo. "The Cardinal." *Renaissance Characters.* Ed. Eugenio Garin. Trans. Lydia G. Cochrane. Chicago: University of Chicago Press, 1991. Pp. 46–97.

Foulché-Delbosc, R. "Le portrait de Mendoza." *Revue Hispanique* 23 (1910), pp. 310–13.

Frigo, Daniela, ed. *Politics and Diplomacy in Early Modern Italy: The Structure of Diplomatic Practice, 1450–1800.* Cambridge: Cambridge University Press, 2000.

Galasso, Giuseppe. "Trends and Problems in Neapolitan History in the Age of Charles V." *Good Government in Spanish Naples.* Ed. and trans. Antonio Calabria and John A. Marino. New York: Peter Lang, 1990. Pp. 13–78.

García Hernán, Enrique. "La curia romana, Felipe II y Sixto V." *Hispania Sacra* 46 (1994), pp. 631–49.

———. *La acción diplomática de Francisco de Borja al servicio del pontificado 1571–1572.* Valencia: OPVI, 2000.

Giannini, Massimo Carlo. "'El martillo sobre el animo': Filippo II e la bolla In Coena Domini nell'Italia spagnola tra religione e sovranità (1568–1570)." Martínez Millán, *Felipe II (1527–1598): Europa y la Monarquía Católica.* Vol. III, pp. 251–70.

Gilbert, Felix. *Machiavelli and Guicciardini: Politics and History in Sixteenth Century Florence.* Princeton: Princeton University Press, 1965; reprint, W.W. Norton and Co.: New York, 1984.

———. "Venice and the Crisis of the League of Cambrai." Hale, *Renaissance Venice.* Pp. 274–92.

———. "Italy." Ranum, *National Consciousness, History, and Political Culture in Early-Modern Europe.* Pp. 21–42.

———. *The Pope, His Banker, and Venice.* Cambridge, Mass.: Harvard University Press, 1980.

Gleason, Elisabeth G. "Confronting New Realities: Venice and the Peace of Bologna, 1530." *Venice Reconsidered: The History and Civilization of an Italian City-State, 1297–1797.* Ed. John Martin and Dennis Romano. Baltimore: Johns Hopkins University Press, 2000. Pp. 168–84.

Goffman, Daniel. *The Ottoman Empire and Early Modern Europe.* Cambridge: Cambridge University Press, 2002.

Gombrich, E. H. "Celebrations in Venice of the Holy League and of the Victory of Lepanto." *Studies in Renaissance and Baroque Art Presented to Anthony Blunt on His Sixtieth Birthday.* London: Phaidon, 1967. Pp. 62–68.

González Palencia, Angel. *Gonzalo Pérez, secretario de Felipe II.* 2 vols. Madrid: Consejo Superior de Investigaciones Científicas, 1946.

———, and Eugenio Mele. *Vida y obras de Don Diego Hurtado de Mendoza.* 3 vols. Madrid: Instituto de Valencia de Don Juan, 1941–1943.

Goody, Jack. *The Development of the Family and Marriage in Europe.* Cambridge: Cambridge University Press, 1983.

Grendler, Paul. *The Roman Inquisition and the Venetian Press, 1540–1605.* Princeton: Princeton University Press, 1977.

Guerzoni, Guido. "Di alcune ignote e poco nobili cause dal soggiorno Bolognese de Kaiser Karl V." Fantoni, *Carlo V e l'Italia.* Pp. 197–217.

Gutiérrez, C. *Españoles en Trento.* Valladolid: Consejo Superior de Investigaciónes Científicas, 1951.

Hale, John R. *Florence and the Medici: The Pattern of Control.* London: Thames and Hudson, 1977.

———. *The Civilization of Europe in the Renaissance.* New York: Atheneum, 1994.

———, ed. *Renaissance Venice.* London: Faber and Faber, 1973.

Hanlon, Gregory. *The Twilight of a Military Tradition: Italian Aristocrats and European Conflicts, 1560–1800.* New York: Holmes and Meier, 1998.

Hay, Denys. "Italy and Barbarian Europe." *Italian Renaissance Studies.* Ed. E. F. Jacob. London: Faber and Faber, 1960. Pp. 48–68.

Hassiotis, Giovanni K. "Venezia e i domini veneziani tramite di informazioni sui turchi per gli spagnoli nel sec. XVI." *Venezia centro di mediazione tra Oriente e Occidente (secoli XV–XVI).* Ed. Hans-Georg Beck. Florence: Leo S. Olschki, 1977. Pp. 116–36.

Headley, John H. *The Emperor and His Chancellor: A Study of the Imperial Chancellery under Gattinara.* Cambridge: Cambridge University Press, 1983.

——. "The Habsburg World Empire and the Revival of Ghibellinism." *Theories of Empire 1450–1800.* Ed. David Armitage. Aldershot: Ashgate, 1998. Pp. 45–79.

Heller, Henry. *Anti-Italianism in Sixteenth-Century France.* Toronto: University of Toronto Press, 2003.

Hernando Sánchez, Carlos José. *Castilla y Nápoles en el siglo XVI: El Virrey Pedro de Toledo.* Salamanca: Junta de Castilla y León, 1994.

Hess, Andrew C. "The Battle of Lepanto and Its Place in Mediterranean History." *Past and Present* 57 (1972), pp. 53–73.

Hillgarth, J. N. *The Mirror of Spain, 1500–1700: The Formation of a Myth.* Ann Arbor: University of Michigan Press, 2000.

Hinajosa, Ricardo de. *Los despachos de la diplomacia pontificia en España.* Vol. I. Madrid: n.p., 1896.

Holt, Mack P. *The French Wars of Religion, 1562–1629.* Cambridge: Cambridge University Press, 1995.

Hook, Judith. *The Sack of Rome 1527.* London: Macmilllan, 1972.

Jacobitti, Edmund E. "Hegemony before Gramsci: The Case of Benedetto Croce." *Journal of Modern History* 52 (1980), pp. 66–84.

Jedin, Hubert. "Catholic Reform and Counter Reformation." *History of the Church.* Vol. V. Ed. Hubert Jedin and John Dolan. New York: Crossroad, 1980.

Jensen, De Lamar. *Diplomacy and Dogmatism: Bernardino de Mendoza and the French Catholic League.* Cambridge, MMass.: Harvard University Press, 1964.

Kagan, Richard L. "Clio and the Crown: Writing History in Habsburg Spain." *Spain, Europe and the Atlantic World.* Ed. Richard L. Kagan and Geoffrey Parker. Cambridge: Cambridge University Press, 1995. Pp. 73–99.

——. "Philip II, History, and the *Cronistas del Rey.*" Navascués Palacio, *Philippus II Rex.* Vol. II, pp. 19–29.

Kamen, Henry. *Philip of Spain.* New Haven: Yale University Press, 1997.

——. *Empire: How Spain Became a World Power 1492–1763.* New York: Harper Collins, 2003.

Keniston, Hayward. *Francisco de los Cobos, Secretary of the Emperor Charles V.* Pittsburgh: University of Pittsburgh Press, 1960.

Kennedy, Paul. *The Rise and Fall of the Great Powers: Economic Change and Military Conflict from 1500 to 2000.* New York: Random House, 1987.

Kettering, Sharon. *Patrons, Brokers, and Clients in Seventeenth-Century France.* Oxford: Oxford University Press, 1986.

Kingdon, Robert M. "The Plantin Breviaries: A Case Study in the Sixteenth-Century Business Operations of a Publishing House." *Bibliothèque d'Humanisme et Renaissance* (1960), pp. 133–50.

——. "Patronage, Piety, and Printing in Sixteenth-Century Europe." *Festschrift for Frederick B. Artz*. Ed. David H. Pinkney and Theodore Ropp. Durham: Duke University Press, 1964. Pp. 19–36.

Kirshner, Julius, ed. *The Origins of the State in Italy 1300–1600*. Chicago: University of Chicago Press, 1995.

Knecht, R. J. *Renaissance Warrior and Patron: The Reign of Francis I*. Cambridge: Cambridge University Press, 1994.

——. *Catherine de'Medici*. London: Longman, 1998.

——. *The French Civil Wars, 1562–1598*. London: Longman, 2000.

Koenigsberger, H. G. *The Practice of Empire: The Government of Sicily under Philip II of Spain*. Emended ed. Ithaca: Cornell University Press, 1969.

——. "Spain." Ranum, *National Consciousness, History, and Political Culture in Early-Modern Europe*. Pp. 144–72.

Kubler, George. *Building the Escorial*. Princeton: Princeton University Press, 1982.

Lane, Frederic C. *Venice: A Maritime Republic*. Baltimore: Johns Hopkins University Press, 1973.

Lea, Henry Charles. *The Inquisition in the Spanish Dependencies*. New York: Macmillan, 1922.

Levin, Michael J. "A New World Order: The Spanish Campaign for Precedence in Early Modern Europe." *Journal of Early Modern History* 6 (2002), pp. 233–64.

Lievsay, John L. *The Elizabethan Image of Italy*. Ithaca: Cornell University Press, 1964.

Liss, Peggy K. *Isabel the Queen: Life and Times*. Oxford: Oxford University Press, 1992.

Lovett, A. W. *Philip II and Mateo Vázquez de Leca: The Government of Spain (1572–1592)*. Geneva: Librairie Droz, 1977.

——. "The Castilian Bankruptcy of 1575." *Historical Journal* 23 (1980), pp. 899–911.

——. *Early Habsburg Spain, 1517–1598*. Oxford: Oxford University Press, 1986.

Lynch, John. "Philip II and the Papacy." *Transactions of the Royal Historical Society*, 5th ser., 2 (1961), pp. 23–42.

——. *Spain Under the Habsburgs*. Vol. I, *Empire and Absolutism 1516–1598*, 2 vols. 2d ed. New York: New York University Press, 1984.

Maggiorotti, L. A. *Architetti e architetture militare*. 3 vols. Rome: La Libreria dalla Stato, 1933–1939.

Mallett, Michael E., and J. R. Hale. *The Military Organization of a Renaissance State: Venice c. 1400 to 1617*. Cambridge: Cambridge University Press, 1984.

Maltby, William S. *The Black Legend in England: The Development of Anti-Spanish Sentiment, 1558–1660*. Durham: Duke University Press, 1971.

——. *Alba: A Biography of Fernando Alvarez de Toledo, Third Duke of Alba, 1507–1582*. Berkeley: University of California Press, 1983.

Mancini, Matteo. *Tiziano e le corti d'Asburgo nei documenti degli archivi spagnoli*. Venice: Istituto Veneto di Scienze, Lettere ed Arti, 1998.

Maravall, José Antonio. *Culture of the Baroque: Analysis of a Historical Structure*. Trans. Terry Cochrane. Minneapolis: University of Minnesota Press, 1986.

March, José M. *Don Luis de Requeséns en el gobierno de Milan, 1571–1573*. Madrid: Ministerio de Asuntos Exteriores, 1943.

Marino, John A. *Pastoral Economics in the Kingdom of Naples*. Baltimore: Johns Hopkins University Press, 1988.

——. "An Anti-Campanellan Vision on the Spanish Monarchy and the Crisis of 1595." *A Renaissance of Conflicts: Visions and Revisions of Law and Society in Italy and Spain*. Ed. John A. Marino and Thomas Kuehn. Toronto: Centre for Reformation and Renaissance Studies, 2004. Pp. 367–93.

Martínez Millán, José. "En busca de la ortadoxia: El Inquisidor General Diego de Espinosa." *La corte de Felipe II*. Ed. José Martínez Millán. Madrid: Alianza Editorial, 1994. Pp. 189–228.

——, ed. *Felipe II (1527–1598): Europa y la Monarquía Católica*. 3 vols. Madrid: Editorial Parteluz, 1998.

Mattingly, Garrett. *Renaissance Diplomacy*. Boston: Houghton Mifflin, 1955, reprint, New York: Dover Publications, 1988.

——. *The Armada*. Boston: Houghton Mifflin, 1959; reprint, Boston: Houghton Mifflin, 1987.

McClung Hallman, Barbara. *Italian Cardinals, Reform, and the Church as Property*. Berkeley: University of California Press, 1985.

McNeill, William H. *Venice, the Hinge of Europe 1081–1797*. Chicago: University of Chicago Press, 1974.

Meinecke, Friedrich. *Machiavellism: The Doctrine of Raison d'Etat and Its Place in Modern History*. Trans. Douglas Scott. London: Routledge and Kegan Paul, 1957.

Menéndez Pidal, Ramón. "The Significance of the Reign of Isabella the Catholic, According to Her Contemporaries." *Spain in the Fifteenth Century, 1369–1516*. Ed. Roger Highfield. London: MacMillan, 1972. Pp. 380–404.

Merriman, Roger Bigelow. *The Rise of the Spanish Empire in the Old World and the New*. Vol. III, *The Emperor*. New York: Macmillan, 1925.

Mitchell, Bonner. *The Majesty of the State: Triumphal Progresses of Foreign Sovereigns in Renaissance Italy (1494–1600)*. Florence: Leo S. Olschki, 1986.

——. *1598: A Year of Pageantry in Late Renaissance Ferrara*. Binghamton: Medieval and Renaissance Texts and Studies, 1990.

——. "Carlos V como triunfador." Navascués Palacio, *Carolus V Imperator*. Pp. 213–51.

Monter, William. *Frontiers of Heresy: The Spanish Inquisition from the Basque Lands to Sicily*. Cambridge: Cambridge University Press, 1990.

Muir, Edward. "Images of Power: Art and Pageantry in Renaissance Venice." *American Historical Review* 84 (1979), pp. 16–52.

——. *Civic Ritual in Renaissance Venice*. Princeton: Princeton University Press, 1981.

Mulcahy, Rosemarie. "Philip II Lover of the Arts." Navascués Palacio, *Philippus II Rex*. Vol. II, pp. 34–44.

Musi, Aurelio, ed. *Nel sistema imperiale: L'Italia spagnola*. Naples: Edizioni Scientifiche Italiane, 1994.

——, ed. *Alle origini di una nazione: Antispagnolismo e identità italiana*. Milan: Guerini ed Associati, 2003.

Nader, Helen. *The Mendoza Family in the Spanish Renaissance, 1350–1550*. New Brunswick: Rutgers University Press, 1979.

Navascués Palacio, Pedro, ed. *Philippus II Rex*. Vol. II. Barcelona: Lunwerg Editores, 1998.

———, ed. *Carolus V Imperator.* Barcelona: Lunwerg Editores, 1999.

Norwich, John Julius. *A History of Venice.* New York: Alfred A. Knopf, 1982, reprint, New York: Vintage Books, 1989.

Nussdorfer, Laurie. *Civic Politics in the Rome of Urban VIII.* Princeton: Princeton University Press, 1992.

Ochoa Brun, Miguel Angel. *Historia de la diplomacia española.* 5 vols. Madrid: Ministerio de Asuntos Exteriores, 1991–1999.

Pagden, Anthony. *Spanish Imperialism and the Political Imagination: Studies in European and Spanish-American Social and Political Theory 1513–1830.* New Haven: Yale University Press, 1990.

Pallotta, Augustus. "Venetian Printers and Spanish Literature in Sixteenth-Century Italy." *Contemporary Literature* 43 (1991), pp. 20–42.

Paris, Louis. *Négociations, lettres, et pièces diverses relatives au règne de François II, tireés du portefeuille de Sébastien de l'Aubespine.* Paris: n.p. 1841.

Parker, Geoffrey. *The Army of Flanders and the Spanish Road, 1567–1659.* Cambridge: Cambridge University Press, 1972; reprint, Cambridge: Cambridge University Press, 1990.

———. *The Dutch Revolt.* Ithaca: Cornell University Press, 1977; reprint, Harmondsworth, UK: Penguin Books, 1985.

———. *Spain and the Netherlands, 1559–1659: Ten Studies.* Glasgow: Collins, 1979; reprint, London: Fortune Press, 1990.

———. *Philip II.* 3d ed. Chicago: Open Court, 1995.

———. *The Military Revolution: Military Innovation and the Rise of the West, 1500–1800.* 2d ed. Cambridge: Cambridge University Press, 1996.

———. *The Grand Strategy of Philip II.* New Haven: Yale University Press, 1998.

———. "The Political World of Charles V." *Charles V 1500–1558 and His Time.* Ed. Hugo Soly. Antwerp: Mercatorfonds, 1999. Pp. 113–225.

———. "David or Goliath? Philip II and His World in the 1580s." *Success Is Never Final: Empire, War, and Faith in Early Modern Europe.* Ed. Geoffrey Parker. New York: Basic Books, 2002. Pp. 16–38.

Parker, Geoffrey, ed. *The Thirty Years' War.* 2d rev. ed. London: Routledge, 1997.

Partner, Peter. *Renaissance Rome, 1500–1559: A Portrait of a Society.* Berkeley: University of California Press, 1976.

Pastor, Ludwig von. *The History of the Popes from the Close of the Middle Ages.* Trans. Ralph Francis Kerr. 40 vols. London: Kegan Paul, Trench, Trubner and Co., 1891–1953.

Pecchiai, Pio. *Roma nel Cinquecento. Storia di Roma,* Vol. XIII. Bologna: Licinio Capelli Editore, 1948.

Pedani, Maria Pia. *In nome del Gran Signore: Inviati ottomani a Venezia della caduta di Constantinopla alla Guerra di Candia.* Venice: Deputazione Editrice, 1994.

Pepper, Simon, and Nicholas Adams. *Firearms and Fortifications: Military Architecture and Siege Warfare in Sixteenth-Century Siena.* Chicago: University of Chicago Press, 1986.

Pierson, Peter. *Philip II of Spain.* London: Thames and Hudson, 1975.

———. *Commander of the Armada: The Seventh Duke of Medina Sidonia.* New Haven: Yale University Press, 1989.

——. "Carlos V, Gobernante." Navascués Palacio, *Carolus V Imperator.* Pp. 101–81.

Preto, Paolo. *I servizi segreti de Venezia.* Milan: Il Saggiatori, 1994.

Prodi, Paolo. *The Papal Prince. One Body and Two Souls: The Papal Monarchy in Early Modern Europe.* Trans. Susan Haskins. Cambridge: Cambridge University Press, 1987.

Quazza, Romolo. *Preponderanza spagnola (1559–1700).* 2d ed. Milan: Casa Editrice Dottor Francesco Vallardi, 1950.

Queller, Donald E. *The Office of Ambassador in the Middle Ages.* Princeton: Princeton University Press, 1967.

——. "The Development of Ambassadorial *Relazioni.*" Hale, *Renaissance Venice.* Pp. 174–96.

Ranke, Leopold von. *The Popes of Rome: Their Ecclesiastical and Political History.* Trans. Sarah Austin. London: J. Murray, 1866.

Ranum, Orest, ed. *National Consciousness, History, and Political Culture in Early-Modern Europe.* Baltimore: Johns Hopkins University Press, 1975.

Redworth, Glyn, and Fernando Checa. "The Courts of the Spanish Habsburgs 1500–1700." Anderson, *The Princely Courts of Europe.* Pp. 41–65.

Rekers, B. *Benito Arias Montano (1527–1598).* London: Warburg Institute, 1972.

Ribot García, Luis Antonio. *La revuelta antiespañola de Mesina: Causas y antecedentes (1591–1647).* Valladolid: Universidad de Valladolid, 1982.

Río Barredo, María José del. "Felipe II y la configuración del sistema ceremonial de la monarquía católica." Martínez Millán, *Felipe II (1527–1598): Europa y la Monarquía Católica.* Vol. I, Part II, pp. 677–703.

Rivero Rodríguez, Manuel. "Felipe II y los 'Potentados de Italia.'" *La dimensione europea dei Farnese, Bulletin de l'Institut Historique Belge de Rome* 63 (1993), pp. 337–70.

——. "La Liga Santa y la paz de Italia (1569–1576)." *Política, religión e inquisición en la España moderna: Homenaje a Joaquín Pérez Villanueva.* Ed. P. Fernández Albaladejo, J. Martínez Millán, and V. Pinto Crespo. Madrid: Universidad Autonoma de Madrid, 1996. Pp. 587–620.

——. *Felipe II y el gobierno de Italia.* Madrid: Sociedad Estatal para la Conmemoración de los Centenarios de Felipe II y Carlos V, 1998.

Robertson, Clare. *Il gran cardenale: Alessandro Farnese, Patron of the Arts.* New Haven: Yale University Press, 1992.

Rodríguez-Salgado, M. J. *The Changing Face of Empire: Charles V, Philip II, and Habsburg Authority, 1551–1559.* Cambridge: Cambridge University Press, 1988.

Roe, John. *Shakespeare and Machiavelli.* Cambridge: D. S. Brewer, 2002.

Romero García, Eladi. *El imperialismo hispánico en la Toscana durante el siglo XVI.* Lérida: Dilagro, 1986.

Roosen, William. "Early Modern Diplomatic Ceremonial: A Systems Approach." *Journal of Modern History* 52 (1980), pp. 452–76.

Rosa, Mario. "The 'World's Theatre': The Court of Rome and Politics in the First Half of the Seventeenth Century." In Signorotto and Visceglia, *Court and Politics in Papal Rome.* Pp. 78–98.

Russell, Joycelyne C. *Diplomats at Work: Three Renaissance Studies.* Wolfeboro Falls: A. Sutton, 1992.

Sahlins, Peter. *Boundaries: The Making of France and Spain in the Pyrenees.* Berkeley: University of California Press, 1989.

Sarrablo Aguareles, Eugenio. "La cultura y el arte venecianos, en sus relaciones con España, a través de la correspondencia diplomática de los siglos XVI a XVIII." *Revista de Archivos, Bibliotecas y Museos* 62 (1956), pp. 639–84.

Saslow, James M. *The Medici Wedding of 1589.* New Haven: Yale University Press, 1996.

Serrano, Luciano. *La Liga de Lepanto entre España, Venecia y la Santa Sede (1570–1573).* 2 vols. Madrid: Junta para la ampliación de estudios é investigaciones científicas, 1918–1920.

Setton, Kenneth M. *The Papacy and the Levant (1204–1571).* 4 vols. Philadelphia: American Philosophical Society, 1976–1984.

Shiels, Eugene. *King and Church: The Rise and Fall of the Patronato Real.* Chicago: Loyola University Press, 1961.

Signorotto, Gianvittorio. "Note sulla politica e la diplomazia dei pontifici (da Paolo III a Pio IV)." Fantoni, *Carlo V e l'Italia.* Pp. 47–76.

——, and Maria Antonietta Visceglia, eds. *Court and Politics in Papal Rome, 1492–1700.* Cambridge: Cambridge University Press, 2002.

Spagnoletti, Angelantonio. *Principi italiani e Spagna nell'età barocca.* Milan: B. Mondadori, 1996.

——. "La visione dell'Italia e degli stati italiani nell'età de Filippo II." Martínez Millán, *Felipe II (1527–1598): Europa y la Monarquía Católica.* Vol. I, Part II. Pp. 893–903.

Spini, Giorgio. "The Medici Principality and the Organization of the States of Europe in the Sixteenth Century." *Journal of Italian History* 2 (1979), pp. 458–73.

Spivakovsky, Erica. *Son of the Alhambra: Don Diego Hurtado de Mendoza, 1504–1575.* Austin: University of Texas Press, 1970.

Sutherland, N. M. *Princes, Politics and Religion, 1547–1589.* London: Hambledon Press, 1984.

Tanner, Marie. *The Last Descendant of Aeneas: The Habsburgs and the Mythic Image of the Emperor.* New Haven: Yale University Press, 1992.

Taylor, Bruce. *Structures of Reform: The Mercedarian Order in the Spanish Golden Age.* Leiden: Brill, 2000.

Tellechea Idígoras, J. Ignacio. *Bartolomé Carranza y su tiempo.* Madrid: Edición Guadarrama, 1968.

Tenenti, Alberto. "Francia, Venezia, e la Sacra Lega." *Il Mediterraneo nella seconda metà del '500 alla luce di Lepanto,* Ed. Gino Benzoni. Florence: Leo S. Olschki, 1976.

——. "La Repubblica di Venezia e la Spagna di Filippo II e Filippo III." *Studi veneziani* 30 (1995), pp. 109–23.

Tocco, Vittorio di. *Ideali di indipendenza in Italia durante la preponderanza spagnola.* Messina: G. Principato, 1927.

Tracy, James D. *Emperor Charles V, Impresario of War: Campaign Strategy, International Finance, and Domestic Politics.* Cambridge: Cambridge University Press, 2002.

Vargas-Hidalgo, Rafael. *La Batalla de Lepanto, según cartas inéditas de Felipe II, Don Juan de Austria y Juan Andrea Doria e informes de embajadores y espías.* Santiago, Chile: Ediciones ChileAmérica CESOC, 1998.

Vázquez de Prada, Valentín. "La embajada española en Francia en la época de Felipe II." *Politica, religión e inquisición en la España moderna.* Pp. 671–90.

Vilar, Pierre. "The Age of Don Quixote." Trans. Richard Morris. *Essays in European Economic History 1500–1800.* Ed. Peter Earle. Oxford: Clarendon Press, 1974. Pp. 100–112.

Villari, Rosario. *The Revolt of Naples.* Trans. James Newell with John A. Marino. Oxford: Oxford University Press, 1993.

Visceglia, Maria Antonietta. "Il cerimoniale come linguaggio politico: Su alcuni conflitti di precedenza alla corte di Roma tra Cinquecento e Seicento." *Cérémonial et rituel à Rome (XVI–XIX siècle).* Ed. Maria Antonietta Visceglia and Catherine Brice. Rome: École Française de Rome, 1997. Pp. 117–76.

——. "Factions in the Sacred College in the Sixteenth and Seventeenth Centuries." Signorotto and Visceglia, *Court and Politics in Papal Rome, 1492–1700.* Pp. 99–131.

Wilkinson-Zerner, Catherine. *Juan de Herrera, Architect to Philip II of Spain.* New Haven: Yale University Press, 1993.

Wolfe, Michael. *The Conversion of Henry IV.* Cambridge, Mass.: Harvard University Press, 1993.

Woodhouse, J. R. "Honorable Dissimulation: Some Italian Advice for the Renaissance Diplomat." *Proceedings of the British Academy* No. 84. Oxford: Oxford University Press, 1993. Pp. 25–50.

Wright, A. D. *The Early Modern Papacy: From the Council of Trent to the French Revolution, 1564–1789.* London: Longman, 2000.

Xavier, Adro. *Luis de Requeséns en el Europa del siglo XVI.* Madrid: Vassallo de Mumbert, 1984.

Zimmermann, T. C. Price. *Paolo Giovio: The Historian and the Crisis of Sixteenth-Century Italy.* Princeton: Princeton University Press, 1995.

Index

Germany, 52, 141

Ghibellines, 115

Giovio, Paolo, 196

Gómez, Alvar, 196

Gonzaga, Ercole, cardinal of Mantua, 70–71

Gonzaga family, 58

Gracián, Antonio, 190–92, 194

Granada, War of, 94

Granvelle, Antoine Perrenot de, cardinal, 58–59, 61, 63, 80, 82–83, 85, 94–95, 109, 183n

Gregory XIII, pope, 102–5, 107–15, 142, 146–47, 165–66, 169, 179, 182, 187, 205

Gregory XIV, pope, 124–26, 143

Gritti, Andrea, 16–18

Guelfs, 115

Guerrero, Alonso, 145

Guicciardini, Francesco, 11, 201, 204

Guise, Henry, duke of, 87, 121–22

Guzmán de Silva, Diego (ambassador to Venice 1571–76), 30–38, 41, 99, 156, 160–65, 170–77, 180–82, 195–94, 196–98

Habsburgs. *See* Charles V; Philip II

Henry II, king of France, 28, 57, 60, 62, 64, 73, 128

Henry III, king of France, 110, 114, 121, 174–76

Henry IV, king of France, 38, 40, 107, 120–30, 132, 205

Henry VIII, king of England, 26

Holy League. *See* Charles V; Philip II; Papacy; Venice

Holy Roman Empire. *See* Austrian ambassadors; Charles V; Ferdinand; Maximilian

Iberia, 4, 203n

Idiáquez, Juan de, 39, 119, 149, 157

In coena domini, 140–41

Innocent IX, pope, 124, 126

Isabella, daughter of Philip II, 117, 128

Isabella, queen of Castile, 207

Isabella, wife of Charles V, 158, 184, 188

Italianità, 4, 202–3

Italian Wars, 1–2, 5, 14–15, 64, 110, 132

Italy. *See* individual territories

Jews, 171–72

Juana, sister of Philip II, 28–29, 144

Juan de Austria, half-brother of Philip II, 31, 34, 36, 83, 92, 94, 96, 98, 100, 102–4, 110, 162, 164–65, 171, 188–89, 199

Julius III, pope, 9, 43, 59–63, 88, 140

Kamen, Henry, 2, 202

Lando, Pietro, 21, 23

Leo X, pope, 58

Lepanto, battle of, 9, 30, 32–34, 100, 104, 114, 161–62, 193

Locatelo Cremones, Vicencio, 197–98

Longjumeau, peace of, 178

Loredan, Pietro, 30

Lorraine, Charles de Guise, cardinal of, 73

Louise of Savoy, 43

Low Countries. *See* Netherlands

Loyola, Ignatius, 147

Machiavelli, Niccolò, 11, 201, 203, 206, 208

Madrid, 34, 39–40, 73, 78, 80, 85, 95, 104, 111, 116, 119, 132, 142–43, 149, 181, 194, 199

Mai, Miguel (ambassador to Rome 1528–33), 45–53, 169, 187, 204

Malta, 83

Mantua, 58, 200

Marcellus II, pope, 64

Margaret of Austria, aunt of Charles V, 49

María Manuela, wife of Philip II, 188

Marlowe, Christopher, 203

Mary Queen of Scots, 118

Mattingly, Garrett, 6

Maximilian II, Holy Roman Emperor, 89

Medici, Catherine de,' 53

Medici, Cosimo de,' duke of Florence, archduke of Tuscany, 5, 9, 58, 63, 86, 89–93, 100, 102, 151, 190

Medici, Ferdinand de,' 5, 131, 201

Medici, Francesco de,' 89

Medici, Lorenzo de,' 11

Medina Sidonia, duke of, 120

Mendoza, Antonio de, 7n, 155, 176–77

Mendoza, Diego Hurtado de (ambassador to Venice 1539–46, to Rome 1546–52), 19–26, 41, 53–63, 92n, 140, 149, 156–57, 159–60, 170–71, 179–80, 184, 187–90, 197, 205

Mendoza, Iñigo de (ambassador to Venice 1590s), 39–41, 130–31, 157, 173